AF576680

# EARLY AMERICAN MODERNS

*Painters of the Stieglitz Group*

# EARLY AMERICAN MODERNS

*by Mahonri Sharp Young*

**WATSON-GUPTILL PUBLICATIONS, New York**

First published 1974 in New York by Watson-Guptill Publications,
a division of Billboard Publications, Inc.,
One Astor Plaza, New York, N.Y. 10036



Manufactured in U.S.A.

Library of Congress Cataloging in Publication Data
Young, Mahonri Sharp, 1911-
Early American moderns.
Bibliography: p.
1. Stieglitz Group. 2. Stieglitz, Alfred, 1864-
1946—Art patronage. 3. Painting, Modern—20th
century—United States. I. Title.
ND212.5.S75Y67 759.06 74-9909
ISBN 0-8230-1598-X

First Printing, 1974

# Contents


*LIST OF COLOR PLATES*

*FOREWORD* 9

*ALFRED STIEGLITZ* 10

*JOHN MARIN* 12

*CHARLES DEMUTH* 14

*MARSDEN HARTLEY* 16

*ARTHUR G. DOVE* 18

*GRADUATES OF THE STIEGLITZ STABLE* 20

- *ALFRED MAURER*
- *MAX WEBER*
- *ABRAHAM WALKOWITZ*

*GEORGIA O'KEEFFE* 22

*COLOR PLATES* 23

*EPILOGUE* 153

*CHRONOLOGY* 154

*BIBLIOGRAPHY* 156

*INDEX* 158

# List of Color Plates


**John Marin**

Plate 1 *Tyrolean Mountains,* 25
Plate 2 *Seaside, An Interpretation,* 27
Plate 3 *Breakers, Maine Coast,* 29
Plate 4 *From the Ocean,* 31
Plate 5 *Red Sun,* 33
Plate 6 *Sunset, Maine Coast,* 35
Plate 7 *Off Stonington,* 37
Plate 8 *Palisades, No. 2,* 39
Plate 9 *Sailboat in Harbor,* 41
Plate 10 *Impression,* 43
Plate 11 *Ship, Sea, and Sky Forms, An Impression,* 45

**Charles Demuth**

Plate 12 *The Drinkers,* 47
Plate 13 *The Nut, Pre-Volstead Days,* 49
Plate 14 *The Circus,* 51
Plate 15 *Columbia,* 53
Plate 16 *Flowers,* 55
Plate 17 *The Tower,* 57
Plate 18 *Aucassin and Nicolette,* 59
Plate 19 *Incense of a New Church,* 61
Plate 20 *Modern Conveniences,* 63
Plate 21 *Paquebot Paris,* 65
Plate 22 *Still Life No. 1,* 67

**Marsden Hartley**

Plate 23 *The Mountains,* 69
Plate 24 *The Mountain, Autumn,* 71
Plate 25 *Desertion,* 73
Plate 26 *Still Life No.1,* 75
Plate 27 *Composition,* 77
Plate 28 *Berlin Ante-War,* 79
Plate 29 *Bowl with Fruit,* 81
Plate 30 *Lilies in a Vase,* 83
Plate 31 *Color Analogy,* 85
Plate 32 *New Mexico Recollections,* 87
Plate 33 *The Window,* 89

**_Arthur G. Dove_**
Plate 34 *Movement. No. 1,* 91
Plate 35 *Nature Symbolized,* 93
Plate 36 *Plant Forms,* 95
Plate 37 *Thunderstorm,* 97
Plate 38 *Waterfall,* 99
Plate 39 *Fog Horns,* 101
Plate 40 *Oil Drums,* 103
Plate 41 *Sand Barge,* 105
Plate 42 *Ferry Boat Wreck,* 107
Plate 43 *Fields of Grain as Seen from Train,* 109
Plate 44 *Cows in a Pasture,* 111
Plate 45 *High Noon,* 113

**_Alfred Maurer_**
Plate 46 *Self-Portrait with Hat,* 115
Plate 47 *Portrait of a Girl with Green Background,* 117
Plate 48 *George Washington,* 119

**_Max Weber_**
Plate 49 *The Two Musicians,* 121
Plate 50 *Still Life,* 123
Plate 51 *The Wayfarers,* 125

**_Abraham Walkowitz_**
Plate 52 *Trees and Flowers,* 127
Plate 53 *Bathers,* 129
Plate 54 *Bathers Resting,* 131

**_Georgia O'Keeffe_**
Plate 55 *Blue No II,* 133
Plate 56 *Light Coming on the Plains No. II,* 135
Plate 57 *Blue and Green Music,* 137
Plate 58 *Dark Abstraction,* 139
Plate 59 *Abstraction,* 141
Plate 60 *Black Iris,* 143
Plate 61 *Black Cross, New Mexico,* 145
Plate 62 *Lake George Window,* 147
Plate 63 *Cow's Skull: Red, White, Blue,* 149
Plate 64 *From the Faraway Nearby, 151*

# Foreword

Alfred Stieglitz, a leading American photographer who owned a photographic gallery, introduced abstract art to America by accident. In 1908, tired of photographic exhibitions, he asked his friend Edward Steichen, who was painting in Paris, if he knew of anything interesting in art that he could show. Steichen suggested drawings by Rodin, and Stieglitz's great career as a dealer began. Matisse came next, and Alfred Maurer and John Marin —American painters who Steichen knew in Paris— followed in 1909. Marsden Hartley walked in off the street with a friend; during the same year Stieglitz held the first Toulouse-Lautrec show in America. In a 1910 group exhibition, he showed Arthur Dove and Max Weber, who were also sent by Steichen from Paris. In 1910, at Steichen's suggestion, Stieglitz introduced Cézanne to America; he also exhibited Henri Rousseau, suggested by Max Weber. In 1911 he gave Picasso his first one-man show anywhere. In 1912 Abraham Walkowitz had a show and suggested an exhibition of children's art, another "first anywhere." Picabia, Brancusi, and Negro sculpture were all American firsts. In 1917 Georgia O'Keeffe's was the last show at the Photo-Secession Gallery at 291 Fifth Avenue before Stieglitz closed it because of the war.

When he reopened at The Intimate Gallery he had an all-American team: Marin, Demuth, Hartley, Dove, and O'Keeffe. These were his Group of Five, whom he exhibited continuously until his death in 1946—except Hartley, who wandered off the reservation. Stieglitz had always admired Demuth's work, but in the beginning he had not wanted to carry someone who would be in competition with Marin. Alfred Maurer, Abraham Walkowitz, and Max Weber had been dropped. Occasionally he gave someone else a show, such as Peggy Bacon or Gaston Lachaise, and he still showed his own photographs and Paul Strand's. But the main events at the Intimate Gallery and later at An American Place were the constantly recurring exhibition of Marin, Demuth, Hartley, Dove, and O'Keeffe.

Never was there such a dealer. He denied that he was one. His gallery was a temple where he preached continuously. By grace and favor, you might be able to buy a picture, but you had to listen to Stieglitz. He did a wonderful job of building up his artists. He supported them in every way—psychologically, professionally, and financially—except for Demuth, who didn't need the money. His estimates of their accomplishments are accepted as fact today. Their connection with Stieglitz makes them into the only true group in the history of American painting.

They were America's early moderns: Marin, Demuth, and Hartley were advanced artists for their day, while Dove may have invented abstract art even before Kandinsky, and O'Keeffe re-invented it for herself. They are all interesting and original painters in their own right, and they were heralded and shepherded throughout life by the hypnotic voice of Stieglitz, one of the most remarkable figures in America art.

# *Alfred Stieglitz 1864-1946*

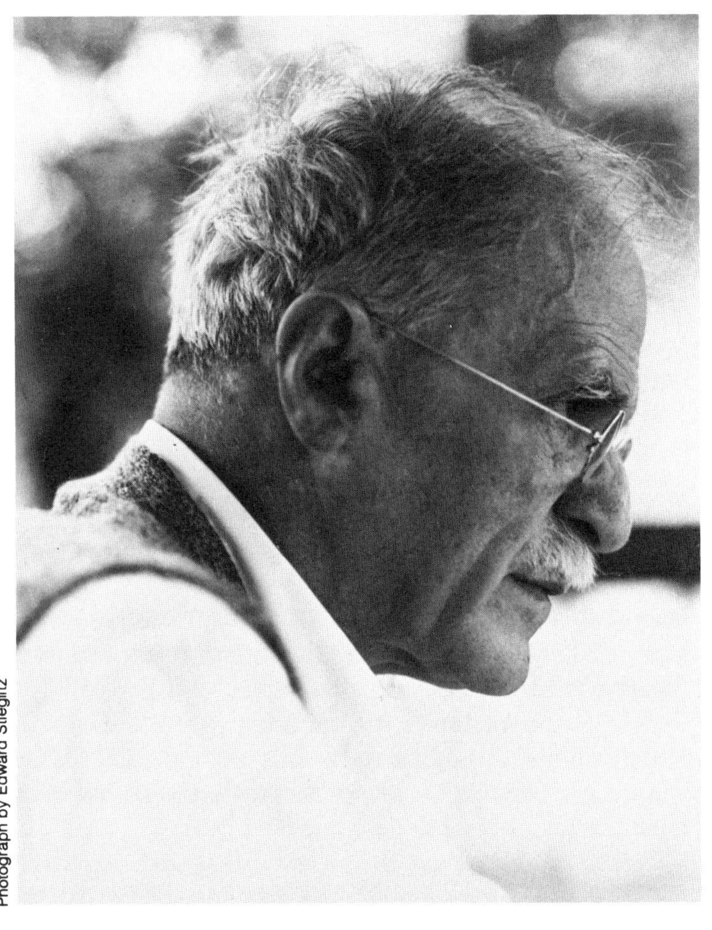

Photograph by Edward Stieglitz

Alfred Stieglitz brought modern art to America: a great photographer, he was the first to show Picasso, Braque, and Matisse in his New York gallery, and the first to show Negro art and children's drawings. His American artists—Marin, Demuth, Hartley, and Dove—pioneered abstraction in America. Along with Georgia O'Keeffe, they made their careers under this great impresario, who also launched Alfred Maurer, Max Weber, Abraham Walkowitz, and many others. As their dealer, backer, leader, philosopher, and friend, Stieglitz pushed them to fame; without him they might never have made the grade. He was almost as important in the history of American art as he thought he was. During his lifetime, he was the all-important figure; now it's his artists who count. His voice is gone but their pictures remain, and while he would be pleased at their present position, he wouldn't be satisfied with his own. Modern art would have happened without him, but the American abstract movement might have had a different shape. A racing man with an eye for a winner, Stieglitz saw to it that his starters won, and all the early American moderns carried Stieglitz's colors. This memorable man and prolific talker, this evangelist, searcher, and seer, sacrificed his own career as a photographer for his painters.

As well as making some of the greatest photographs that art form has produced, Stieglitz ran the most influential photographic magazine in the country. His Photo-Secession Gallery at 291 Fifth Avenue, which brought modern art to America, was founded to advance photography. "Secession" had a revolutionary ring in those days, but Stieglitz never seceded from anything except his one attempt at business. He hated business and always resented the suggestion that he was a dealer. He cared more for being a prophet than he did for photography, which didn't suffice him. He had no desire to paint, or to follow his friends Steichen, Sheeler, and Man Ray into commercial photography. His artists gave him a second career.

Actually, the photographic battle was already won. Stieglitz moved fast to the front ranks of his profession, becoming a leader of the heroic period in American photography. Indeed, victory came so soon that it left Stieglitz without a mission. He found a new cause in modern art and brought it to America, but modern art turned out to be too big for one man to handle. Stieglitz had a message for America to which America wouldn't listen.

He introduced the School of Paris to the States, but when Cubism made its big hit at the Armory Show of 1913, Stieglitz turned against the French and discovered specifically American qualities in Marin, Hartley, Demuth, and Dove, who had all been trained in Europe. The Stieglitz magic worked on writers as well as artists; Paul Rosenfeld, Alfred Kreymborg, Waldo Frank, and Lewis Mumford all fell under his spell. With his lack of a definite doctrine, Stieglitz was like a Japanese teacher who produces illumination by jolts, contradictions, and rudeness. Yet the atmosphere of excitement and ferment that the man generated, and his own dedication and enthusiasm, were hard to believe. His message, never clear, has now vanished—but when a dealer tells a client that a picture was painted for him alone, that's pure Stieglitz. He was a hypnotist and American Gurdieff, and those who remember him, believe in him still.

Stieglitz proclaimed himself the leader of the group. Fiercely independent, he demanded subservience; living for his artists, he demanded that they live for him. All opinions were valid as long as they were his; you were free to disagree somewhere else. Disdainful of money, this extraordinary salesman denied that he was selling. He talked people down. He talked all the time and never listened. By helping others he sustained himself; while keeping everyone afloat, he asked only adulation in return. He seriously believed that he was an incarnation of the struggle toward truth; he felt only exasperation for the unheeding Americans who didn't hear his message. Consequently, there wasn't much laughter around Stieglitz.

Stieglitz proclaimed that he was born in Hoboken, that he was an American, that photography was his passion, and the search for truth his obsession. His father, the only Jewish member of the New York Jockey Club, retired early to play billiards and keep open house at Lake George, where thirty people sat down to supper. Stieglitz loved race horses and Lake George all his life, but he never attained the standing of his father, a friend of men like J.P. Morgan and Leonard Jerome. In 1881 his father took the family to Berlin to give the boy an education, and Alfred heard the opera *Tristan und Isolde* a hundred times. When he discovered a camera shop in the Klosterstrasse, his life was made, and soon his photographs won medals in all the shows.

Returning to New York in 1890, he started a lithography business and married Emmeline Obermeyer, but neither venture was a success. The nasty New York streets were a shock after Berlin; this was the America that Bernard Berenson and Gertrude Stein had left. Dropping his business as soon as he could, he photographed the snow in the city, emigrants in steerage, and workhorses in the night. His magazine *Camera Work,* which he started in 1902, is a record of photography and modern art up to our entrance into World War I. The watercolors of Rodin and Cézanne, and works by Brancusi and the American painters in this book, were first shown in his Photo-Secession gallery and published in his magazine. World War I was a difficult time for a man who had loved Germany, and Stieglitz closed down both enterprises. He had no gallery of his own again until after the War, and he never had another magazine, but his flow of talk continued. For a while during the War he held forth to people at the Far East Tea Garden, a Chinese restaurant on Columbus Circle, with the street lights blinking across Central Park.

In 1916 he met Georgia O'Keeffe, which changed everything. She came to New York to live in 1918 and they were married in 1924. O'Keeffe was the great love of his life and Stieglitz photographed her continually. They worked together at borrowed galleries, hanging shows of his artists' work.

His second place of business (if that term may be used) was the Intimate Gallery, which Stieglitz opened at the Anderson Galleries in 1925. He founded his other great gallery, An American Place, in 1929, and this lasted through another world war. These were sacred spots which stood for the divinity in man. Stieglitz's need to talk didn't diminish. He dominated all his artists except Hartley, with whom he quarreled, and possibly O'Keeffe. As before, the pictures weren't for sale, although under certain circumstances, pictures might be bought. If you asked Stieglitz what An American Place was, he asked you what was life itself. Outside this laboratory, this cathedral, was death.

When Stieglitz died in 1946, the group fell apart. Dove died the same year; Demuth was already dead; Hartley had left the fold; and Marin took up with another dealer. As Stieglitz wished, Georgia O'Keeffe gave away his great collection of the work of these artists to museums, wound up the gallery, and moved permanently to the Southwest. Stieglitz wouldn't approve of what has happened in painting since his death, though he did as much as any man to bring it about.

# *John Marin* *1870-1953*

John Marin was born on December 23, 1870, in Rutherford, New Jersey, just behind the Palisades. His mother died shortly after he was born. His father, a public accountant, was constantly on the road and so young Marin was brought up by his grandparents in Weehawken, with the New York skyline towering across the river. Later he lived with his aunts in Union City. A real Jersey boy, Marin spent all his life near the Palisades during the great days of the ferry boats. This was surely a picturesque environment: one ferry in the river and another creaking in the slip; gulls squealing overhead; driftwood swirling in the greasy water. The hot dog carts on the New York side have never changed.

Marin said that his ancestors were the best English ale, Dutch bitters, Irish gin, French vermouth and plain scotch. However, his father's surname was French and originally may have been Spanish, while his mother's family had been in this country a long time. Marin's father was always prosperous and sent money home. The only thing Marin liked about school was geometry. He went to Stevens Institute of Technology in Hoboken for a year, and then worked in an architect's office as a draftsman. He designed a half-dozen houses in Union City, but he preferred to sketch the Jersey meadows and the beechwoods along the Palisades. When he was twenty-eight, he wandered off to the Pennsylvania Academy of the Fine Arts in Philadelphia. He didn't learn much from dissecting old tramps under Thomas Anshutz, whom he rather took to despite his caustic teaching. To please his aunts, he studied at the Art Students League in New York, but the lessons weren't of much use. He was a kid until he was thirty.

When he was thirty-five, his father sent him to Paris, where he was taken in by his step-brother Charles Bittinger, who later became a successful Navy painter and portraitist. Living on the Rue Campagne-Première, he met a lot of artists through Arthur Carles (a fellow student at the Pennsylvania Academy), including Alfred Maurer, Max Weber, and Edward Steichen, who was still a painter. Carles went to Gertrude Stein's parties but Marin didn't, since he wasn't one to push himself forward. The new ideas about painting never touched him.

As a boy, he had become interested in art through the drawings in the magazines, and his great admiration was for Edwin Austin Abbey, whom Van Gogh called the cleverest of them all. In Paris, with his step-brother's help, Marin taught himself to etch the cathedrals of France. He admired the etchings of Charles Meryon, the half-English friend of the French art critics, the Goncourts. Whistler's influence upon Marin was so strong that he didn't mention it, just as he didn't talk about Cézanne's influence later. Marin's etchings sold, and for the first time he earned some money as an artist.

By now, his extraordinary appearance and personality were already fully developed. Paul Rosenfeld said that Marin's lean and swarthy face with its sharp nose reminded people of a wizened apple. He had the curious personal dignity of a Yankee farmer, but when he got excited, became as tense and high-spirited as his future watercolors. Even the critic, Henry McBride, who saw him in Venice where Marin visited his father and stepmother, mentioned his hatchet face.

After seeing Marin's watercolors in Paris, Steichen sent them along to Stieglitz in New York, who exhibited them in 1909 along with fifteen oils by Alfy Maurer. In 1910 Marin went back to the States for good, and Stieglitz gave him a one-man show of forty-three watercolors, twenty pastels, and eight etchings. Elizabeth Luther Carey mentioned Marin's debt to Cézanne and Hartley was reminded of Whistler; in fact, he always expected the ghost of Whistler to materialize out of 291 Fifth Avenue.

At forty-two, with his watercolors selling, Marin married an old sweetheart and settled down in the Palisades. He was fascinated by New York, with its piles of great houses one upon another, but he always came home at night. From the first, his wife went along on his painting trips. In 1914 Marin's son was born. And in the same year, Marin discovered Maine.

Though he impressed McBride as one who was here upon a secret errand, Marin had his own toughness, which he needed in dealing with Stieglitz. He wrote one of his gnarled little poems about Stieglitz and 291: "Well guarded it/by He—who jealously guards/its innocence, purity, sincerity,/subtly guarded it/so that—it seems—not at all guarded/no tyrant—yet tyrant of tyranny."—(John Marin, *Selected Writings,* p. 13.)

Marin had that disregard for others that an artist must have to survive. He didn't care who supported him, Stieglitz or his father. His aunts and his wife took care of

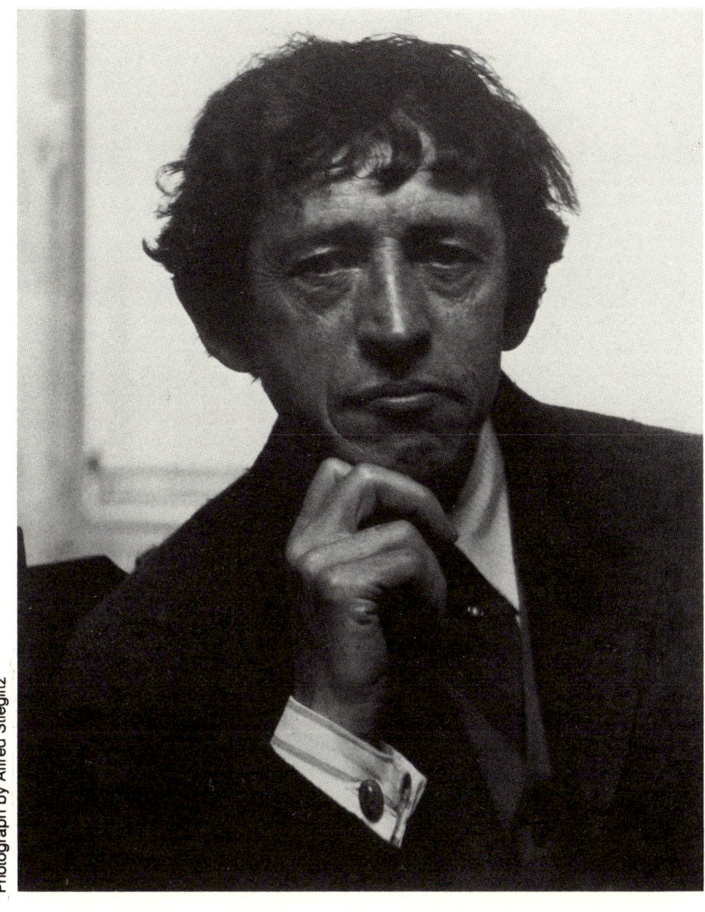

Photograph by Alfred Stieglitz

him, and his inability to handle the world made other people handle it for him. Life within the Stieglitz circle was perfect for Marin. It provided all the artists he needed to talk with, and they didn't think he was a fool. At Stieglitz's Saturday afternoons, he wandered silent among the grotesque people. Without Stieglitz, Marin might have been defeated; before Stieglitz, he was a lost boy.

New York and New Jersey were Marin's winter life, but the best of the year was in Maine with the sea and the islands. Many of the people who love Marin now, love him because of Maine. Summer visitors such as Marin, see Maine as the natives never see it: without the poverty and the interminable winters. Marin had lots of artist friends in Maine, including Abraham Walkowitz, Paul Strand, the photographer, and the etcher Ernest Haskell, who might have been a hermit. Wrong-headed and unpredictable, Haskell would tell you the truth to your face, which is unpardonable.

At Westport, fifteen miles from Bath, Marin lived on berries and fish in a five-dollar-a-month shack, built on a ledge fifteen feet above high tide. He often sailed out to Ragged Island with the Haskells; indeed, Haskell said that Marin painted and fished as though he *believed* in painting and fishing. In 1915 Marin bought a particularly wild offshore island which turned out to have no fresh water. At his next place in Stonington, Marin dug clams, picked berries, caught fish, and bought a power boat that leaked like hell. "My boy is brown and well, full of life. My wife is brown and well. I am brown and well." (MacKinley Helm, *John Marin,* p. 40.)

In 1919, while Stieglitz was still floored by the War, Charles Daniel, a former saloon-keeper who started his gallery after the Armory Show, gave Marin a retrospective and brought him his first real patron, Ferdinand Howald. Many of the Marins owned by Howald are reproduced in this book; Howald bought more than thirty watercolors, but far fewer than Stieglitz, who ended up with two hundred. When Stieglitz opened his Intimate Gallery at the Anderson Galleries in 1925, Marin returned to the fold, which in fact he never had left. He painted mainly in the summer. During the winter in New Jersey, he puttered around in his studio and worked a bit on his oils, which he didn't show because people didn't think they were very good. Stieglitz often got a thousand dollars for a watercolor, and in 1927 he sold *Back of Blue Mountain* to Duncan Phillips for $6,000, which may have been a bit inflated. Stieglitz told Phillips that he thought he had finally gotten a glimpse of the spirit of the gallery.

In 1929 and 1930 Marin stayed with Mabel Dodge Luhan in Taos, New Mexico, where he was a lamb among tigers, but a wary lamb at that. He had no real trouble in the Depression. During 1932 he bought a house in Cape Split in Washington County, the first Maine home he had ever owned. The water was so close to his house that he felt he was on a boat, and he ate fish morning, noon, and night. In 1936, when Marin was in his middle sixties, Stieglitz organized a sensational retrospective at the Museum of Modern Art. Hartley wrote in the catalog: "You will never see watercolors like those of John Marin so take a good look." (Helm, p. 74.) From here on out, Marin was a famous figure. After his wife died in 1945, and Stieglitz in 1946, Marin's son assumed his support. Occasionally, Marin got annoyed at modern art or the modern world, but he had a serene old age. He could still climb a tree, still play Bach, and he was pleased with his fame. When he died in 1953, he said he had had delight. And he has given it to many.

# *Charles Demuth* *1883-1935*

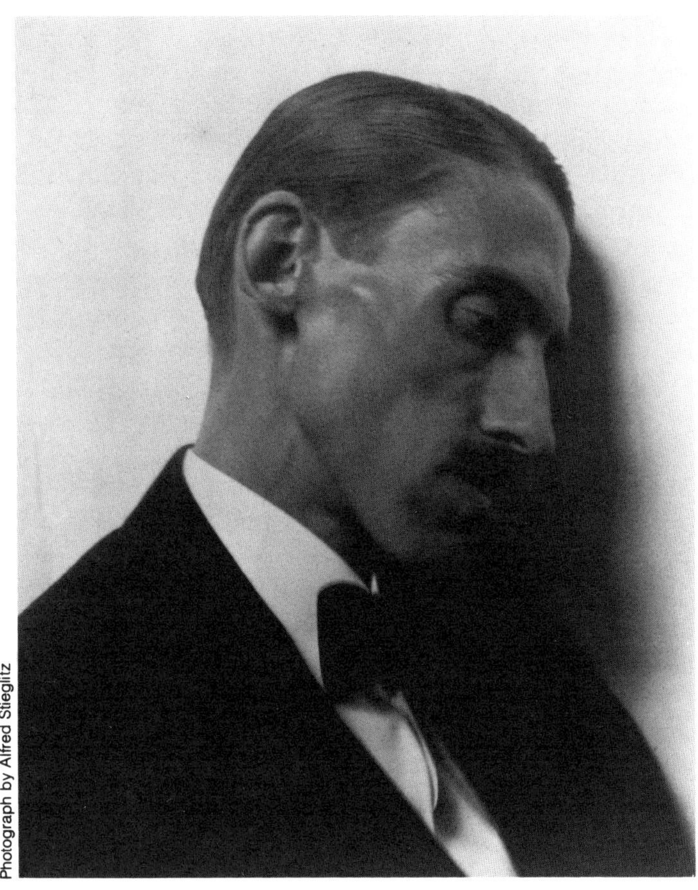

Photograph by Alfred Stieglitz

Charles Demuth was born in 1883 in Lancaster, the center of the Pennsylvania Dutch country, where his family owned a tobacco store that was one of the oldest businesses in the United States. Demuth kept up his Lancaster connection all his life; he never had a home of his own. The most important figure in his life was his mother, whom he called "Augusta the Ironclad" and "a ship under full sail." (Emily Farnham, *Charles Demuth: Behind a Laughing Mask*, p. 137.)

Never strong, Demuth limped from boyhood. His family didn't object to his becoming an artist, and he spent two years as a day student at Franklin and Marshall Academy, one of the oldest schools in the country. Then he went on to the Pennsylvania Academy of the Fine Arts in Philadelphia. Wherever he went, and he traveled a lot in his short life, the brick houses of Lancaster and the flowers from his mother's garden were in the back of his mind.

In Philadelphia, Demuth made a friend of William Carlos Williams, who was already dividing his time between medicine and poetry. Demuth impressed his friends more than he impressed his teachers; with his distinguished appearance and great charm, he got along well with Arthur Carles, Charles Sheeler, George Biddle, and Franklin Watkins. In many ways he was a Philadelphia artist, and he kept in touch with the town all his life.

Around the Academy there was a lot of talk about Paris. Demuth made his first trip abroad in 1904, and found it very different from Lancaster; there was wine twice a day, and there was the incredible feeling that art was important. Demuth liked it so much he considered spending his life there. Like most American artists, he saw only other Americans, but that was what he went there for, to be an American in Paris. He was conscious of the new things that were happening in French art, but mainly he saw his Philadelphia friends and lived the good life. This was not a question of work, for you could always paint in America; the important thing was to absorb what was in the air. The Americans learned from walking along the Seine, staring over at Notre Dame, looking in the bookstores, and talking to each other. It doesn't sound like much, but it was a whole way of life, which lasted until the Crash in 1929. Paris was the best part of being American, and the artists were never more American than when they were sitting on the terrace of the Dôme, with the miraculously cheap drinks in front of them. This life had made Marin, and it did the same for Demuth.

While in Paris, Demuth met Gertrude Stein, but he was more influenced by Cézanne than by Stein's Cubist friends, whose work was rigid and too drab for him. Demuth also met Marsden Hartley in Paris, and they shared many tastes—artistic, alcoholic, and homosexual. They were both far happier in Europe. When Demuth came back just before the War, he was met at the dock by his mother, but he soon moved off to Provincetown on Cape Cod. Both Hutchins Hapgood, who had known Gertrude Stein in Florence, and Eugene O'Neill, drinking and writing his first plays, were there. Lots of people who were well-known at the time were also there, like Susan Glaspell, the novelist, and her husband George Cram Cook, who ended up as a Greek shepherd at Delphi. Provincetown was Greenwich Village's summer resort, and Demuth visited both as often as he could. His life alternated between invalidism in Lancaster and wild sprees on the town in New York City. A witty man at a party, Demuth drank as much as he painted, but almost all of his work was good.

In New York, Hartley introduced Demuth to Stieglitz, but Stieglitz didn't want to carry someone whose watercolors competed with Marin's. Hartley then took Demuth over to Charles Daniel who served as a backup for Stieglitz, handling the Stieglitz artists when Stieglitz was without a gallery, and handling clients like Ferdinand Howald, who wouldn't put up with Stieglitz. Though he didn't join the group until later, Demuth was very much under Stieglitz's influence, and ended up as a member of the inner circle.

Demuth, like Marin, had no trouble selling. McBride praised him and people liked his work, which was original and pleasing. During the War, when he couldn't go to Europe, Demuth went to Bermuda, sometimes with Hartley or sometimes with others, for this diffident man never lacked friends. The quiet life in his mother's sheltering arms alternated with fearsome binges in Greenwich Village. One night, when Demuth and his old friend Eugene O'Neill were at Romany Mary's restaurant, a friend of theirs took an overdose of heroin and died in front of them. Demuth, who had been taking heroin himself, was scared to death; O'Neill drank himself senseless in the Hell Hole, their favorite saloon.

In 1921 Demuth went back to Paris for his last trip. Always a great reader, he had done a series of illustrations to Zola's *Nana* and another to Henry James' *Turn of the Screw*. A great admirer of Proust, he wanted to illustrate *Remembrance of Things Past*, but the novelist was too near death to see him. This was a pity, for Demuth would have done a great job. While on this trip, he discovered that he was diabetic just in time to be saved by insulin.

Though Demuth didn't need financial backing the way the others did, Stieglitz wrote to Demuth that his fight for O'Keeffe and Marin was his fight for him as well. He considered Demuth among the "A-1 men." Demuth exhibited with him and stayed with him for the last ten years of his life, and after Demuth's death, Stieglitz continued to carry his work. Next to his mother, Stieglitz was the greatest force in Demuth's life, and as a tribute he wrote Stieglitz one of those twisted little poems that flourished in this atmosphere.

> "For no reason, perhaps a very good reason . . . as I start to write this,—I have been thinking, when really not thinking, of lighthouses and fog.
>
> Lighthouses and fog—a lighthouse and many fogs. There really-are not many lighthouses, and fogs seem to be always rolling in from most distinguished shores and seas.
>
> Lighthouses are fixed. Sometimes they seem to have moved but—they really haven't. Lights in lighthouses sometimes move but they do not move as lights in a political street parade move. Lights in lighthouses sometimes wink, and I've seen them myself twinkle."
>
> "But you said you were writing about Stieglitz—"
>
> "Well, I am writing about Stieglitz—here, this is what I have been doing,—writing about Stieglitz!" (Charles Demuth, *America and Alfred Stieglitz*, p. 246.)

When Demuth died in 1935, still talking about illustrating Proust, his old friend William Carlos Williams believed that he had intentionally stopped the insulin.

# *Marsden Hartley* *1877-1943*

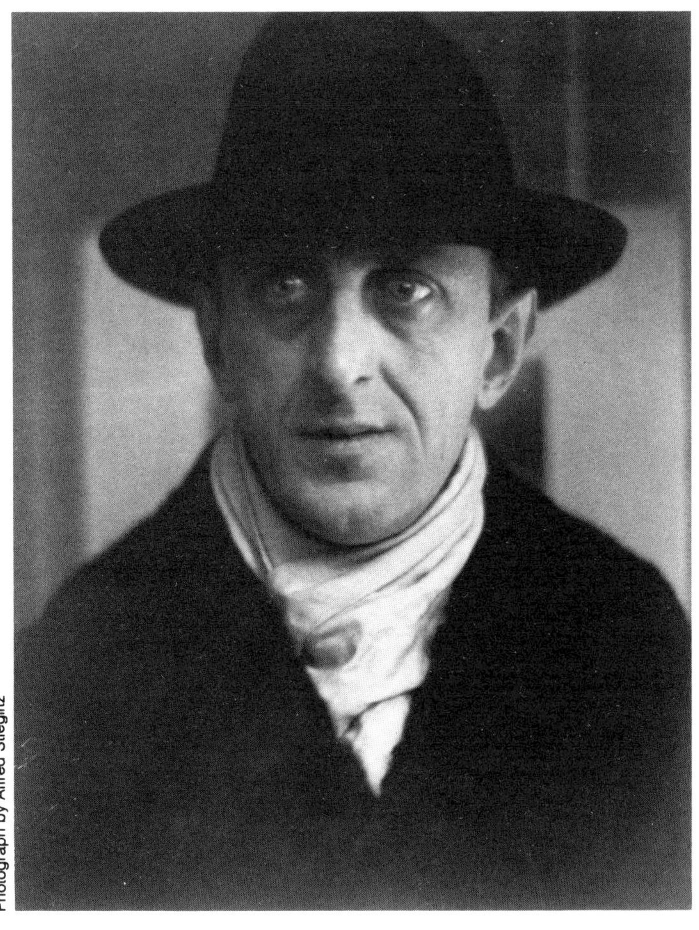

Photograph by Alfred Stieglitz

Marsden Hartley was born in Lewiston, Maine. This "gaunt eagle from the hills of Maine," as Jerome Mellquist called him, was a great "Maine-iac" all his life though he wasn't exactly rooted in hilly soil. Lewiston is a milltown on the Androscoggin River, and Hartley's father was a cottonspinner from Lancashire. Unlike Marin and Demuth, he was a poor boy, the youngest of nine children, and he had a rough time all his life. Stieglitz and Daniel helped as much as they could, but Hartley wasn't an easy man to help.

While still a boy, Hartley moved to Ohio with his family, and adopted his first name from that of his father's second wife. He went to the Cleveland School of Art, the New York School of Art, and the National Academy of Design. The most important influences on his art were *Jugend*, the German satirical magazine and Segantini, the Italian painter of Alpine landscapes, whose dark mountains recurred in Hartley's pictures throughout his life. During his early days in New York, he used to see Albert Pinkham Ryder on the street and in Kiel's bakery, where Hartley ate for a quarter with Alanson Hartpence, who later was Daniel's assistant at the gallery. No praiser of poverty, Hartley pointed out that Degas and Manet were rich, and that anybody, let alone an artist, would have been glad of Cézanne's income. Ryder made Hartley feel like a bondholder, because Ryder lived on thirteen cents a day. When in the early 1900's he went back to Maine to paint, Hartley lived on four dollars a week, yet he loved elegance and alcohol.

He showed his Maine paintings to John Sloan, Maurice Prendergast, and William Glackens in New York, but he was a non-starter until he was taken to see Stieglitz by Seumas O'Sheel, a young Irish poet. Stieglitz told Hartley that if he wanted to send some pictures to the Gallery, he would look at them. After a few days, Stieglitz said that he didn't know what he thought of those pictures any more than he did at first, but he would give Hartley an exhibition in two weeks. This was Hartley's initiation into a most remarkable experience; Hartley felt he had the right to call it unique, for here was one man who believed in another man over a space of more than twenty years. In 1912, with the help of Arthur B. Davies, Stieglitz put up the money for Hartley to go abroad for a few months, which later stretched into years.

In Paris, Hartley had his letters sent to him in care of Gertrude Stein. Stieglitz scolded him for listening to her; she thought he should have twelve hundred dollars a year. Hartley agreed that some rich American should be willing to put up the money. Stieglitz saw to it that Hartley had his few months in Germany, believing that Hartley loved Berlin, as Stieglitz did, for the neatness, the propriety, and the efficiency. Actually, Hartley was a drinking man and Berlin was a homosexual paradise. Besides, the Germans liked his work and Hartley thought of staying on there, if he could make a living, as Demuth thought of staying in France. As a friend of Kandinsky's and exhibitor with the *Blaue Reiter* group, Hartley was genuinely close to foreign artists.

When Hartley came back to New York for a visit, he found it horrifying, as Stieglitz had on his own first return, although by now Stieglitz thought New York was the most remarkable place on the globe. He hoped that Hartley would be able to make a go of it in Germany, for he didn't see much hope for modern art in the States in the short run. Hartley lingered in Germany as long as he could, until the end of 1915. When he came back, he lived in Provincetown and Greenwich Village, and went to Bermuda for long painting trips with Demuth.

After the Armistice, Hartley went right back to Europe. Robert McAlmon, an early friend of Hemingway's, saw a lot of Hartley in Berlin during the winter of 1922-23. Inflation made Germany a paradise for Americans, since the dollar bought ten or twenty times as much in Germany, and cocaine cost ten cents a snort. Hartley was beamingly merry because for the first time he could live as he liked, going to night clubs in evening dress with an orchid in his lapel. Paris was also incredibly cheap, for prices were far lower than now, with the franc at fifty to the dollar. Hartley scrounged from Stieglitz, Daniel, and such unlikely patrons as William C. Bullitt, Franklin Roosevelt's friend. For a while he lived at Aix-en-Provence, starting to paint where Cézanne left off. After the Crash, when everybody left, he hurried home.

During the Depression, Hartley discovered America. Mexico was too explosive and Nova Scotia was too far, so he ended up in Maine. Here, he painted and wrote poems until his death in 1943. "Sea dove in a shroud/of sand, all shiny with/thick clips of sun/sea dove in a shroud/of sand, and the last word/spoken—alone." (Scribner Ames, *Marsden Hartley in Maine.)*

# Arthur G. Dove 1880-1946

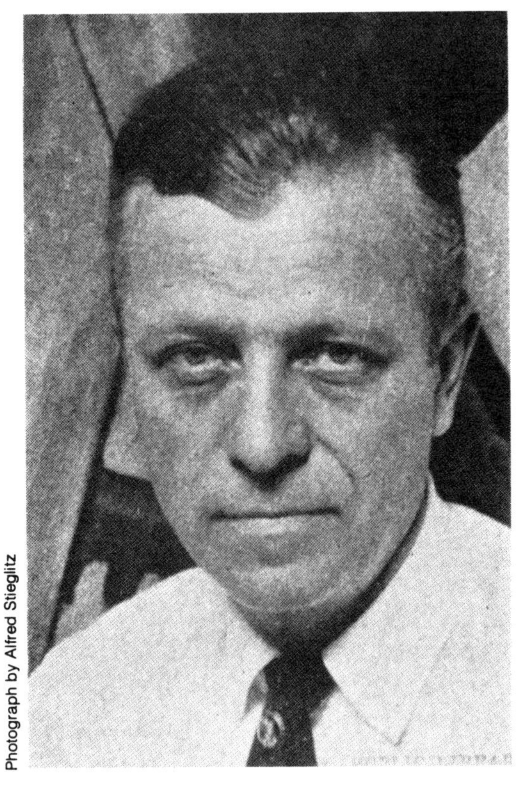

Photograph by Alfred Stieglitz

Dove was an upstate New Yorker born in Canandaigua. His father was a contractor who built part of Hobart College at Geneva, where Dove went for two years before studying law at Cornell. Dove was never forgiven by his father for becoming a painter. After Cornell, Dove made the rounds of the advertising agencies in New York with his portfolio under his arm, and started drawing illustrations for the magazines. Dove was the only man of the Stieglitz group who worked as a commercial artist. Married to a hometown girl, he could have settled down to commercial success, but he quit in 1907 and went to Paris to paint. He was right to go, for otherwise we would never have heard of him; except for Norman Rockwell, the *Saturday Evening Post* artists have been forgotten.

Dove's great friend in Paris was Alfred Maurer, who was making the difficult style change to abstraction. Maurer and the other artists liked Dove's work (which is more important than critics realize). Dove showed in the *Salon d'Automne* and got his name in the papers. This is the kind of recognition that encourages an artist to think he can make it. When his money ran out, Dove went back to the States; from then on it was never easy.

Steichen had sent Maurer and Marin to Stieglitz, and they sent Dove. As in most groups, things weren't always quiet in the Stieglitz Stable. Steichen thought Hartley was far from genuine and after Stieglitz died, Georgia O'Keeffe got rid of his collection of Hartley's pictures for a song. The fiercely independent Dove was the most faithful of all the Stieglitz painters. Stieglitz said that Hartley didn't know what 291 was all about, but Dove never questioned. For him, Stieglitz was always the great voice.

When Dove was asked what Stieglitz meant to him as an artist, he answered: "Everything." He valued Stieglitz's opinion as one who has always known. He didn't think he could have existed as a painter without the battle Stieglitz fought day by day for twenty-five years. For him, Stieglitz was without a doubt the one man who had done the most for art in America. In 1910 Stieglitz showed some of Dove's pictures at his gallery, and in 1912 gave him "The Arthur G. Dove First Exhibition Anywhere." Dove's pictures were eyecatchers and they made news but not money. His father helped occasionally but not as much as he could have; unlike Marin, Dove never caught on. He had only one great patron, Duncan Phillips; even Ferdinand Howald bought only two of his pictures. In 1910, when his son was born, Dove moved to Westport, Connecticut, and when his father wouldn't give him the hundred dollars a month he needed to live, he tried farming. This didn't give him much time to paint, but he lived his own life and paid the price.

In 1920 he left his wife and home for good and went to live on a boat. He had a series of boats, from scows to a forty-two-foot Bermuda racer that belonged to his old friend William S. Hart, the stone-faced sheriff of the silver screen. He took up with another woman, a painter herself, whom he married when his first wife died. He lived on Hart's boat for seven years, tying up in the winter at a yacht club on Long Island Sound. There was so little room that Dove's pictures got smaller and smaller. Things were pretty thin, with barely enough money for groceries, but he knew what he was doing.

In 1932, after his father died, he and his second wife moved back to Geneva. His father had been well off, and Dove had every reason to think he would inherit a sizeable amount of money. Instead, he inherited the mortgage and the family farm, on which he labored for six years. In 1938 he gave up and went back to Long Island to live until his death in 1946.

Dove died the same year as Stieglitz, as though he refused to survive his death. Even Dove's second wife considered Stieglitz the greatest man she had ever met.

# Graduates of the Stieglitz Stable

Many other Americans exhibited with Stieglitz—Arthur Carles, Oscar Bluemner, Elie Nadelman, Gaston Lachaise, Macdonald Wright, and many who are now unkown. Alfred Maurer had his first American exhibition at 291 in March 1909; Max Weber and Abraham Walkowitz had their first comprehensive exhibitions in 1911 and 1912 respectively.

**Alfred Maurer** (1868-1932), the son of a Currier and Ives artist whose paintings are still popular on calendars, studied at the National Academy of Design, went to Paris to study in 1897, and stayed there pretty much until 1914. Success came easy to him and he won first prize at the Carnegie International in 1901, a tremendous honor in those days. As a young man in Paris, he was very much the gay blade, with a house on the Marne and a girl on each arm. He had a wonderful time. Maurer was an early friend of the Steins, and once a week for years he had dinner at a creamery with Leo Stein and Mahonri Young, both great talkers. When modern art came to Maurer, it was a conversion. From then on, he painted like a wild man. He was never again the gay, light-hearted Alfy his friends had known.

Maurer was the only one of the Stieglitz group who achieved success as a realistic painter, and the only one who sacrificed his career to abstractionism. When war broke out in 1914, he came back to New York from Paris to live with his father, who thought his son had lost his mind. The old man lived to one hundred, and Alfy committed suicide shortly after he died. He was never dependent upon Stieglitz, financially or psychologically, and after the first shows at 291, he exhibited with Erhard Weyhe, the great bookseller.

Although Stieglitz respected Maurer as an artist, he didn't like him well enough to become his agent or patron. Georgia O'Keeffe said nothing happened that was unfriendly between Maurer and Stieglitz; Maurer was just forgotten when he wasn't around.

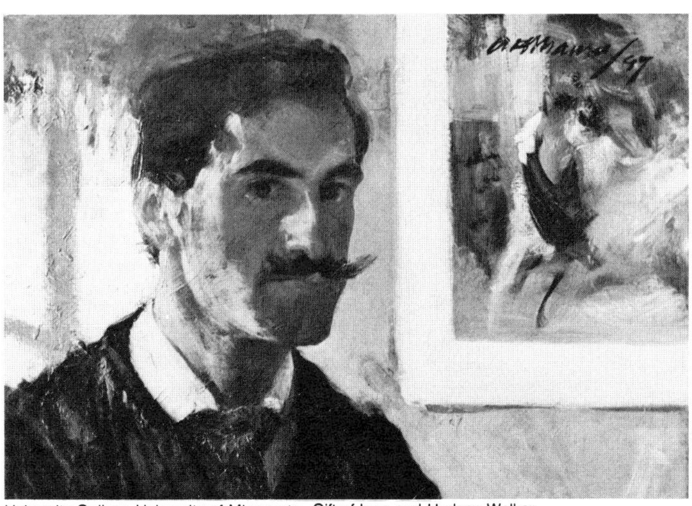

University Gallery, University of Minnesota Gift of Ione and Hudson Walker

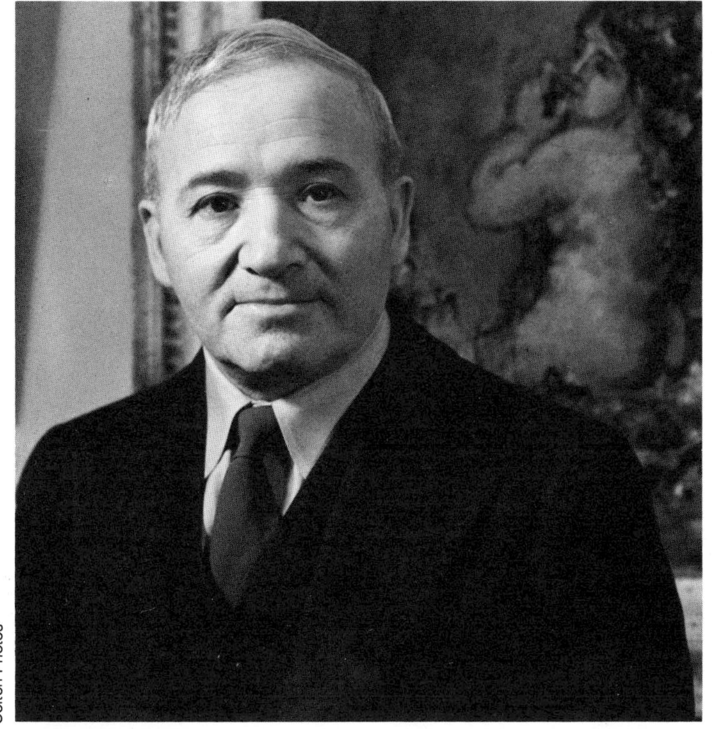

Colten Photos

**Max Weber** (1881-1961) was born in Russia and came to America ten years later. He graduated from Pratt Institute, the great commercial art school. One of his teachers was Arthur Wesley Dow, a man particularly interested in Far Eastern painting and the wisdom of the Orient. When Weber went to Paris in 1905, he studied Persian miniatures, Coptic textiles, and Oriental sculpture as much as he did painting, or so he said. But they were not nearly so important an influence upon him as Cézanne, whom he discovered for himself at the *Salon d'Automne* in 1906. Matisse, with whom he studied for two years, was also interested in Persian miniatures, and his theories fitted Dow's. Weber, however, was an impressionable young man who turned at every wind. He met Picasso, took easily to primitive art, and became a friend of Henri Rousseau. He exhibited at 291 the year after he got back, arranged the first show of Henri Rousseau in 1910, and had his own first one-man show in 1911. Stieglitz admitted that he learned a great deal about modern art from Weber, rather than the other way round. We usually think of Stieglitz as always giving, but he learned about modern art from Steichen and Max Weber.

Weber was interested in many things, far more than Stieglitz; he was fascinated by American Indian art and by Mexico. Considered an eclectic at the time, his work followed the course of French art, passing through the phases of Cubism before he hit his own style—a lyric lament for his own people and his East European origins. He was a great help to Stieglitz, but he wasn't sufficiently in tune with 291; he had his own mystic interests and turned away from Stieglitz to an independent career of his own.

**Abraham Walkowitz** (1878-1965) was no mirror of the styles; his view of art and the world was always personal, and it was fortunate for him that he was considered modern in spirit. Born in Russia three years before Weber, he came to the States in 1889 and studied, like Hartley, at the National Academy of Design. His works were first exhibited at the Educational Alliance in New York in 1900, and at University Settlement House in 1902. He went to Paris in 1906, and like Max Weber he was swept off his feet by Cézanne and met Picasso and Henri Rousseau. The great event of his life was watching Isadora Duncan dance. He came back to New York in 1907, and exhibited with Stieglitz from 1912 until 291 closed. He learned his modernism from Stieglitz during this period. A mild man, and never as abstract an artist as Maurer or Weber, Walkowitz didn't venture very far down the road to Cubism. His association with Stieglitz was important, but the tremendous personality of Isadora Duncan dominated his art for years. Toward the end he wandered about New York practically blind, eager to talk about the old days.

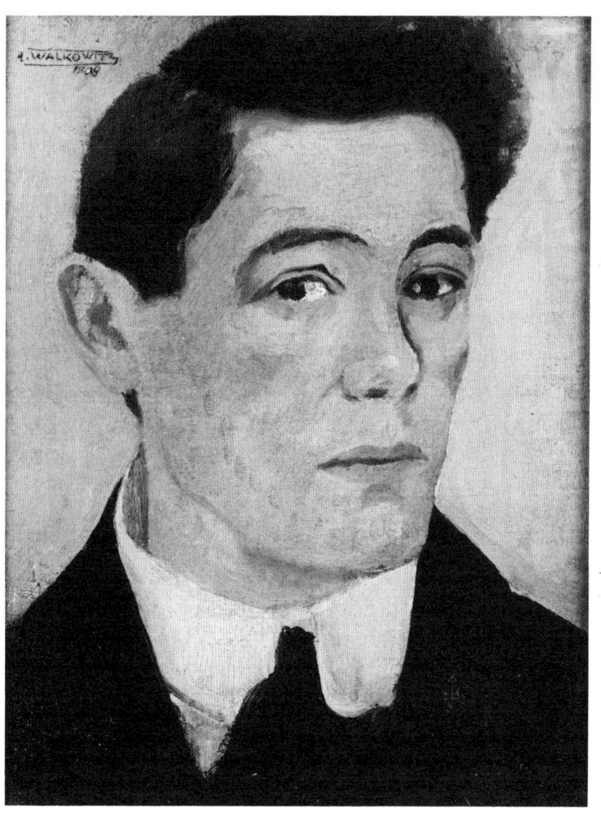

The Brooklyn Museum Gift of Abraham Walkowitz

# Georgia O'Keeffe b. 1887

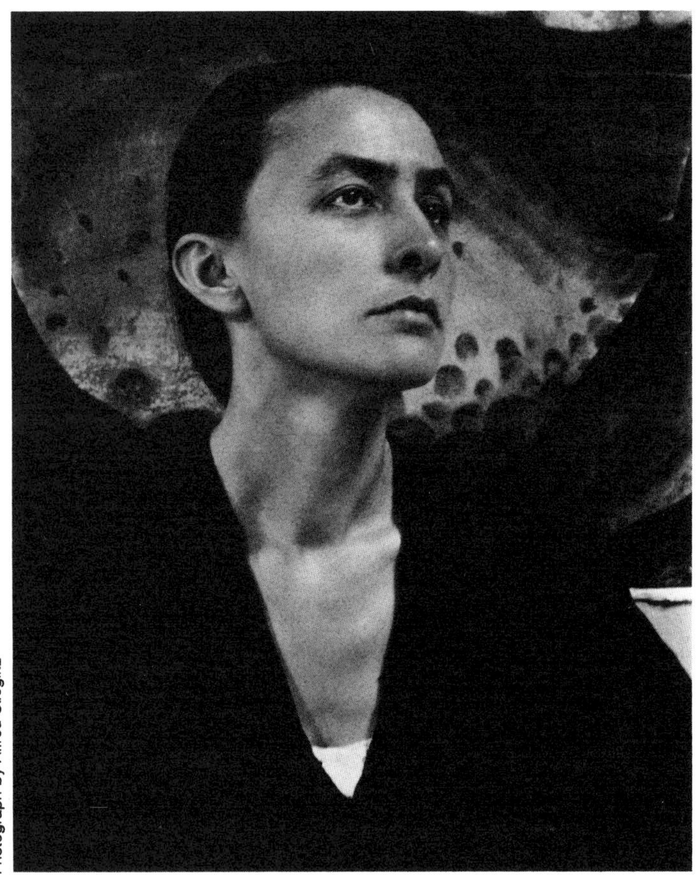

Photograph by Alfred Stieglitz

Georgia O'Keeffe, the only living member of the Stieglitz group, and the only woman, was the last to join. The only one not trained abroad, she was the most American of the lot. Despite her closeness to Stieglitz, she drifted farthest from the fold. Since his death, she has become identified with New Mexico and another way of life. Born in Sun Prairie, Wisconsin, she went to the Art Institute of Chicago on Michigan Avenue in 1904 and 1905, when the others were going to Paris. In 1907 and 1908, while Stieglitz was holding his pioneering exhibitions of Picasso and Matisse, she studied at the Art Students League, and once she ventured down Fifth Avenue to see the show of Rodin drawings at 291. At Teachers College she studied with Arthur Wesley Dow, who had known Gauguin and the mystery of the Orient, and she absorbed his theories.

In 1915, while O'Keeffe was teaching art in West Texas, a friend in New York showed some of her drawings and watercolors to Stieglitz, and the next year he included some of her work in a group exhibition. When O'Keeffe heard about this, she stormed into 291 and demanded an explanation. It was a grand scene, with the old master at his best; O'Keeffe came to protest and stayed for thirty years. Her first one-man show at 291 in 1917 was the last show for the gallery before it closed. When she came back to New York to see the show, it had already been taken down, but Stieglitz rehung it for her. In 1918, Stieglitz backed her for a year in New York, and she quit her teaching job. O'Keeffe had breezed into the gallery at the right time, for Stieglitz was at the end of his rope, depressed by the War, with his beloved gallery sinking under him. O'Keeffe was a new beginning for him. He photographed her thousands of times.

She didn't share his feeling for New York, and Maine had no particular meaning for her, but she went where he went. Stieglitz loved his boyhood home at Lake George, where he photographed the clouds or just looked out the window, but the Adirondacks aren't for everybody. In 1923 Stieglitz put on a big exhibition of one hundred of her paintings at the Anderson Galleries, and in 1924 they were married.

Georgia O'Keeffe was the only one of the Stieglitz painters whose work wasn't bought by the Columbus collector, Ferdinand Howald. It wasn't for lack of trying. Stieglitz had recommended Hartley's book *Adventures in the Arts* to Howald and on one occasion, he sent three framed Marins on approval, but Howald didn't like to have things picked out for him. When Stieglitz sent Howald an O'Keeffe painting on approval and he returned it, she said it was fine by her. She was glad to have it back. She would rather tear it up and throw it out the window than have Howald keep it, if he didn't like it.

In 1929 she visited Mabel Dodge Luhan in Taos and fell in love with the country. From this time on she spent her summers in New Mexico, which Stieglitz didn't like because it was so far from a doctor. In 1934 she rented Ghost Ranch, which she later bought, along with another house in Abiquiu. After Stieglitz died, she wound things up in New York, gave away his collection as he wished, and closed An American Place for good. Since then she has spent her life in the bright sun and the bitter cold, far from gallery talk and city streets.

# Color Plates

## *John Marin*

*Plate 1*
TYROLEAN MOUNTAINS, 1910
*Watercolor, 14 1/2" X 17 3/4"*
*The Columbus Gallery of Fine Arts, Columbus, Ohio*
*Ferdinand Howald Collection*

This watercolor was painted in 1910, the year Marin came back from Europe and had his first show in Stieglitz's gallery. He hit his stride when he was in his forties. He may have seen some German Alpine painting, but Marin had a great capacity for working things out for himself. Once he found his style, he stuck to it; he had a vision all his own, and that's what's good about him. It's surprising that he came to these blotting-paper effects straight from his angular etchings of French cathedrals.

Despite the uncertainty about the European origins of his style, he was an amazingly original artist. You'd never miss a Marin across the room, even starting this early. And his paintings are remarkably varied, considering how limited his vocabulary was—ships, sea, sun, sky, pines, rocks, and a few mountains.

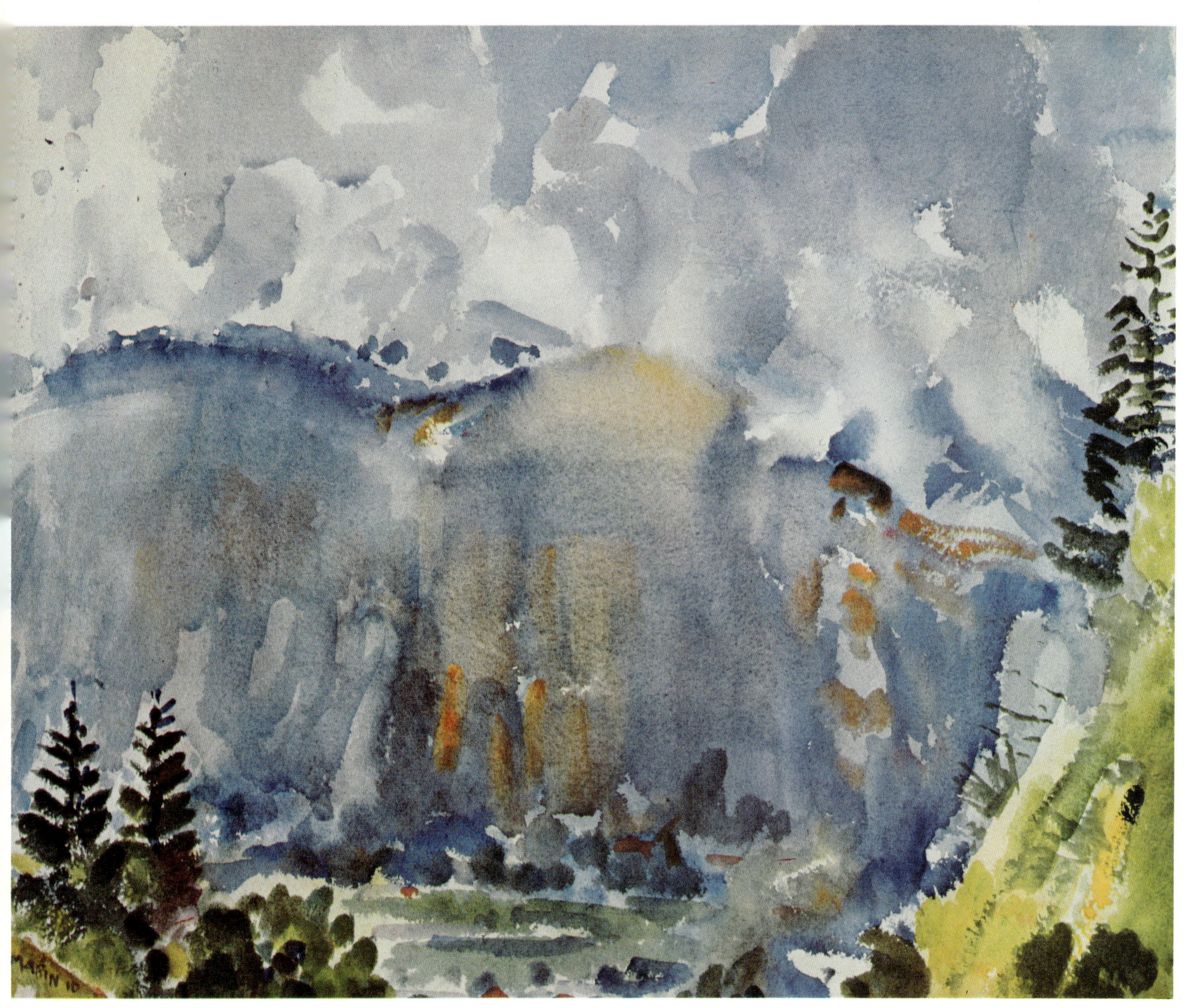

## *John Marin*

*Plate 2*
SEASIDE, AN INTERPRETATION, 1914
*Watercolor, 15 1/2" X 18 5/8"*
*The Columbus Gallery of Fine Arts, Columbus, Ohio*
*Ferdinand Howald Collection*

There's nothing particularly interpretive about this picture. The Stieglitz painters picked up his literary tone, and their words were portentous, in contrast to the freedom of their work. Marin is thrashing around a bit in this painting. The straight horizon across the middle of the picture is too heavy; it cuts the composition in two and it makes too much of a right angle with the tree in the foreground.

In calling the watercolor an interpretation, Marin was just trying to hold his end up as a literate painter, in the spirit of the group. Actually, he is surprisingly uninterpretative, and you'll go far before you find a symbol. W.H. Auden said that fairy stories mean what they say, and nothing more; that seems to be true of Marin's world—a tree is a tree. At his best, Marin reminds you of eternal verities, and he transfers his experiences directly to the viewer. Putting on a fancy title now and then made him feel like one of the Stieglitz boys.

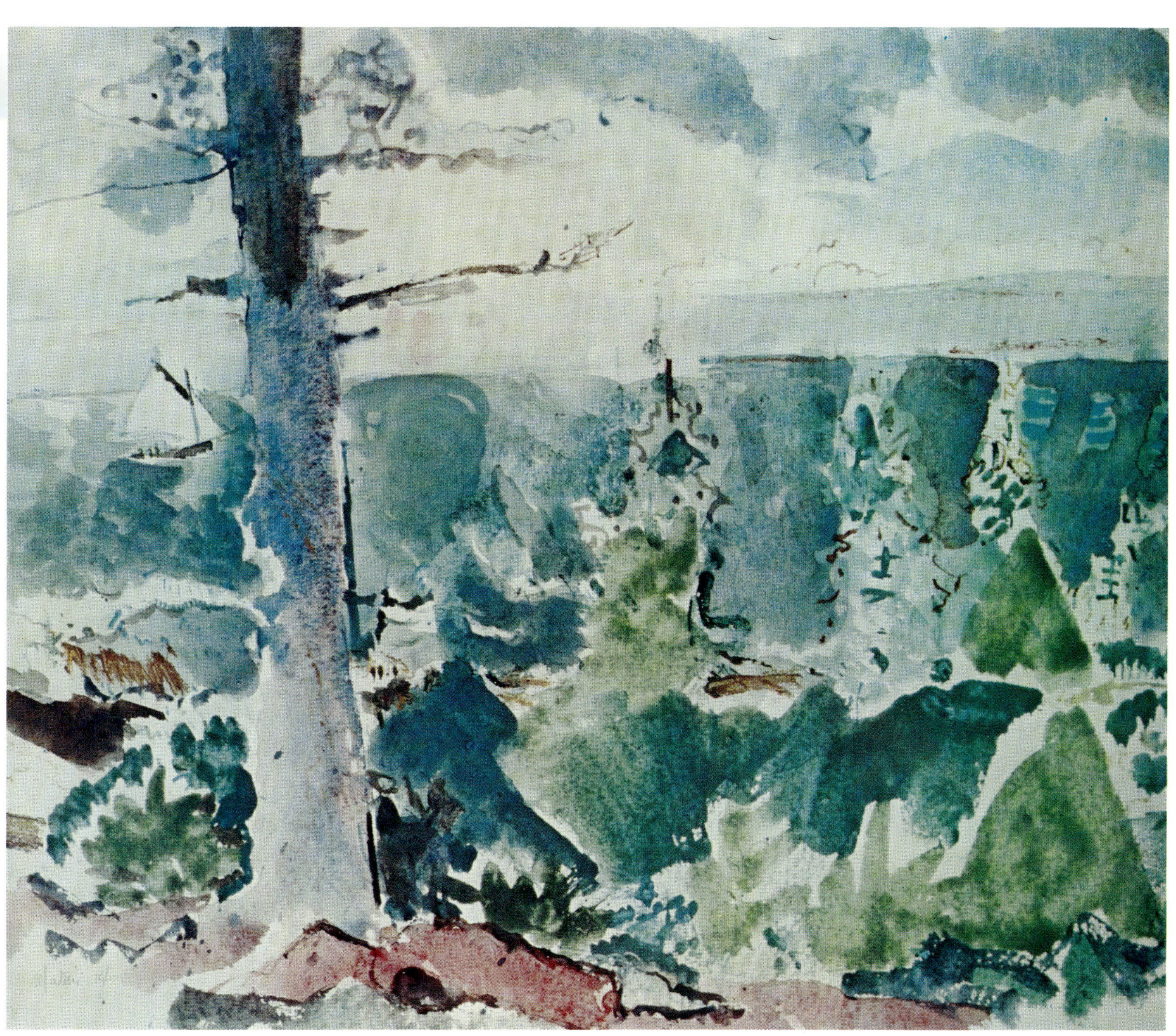

## *John Marin*

*Plate 3*
BREAKERS, MAINE COAST, 1917
*Watercolor, 15 7/8" X 18 5/8"*
*The Columbus Gallery of Fine Arts, Columbus, Ohio*
*Ferdinand Howald Collection*

Marin painted with both hands, and people said he looked like his watercolors. Certainly this painting is sufficiently jumpy, nervous, and excited. Marin liked to be close to the sea, almost in it. For people now, he conveys the feeling of the sea better than the professional surf painters, like Frederick Waugh, who were a great deal more popular than Marin at the time. But Marin's watercolors have always had their admirers, who saw in them immediately exactly what we see today. The originality of Marin's paintings never stood in their way.

There is much more action in Marin's *Breakers* than in the paintings by old-line surf-painters. There's a lot more going on in Marin. Maybe his action even gets a bit out of control, with a wild sense of things crashing and breaking apart. These waves aren't made of blue steel, they're made of foam and frenzy.

The surf is a surprising subject for watercolor, since use of this medium was usually limited to painting subjects for old ladies. Marin pushed watercolor about as far as it could go. His waves explode all over the place. Marin's ocean didn't have many calm days, since on those days he went off fishing, or took to the woods, which he didn't paint nearly as well as he did the sea. Every now and then things had to quiet down.

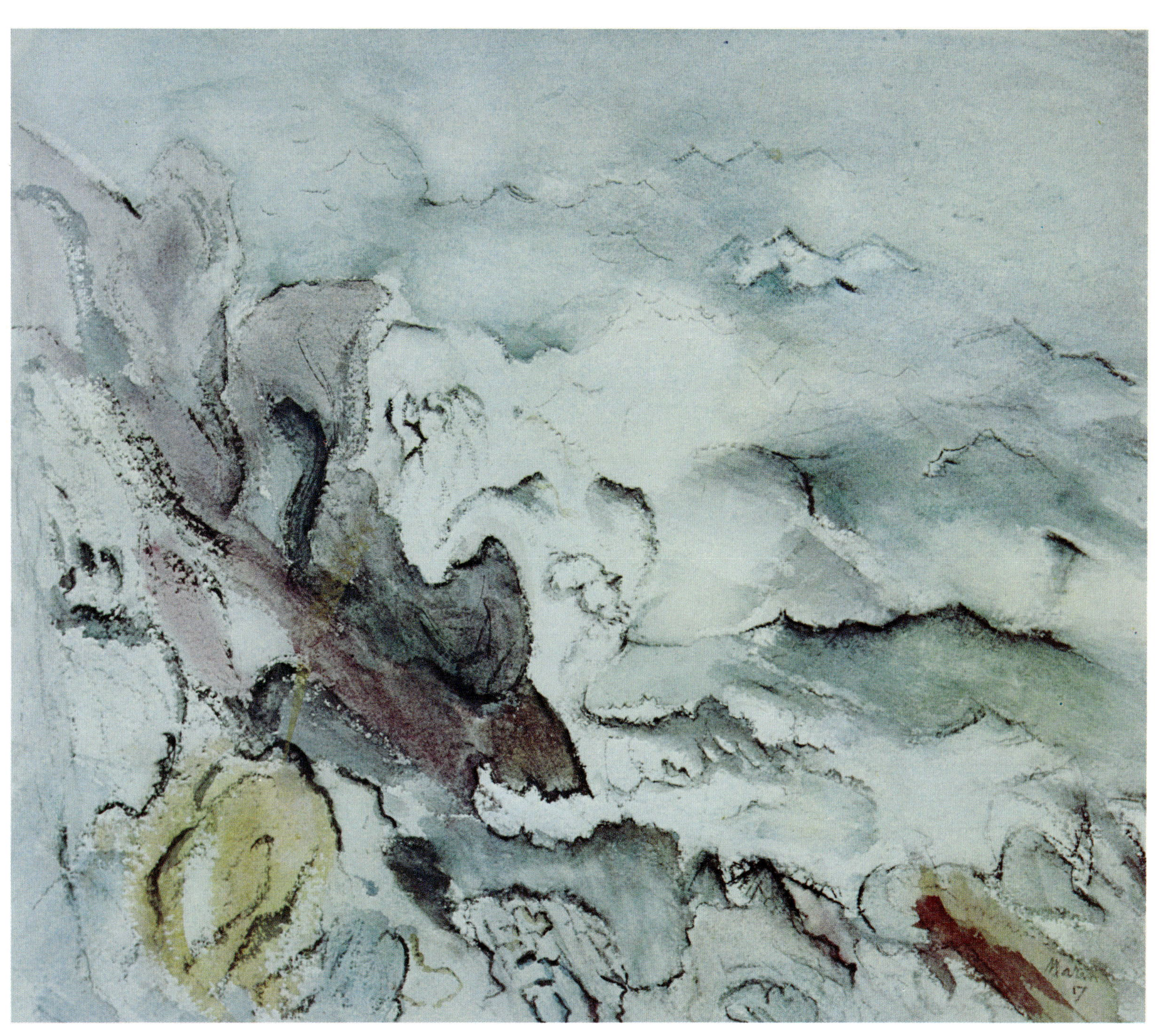

## *John Marin*

*Plate 4*
FROM THE OCEAN, 1919
*Watercolor, 16 1/8" X 19"*
*The Columbus Gallery of Fine Arts, Columbus, Ohio*
*Ferdinand Howald Collection*

The horizontal mass in the center of this painting is overwhelming. Marin tried to give more significance to this island than it can carry; as a matter of fact, the island seems less substantial than the dark sea around it. The sea itself is soggy and lacking in zip and zing. From the title, Marin seems to be trying to say that things look different from the sea, but his point doesn't come across too well.

This is a rather static Marin, not particularly characteristic of him. Ferdinand Howald, the man from Columbus, Ohio, who bought all these Marins, was one of those collectors who ruminate, and like to think they select paintings for profound reasons, when maybe it's just that something appealed to them that day. Howald was a very calm man and perhaps this painting's stillness appealed to him.

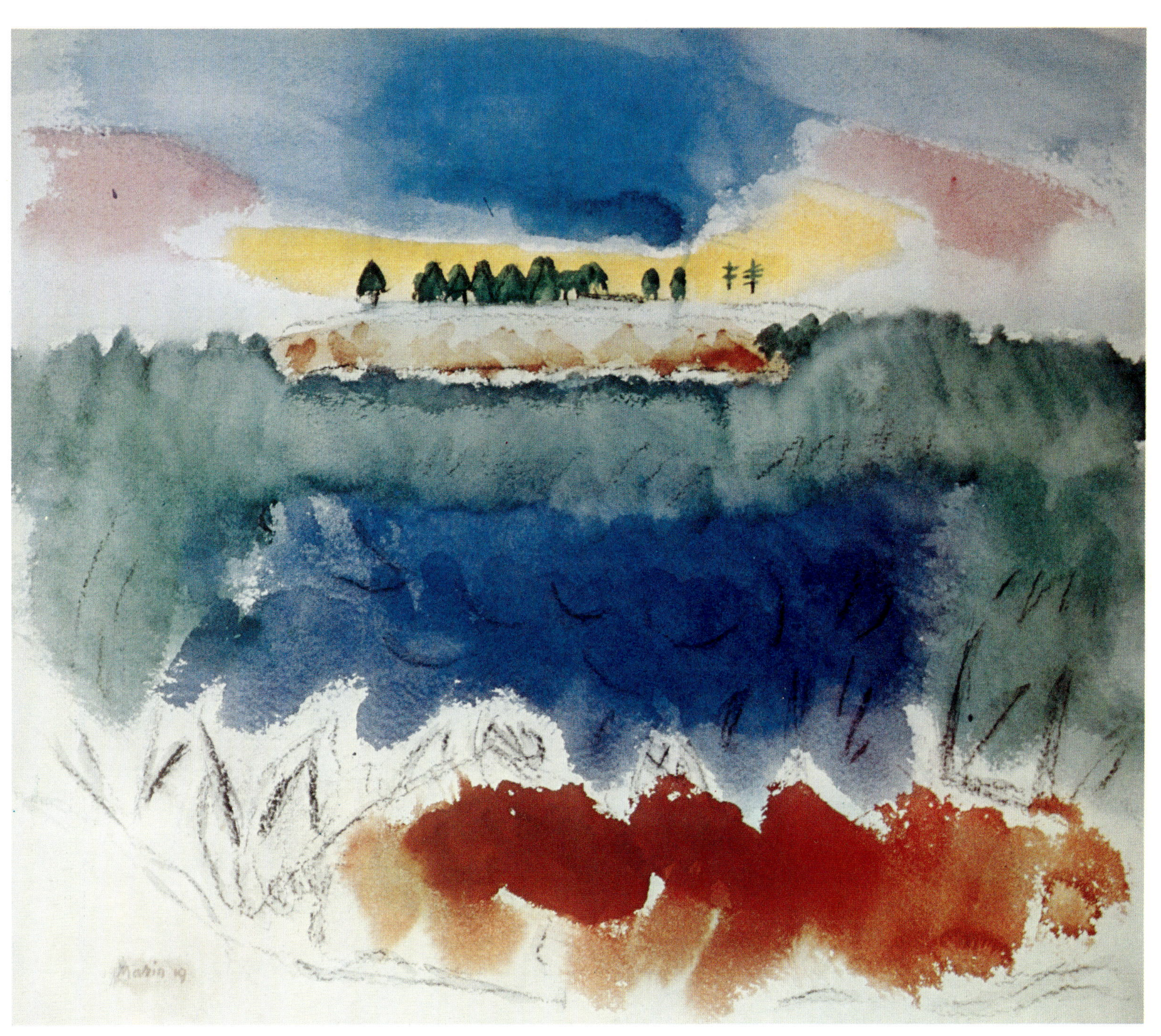
Marin 19

## *John Marin*

*Plate 5*
RED SUN, 1919
*Watercolor, 16 1/8" X 19"*
*The Columbus Gallery of Fine Arts, Columbus, Ohio*
*Ferdinand Howald Collection*

Marin liked strong color and violent effects. This wild and wooly watercolor looks as though Marin just dashed it off. His technique is far removed from the careful control of most watercolor painters. He tried to convey the drama of the sea and sky, and to a surprising extent he succeeded. Marin genuinely enjoyed stormy weather, but not enough to stay in Maine in the winter. Storms at sea are occasions for glee, as long as you're not in a boat.

Marin's output isn't that huge—he did just 3,000 paintings, the vast majority watercolors, during a very long life. Obviously, he loved what he was doing and was all wrapped up in his material, as was Turner at his amazing best. Marin's paintings have that quality of being a direct imprint of reality, of experience. He really *enjoyed* a squall or a sunset, and his directness makes Winslow Homer seem contrived.

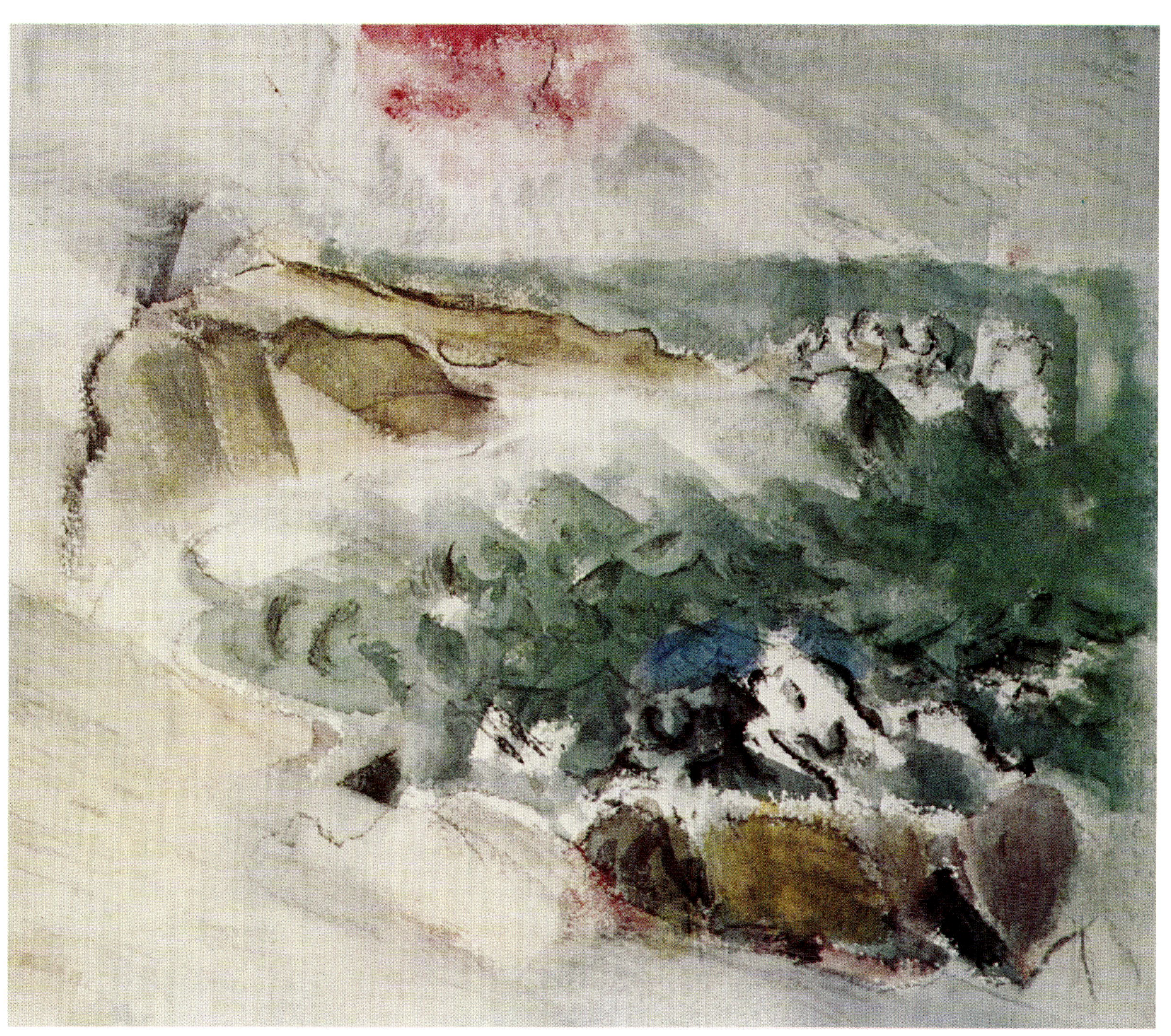

## *John Marin*

*Plate 6*
SUNSET, MAINE COAST, 1919
*Watercolor, 16 1/4" X 19 1/4"*
*The Columbus Gallery of Fine Arts, Columbus, Ohio*
*Ferdinand Howald Collection*

Nobody had ever painted a sunset like this. For Marin, this was what Maine was all about. There aren't any people in his pictures, just an occasional boat. He felt at home with nature, and he shared his elation through his paintings. Certainly Marin was exhilarated by this sunset. There's not much exhilaration in modern art, but Marin got his enthusiasm across very well. That's what he thought the artist was for.

This is one of his best. Where most watercolors are pale, this one is violent. And it's completely his own style, with a freedom and a force that nobody has come close to. Actually, Marin was a lot more free than painters are now. We like to talk about the direct technique of Abstract Impressionism, but many paintings of the fifties are conscious and contrived. This is one of Marin's triumphs, brilliant and hard-hitting.

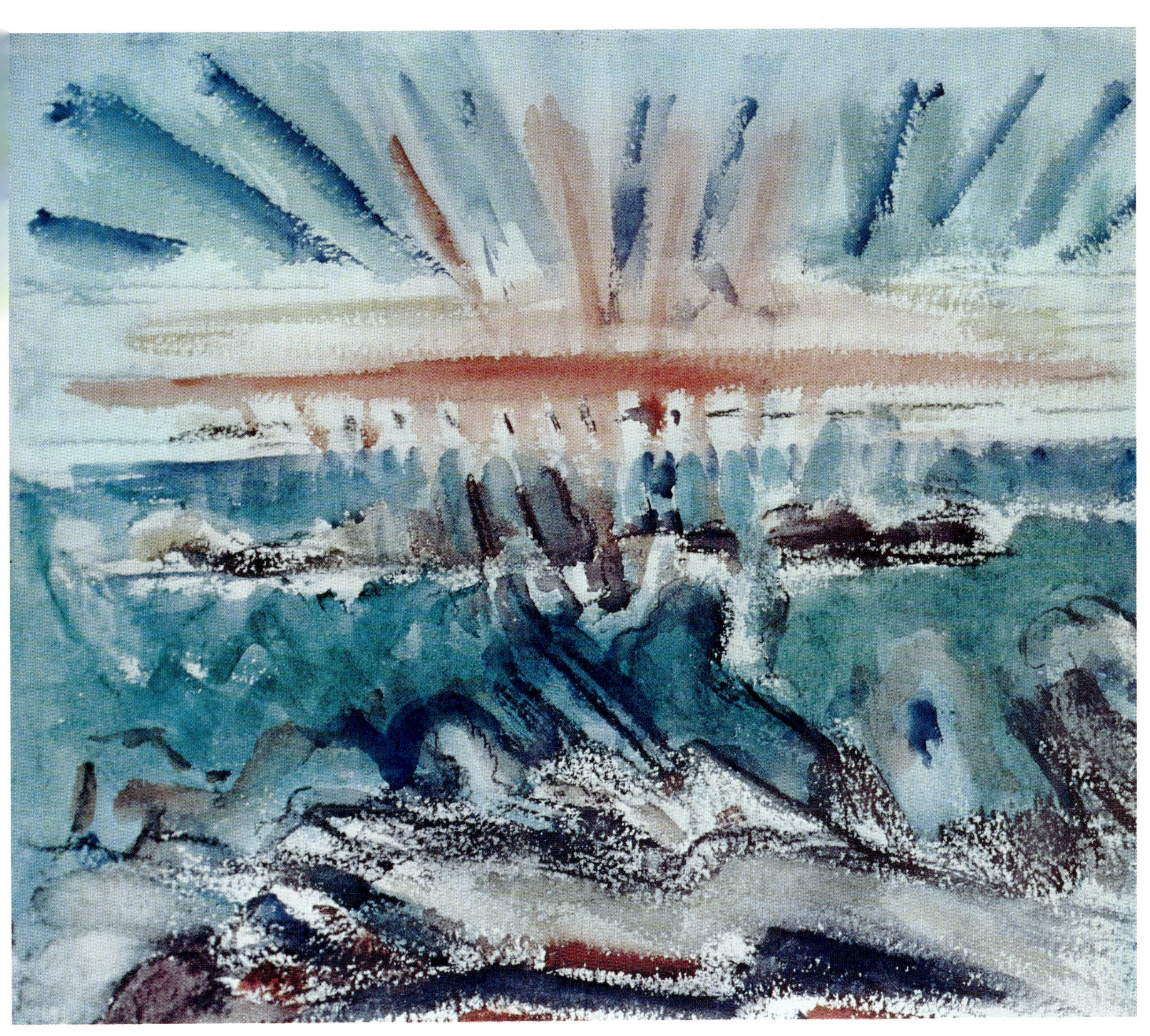

## *John Marin*

*Plate 7*
OFF STONINGTON, 1921
*Watercolor, 16 3/8" X 19 1/2"*
*The Columbus Gallery of Fine Arts, Columbus, Ohio*
*Ferdinand Howald Collection*

Marin's Maine was the coast with its fringe of islands, and he would have been a different artist if he'd never gone there. That bar in the sky isn't a cloud; it's there to stop the picture from running off the paper. He loved the little trees in the distance, but his real subject was the fight between the rocks and the water.

Marin's unusual picture structures give more life to a landscape than was there in the first place. His compositions jump all over the place; that's one of their great virtues. He certainly invented his own kind of Maine; the country you see on your summer vacation is far more placid.

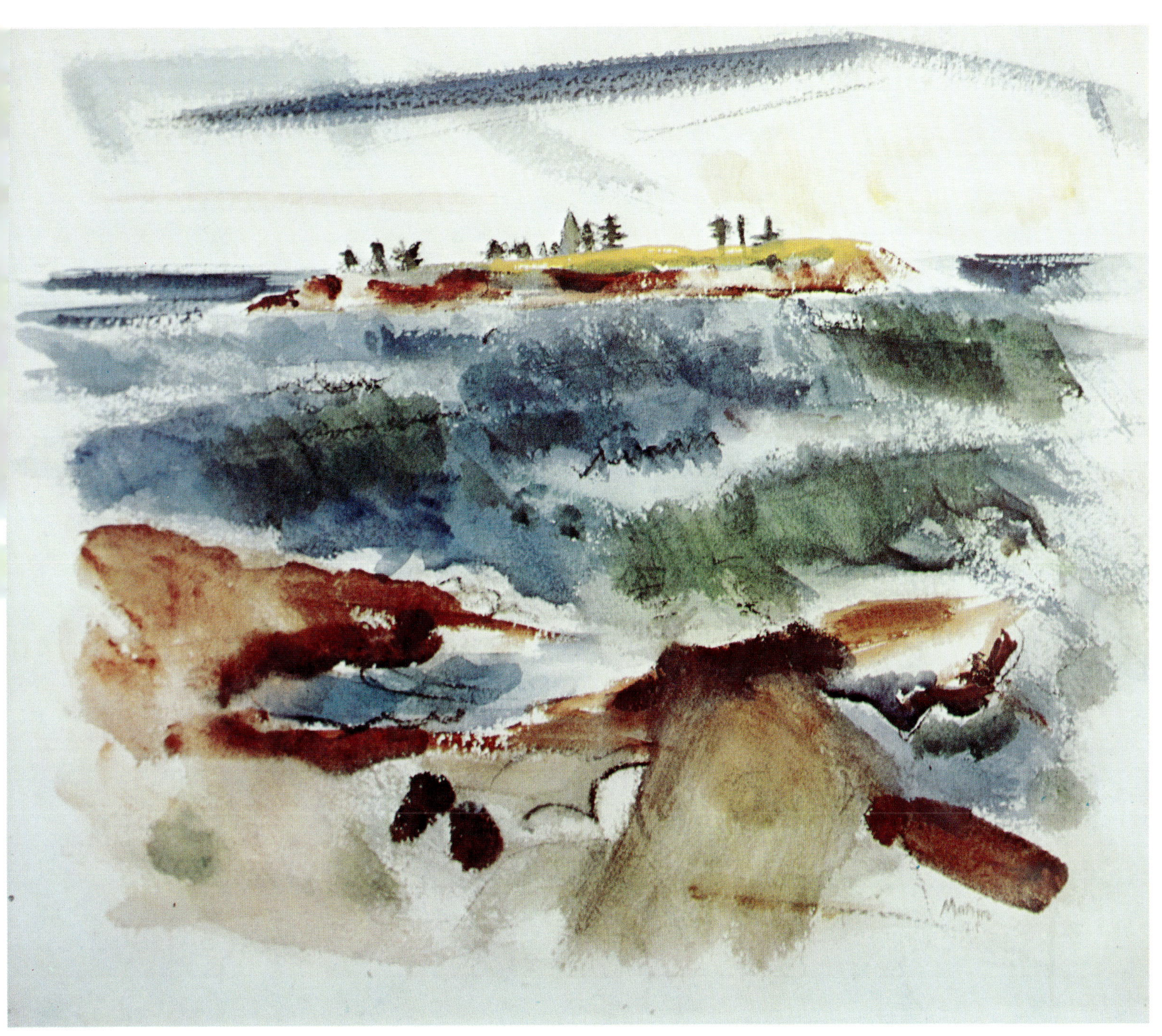

## *John Marin*

*Plate 8*
PALISADES, NO. 2, 1922
*Watercolor, 16" X 19 1/8"*
*The Columbus Gallery of Fine Arts, Columbus, Ohio*
*Ferdinand Howald Collection*

Marin lived along the Palisades, across from New York City, all his life, but he didn't do justice to their grandeur. Perhaps they were too familiar. His cliffs lack the dignity of the original. Here he has the Palisades jumping around in a squall, which is far from the fact. The Palisades are stern and forbidding, but Marin makes them look irresponsible. He did a lot of watercolors of the Palisades, but he never really got the hang of them.

For all his air of improvisation, Marin wasn't a sketch artist; he didn't dash these off on the spot and slip his pad back into his pocket. He worked hard for his spontaneity. Perhaps his view of the Palisades isn't what *you'd* see, but it certainly is lively.

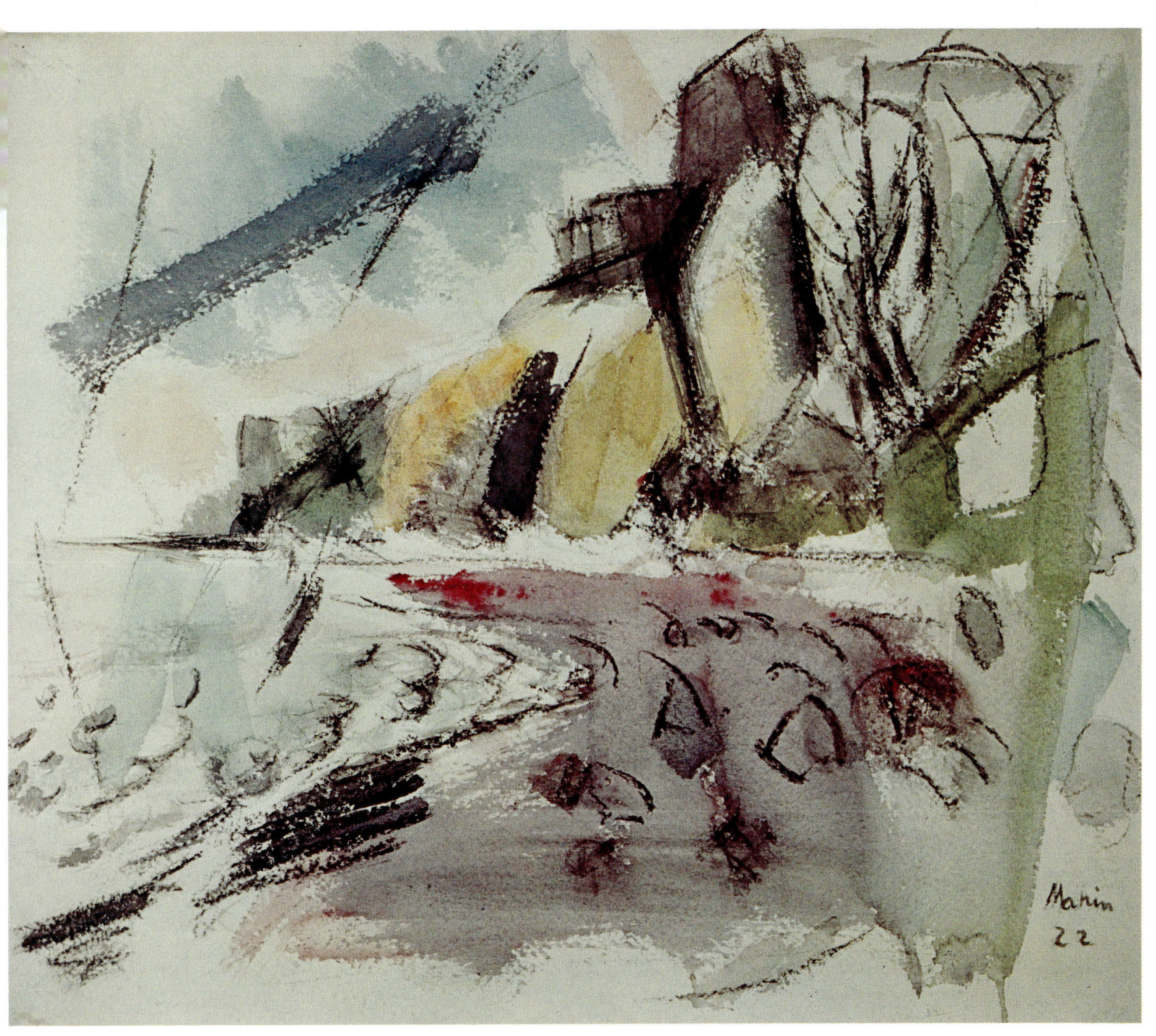
Marin
22

## *John Marin*

*Plate 9*
SAILBOAT IN HARBOR, 1922
*Watercolor, 13 1/2" X 17"*
*The Columbus Gallery of Fine Arts, Columbus Ohio*
*Ferdinand Howald Collection*

Here Marin's interior frame takes over the picture, and we're seeing the captured boat through a porthole. Marin was more interested in the composition than in the objects; he was trying to capture an essence. It's hard to say what this angular shape means, but it gives a menacing sense of drive to a calm ship and a calm sea. Marin could get excited when there was nothing to get excited about, and we go along with him.

This watercolor comes off very well; in fact, it's one of the most effective he ever painted. Ferdinand Howald knew what he was doing when he picked this one; Marin was going strong, and he couldn't miss.

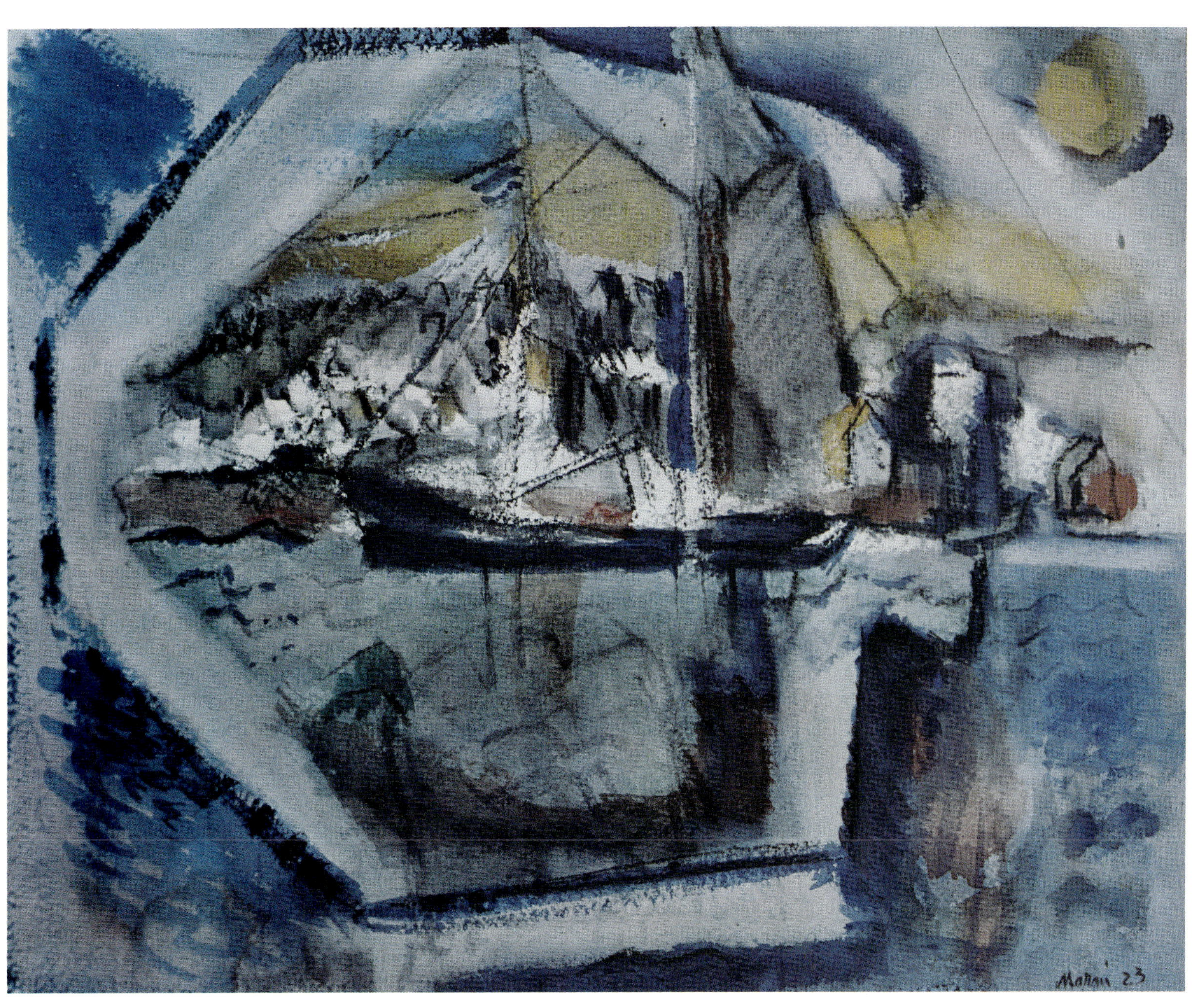
Marin 23

## *John Marin*

*Plate 10*
IMPRESSION, 1923
*Watercolor, 17 1/2" X 21 1/4"*
*The Columbus Gallery of Fine Arts, Columbus, Ohio*
*Ferdinand Howald Collection*

Marin's work is more immediate than the careful piling-up of effects of the real Impressionists. By *impression*, he meant a rapid glimpse of the sea and sky. This painting gives a splendid sense of the storm breaking up; maybe it's the view from Marin's window, where he was snug and safe.

Marin must have enjoyed looking at this picture in the winter, when he was cooped up on the Jersey side of the Hudson. This was the Maine that he loved; he wasn't too happy away from the sea. He didn't really have any business painting in New Mexico, and he knew it. For the most part, Marin had the good sense to stick to what he did best. He had a narrow talent and a narrow subject, but he made something big out of both of them.

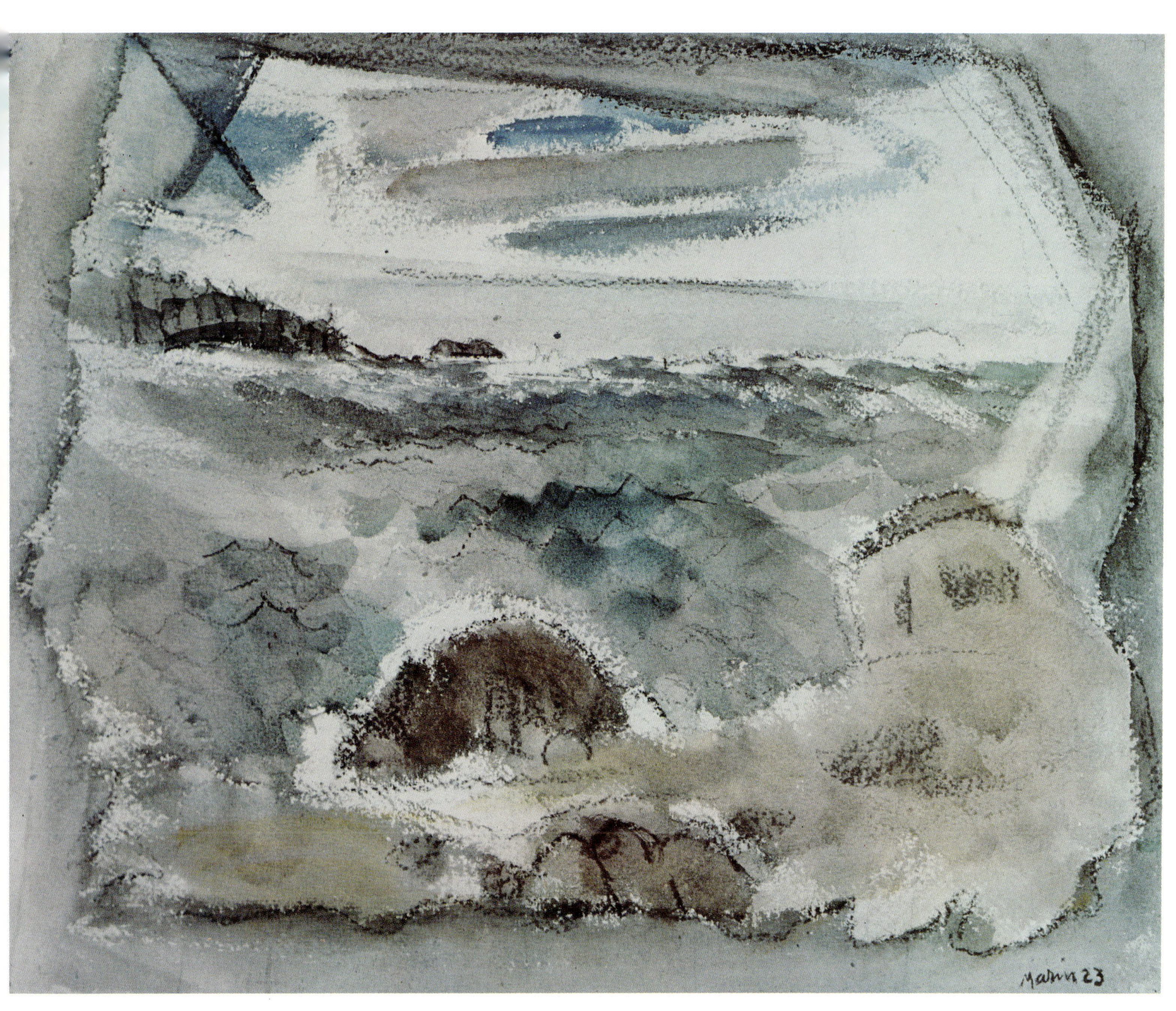
Marin 23

## *John Marin*

*Plate 11*
SHIP, SEA AND SKY FORMS, AN IMPRESSION, 1923
*Watercolor, 17″ X 13 1/2″*
*The Columbus Gallery of Fine Arts, Columbus, Ohio*
*Ferdinand Howald Collection*

This is another one of his hits, a winner. It's vibrant and full of life. These paintings never bore you, that's for sure. There's too much life; too much going on.

A sailing ship at sea in rough weather; that's exciting every time. The sky forms, which he put in afterwards, became strikingly important in his work. Those bare clouds don't mean a thing, but they gave him a dramatic shape. They contain the action; they *are* the action.

Marin jumps at his subject, and it jumps at him. He doesn't seem to have had preconceived ideas of how things should look. He seems to have painted them bang-off, as though the whole thing just occurred to him, but it wasn't all that easy.

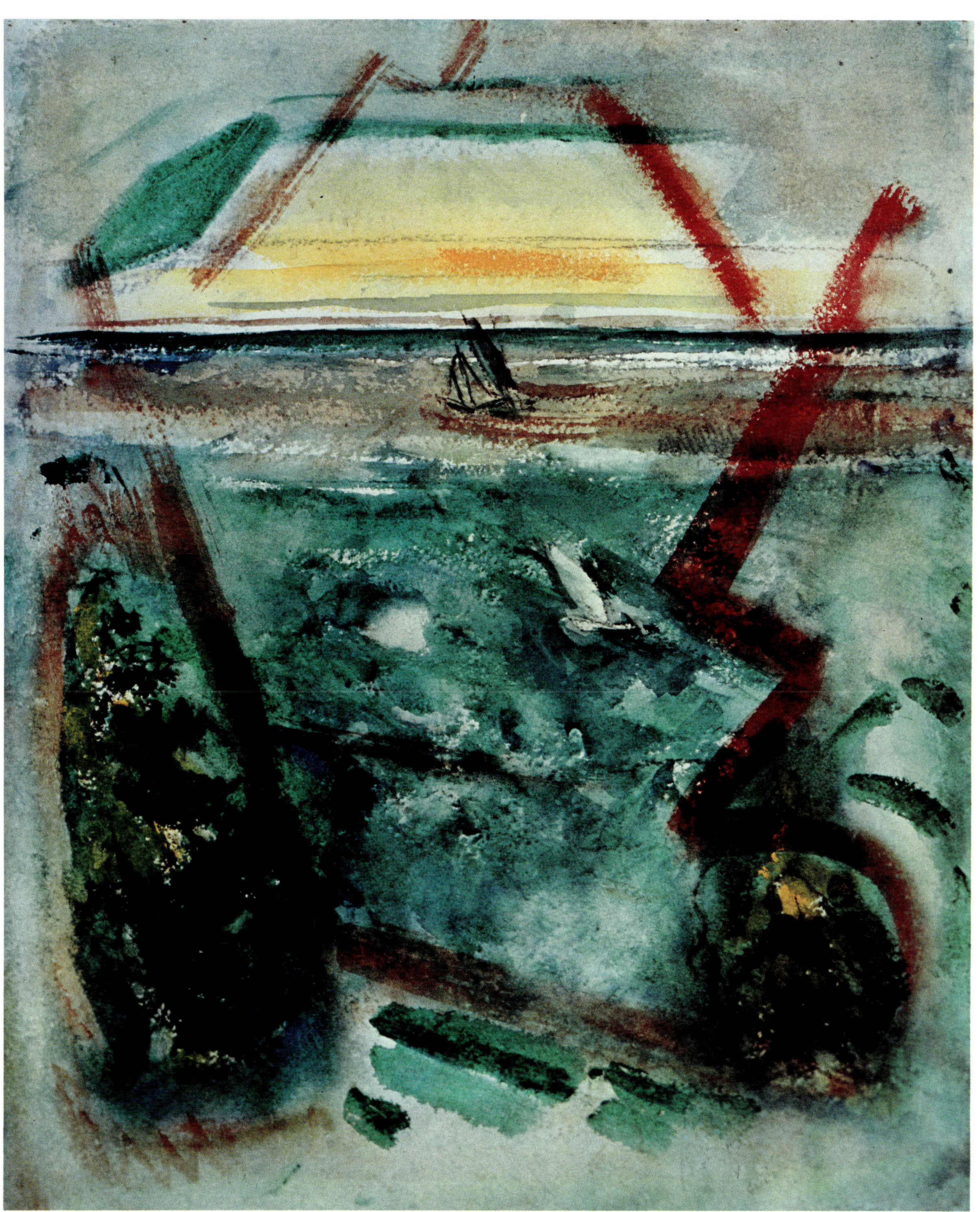

## *Charles Demuth*

*Plate 12*
THE DRINKERS, 1915
*Watercolor, 10 3/4" X 8 1/4"*
*The Columbus Gallery of Fine Arts, Columbus, Ohio*
*Ferdinand Howald Collection*

Drinking was a subject that Demuth understood. He behaved pretty well in Lancaster despite the availability of Lancaster rye, so the scene in this watercolor is probably New York. Liquor wasn't particularly a problem to Demuth. It gave him a chance to get away from his mother and his limp, and it shook off his repressions. There's a sinister air about this saloon; they weren't all cheerful places. His favorites in New York were the Hell Hole and Jimmy the Priest's. The alcoholic expansion is convincing, and so is the superior barkeep, but the man on the right has his head on backwards.

Demuth was the only one of the Stieglitz bunch who had an eye for drama; his paintings often seem to tell a story when there isn't one. Maybe there were stories he didn't tell. He had them, heaven knows, for he was a secretive type, not exactly all on the surface. He was a private artist, just as he was a private person, and he didn't want to give too much away. But he was good at suggesting that there was more than met the eye, or that something had just happened or was about to happen. He liked it that way.

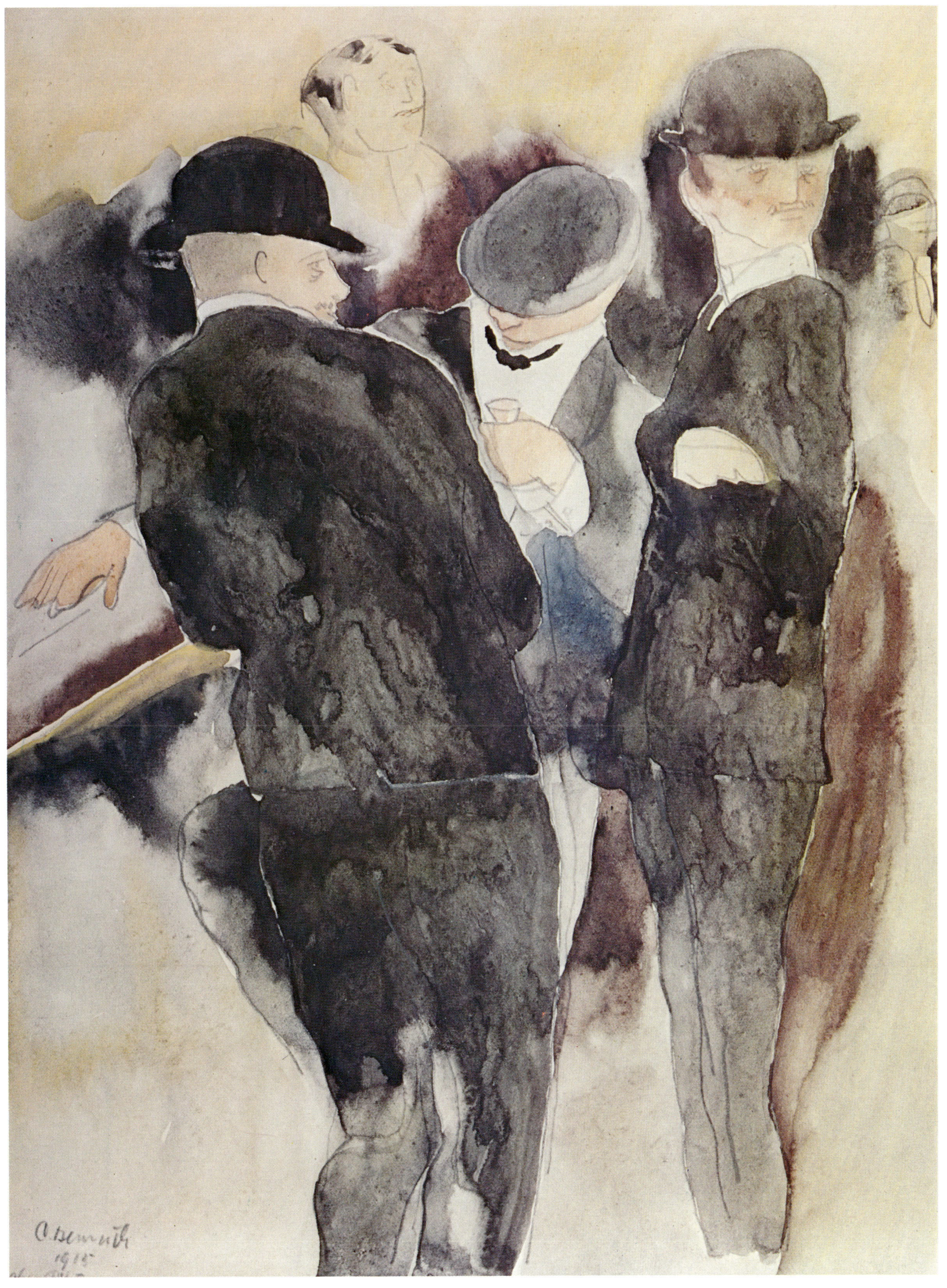

## *Charles Demuth*

*Plate 13*
THE NUT, PRE-VOLSTEAD DAYS, 1916
*Watercolor, 10 9/16" X 7 13/16"*
*The Columbus Gallery of Fine Arts, Columbus, Ohio*
*Ferdinand Howald Collection*

The crackpot at the bar isn't a happy drunk, and neither was Demuth. The only people who have their heads on straight are those behind the bar, and they're not drinking. There's a story here, but we don't know what it is. Things are going badly for the nut, and he'll have trouble getting out of this one.

Gertrude Stein was impressed by Demuth because he was one of the very few people who was interested in the plays she was writing. He was always talking about them, she said, which doesn't seem like him, but then, her memory wasn't too good since she insisted that she had never seen him after World War I. His interest in her early work is understandable. Here was somebody trying to say subtle things in an oblique way. It was Gertrude Stein's early work that he knew, and it is doubtful that he would have been so taken by the public performer she later became. Her world wasn't Demuth's world at all. He was a lurker in the shadows, and so are the people he painted—queer birds and shifty types in desperate bars.

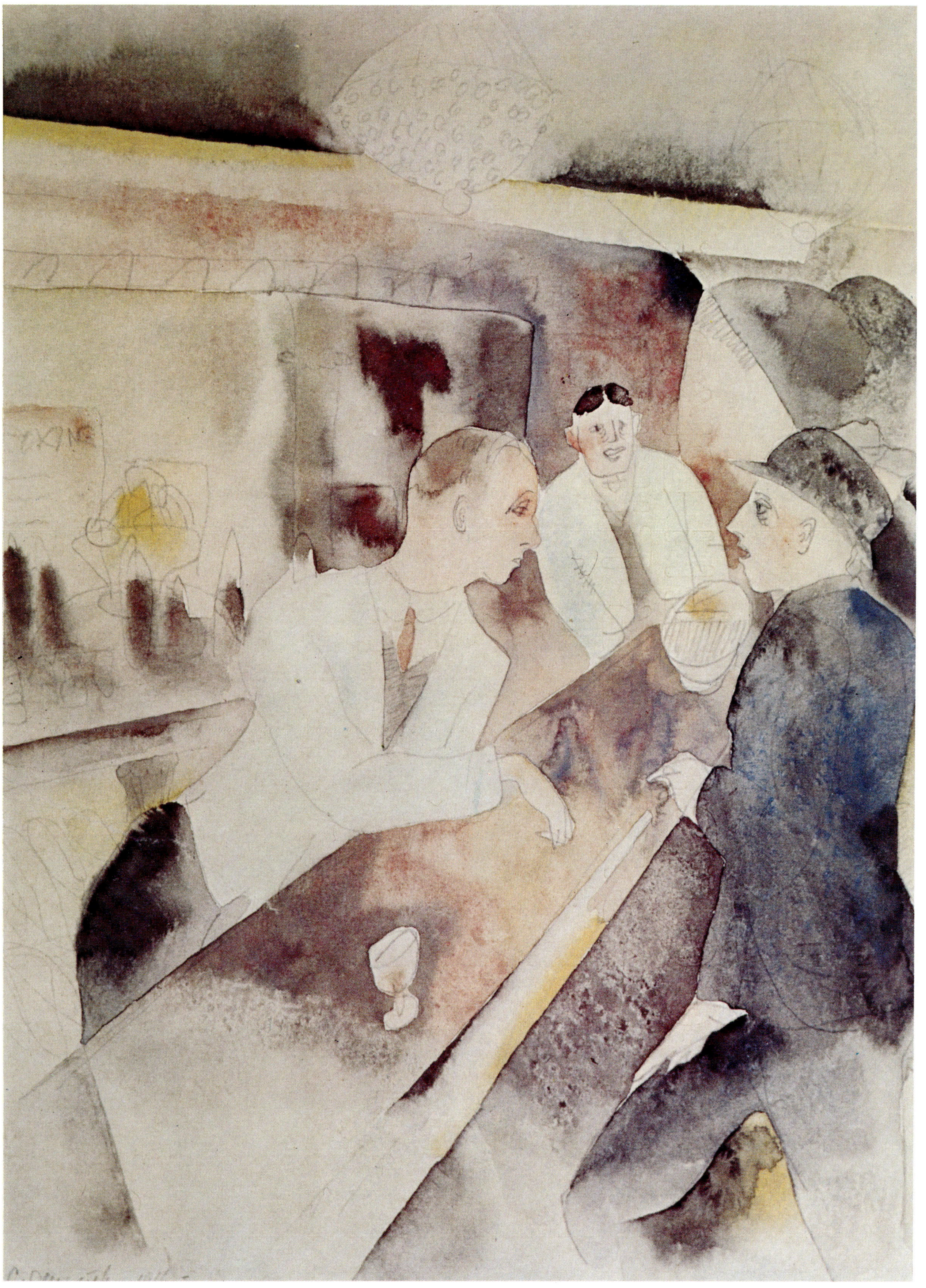

*Charles Demuth*

Plate 14
THE CIRCUS, 1917
*Watercolor, 8" X 10 5/8"*
*The Columbus Gallery of Fine Arts, Columbus, Ohio*
*Ferdinand Howald Collection*

Demuth drew a lot of circus and vaudeville performers, favorite subjects with artists from Daumier through Degas. Demuth caught the suspense very well, and the strain. He was interested in what the acrobats were doing rather than the spectacle; it was deadly serious for them, and so it was to Demuth. He understood the fear of falling. These strange people fascinated him the way they did Lautrec.

This is no Barnum and Bailey world, with oompah bands and daring young men on the flying trapeze. It's the one-ring world of the French circus, where you can see the performers tremble and sweat. It's a faintly sinister world, or Demuth made it so. French clowns—even the Fratellini, famous in Demuth's time—have a highly disquieting side, with their sinister smiles, their very real kicks in the pants, and their appalling practical jokes.

Demuth was not a spectacle man, he did not care for the hurrah and the roar of the crowd. It was the psychological strain that fascinated him; he knew how he would feel if he was up there.

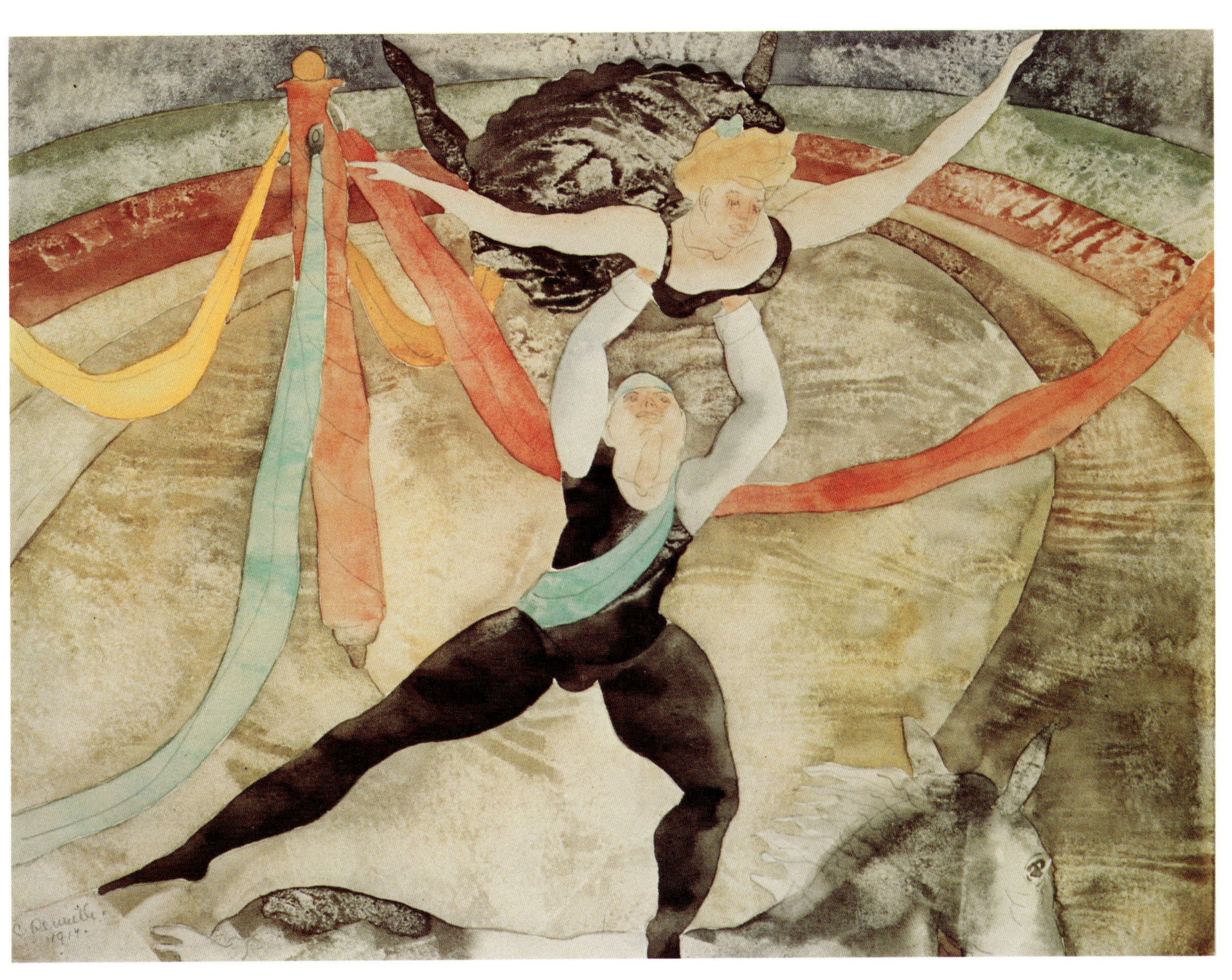

***Charles Demuth***

*Plate 15*
COLUMBIA, 1919
*Watercolor, 11 15/16″ X 8″*
*The Columbus Gallery of Fine Arts, Columbus, Ohio*
*Ferdinand Howald Collection*

Columbia looks as though she started out as Marianne or La Belle France. Demuth didn't take kindly to the patriotic hullabaloo of the Great War. Columbia, the Army, and the Navy all look the worse for wear, as though they had been out on the town. Demuth was a witty man, and a great one for private jokes; this lady is no "gem of the ocean," nor does she have anything to do with Columbia, Pennsylvania, next door to Demuth's hometown.

This is Demuth's nightlife side, prowling about in odd corners, and this may well be a vaudeville turn. Demuth could see humor where there wasn't any; in fact, that's where he preferred to find it. He liked stray spots of light in unaccustomed places, and he could find mystery in center stage. The world struck him as menacing, and in the beginning, he liked it. Later, when the menace to his health was real, he didn't like it a bit.

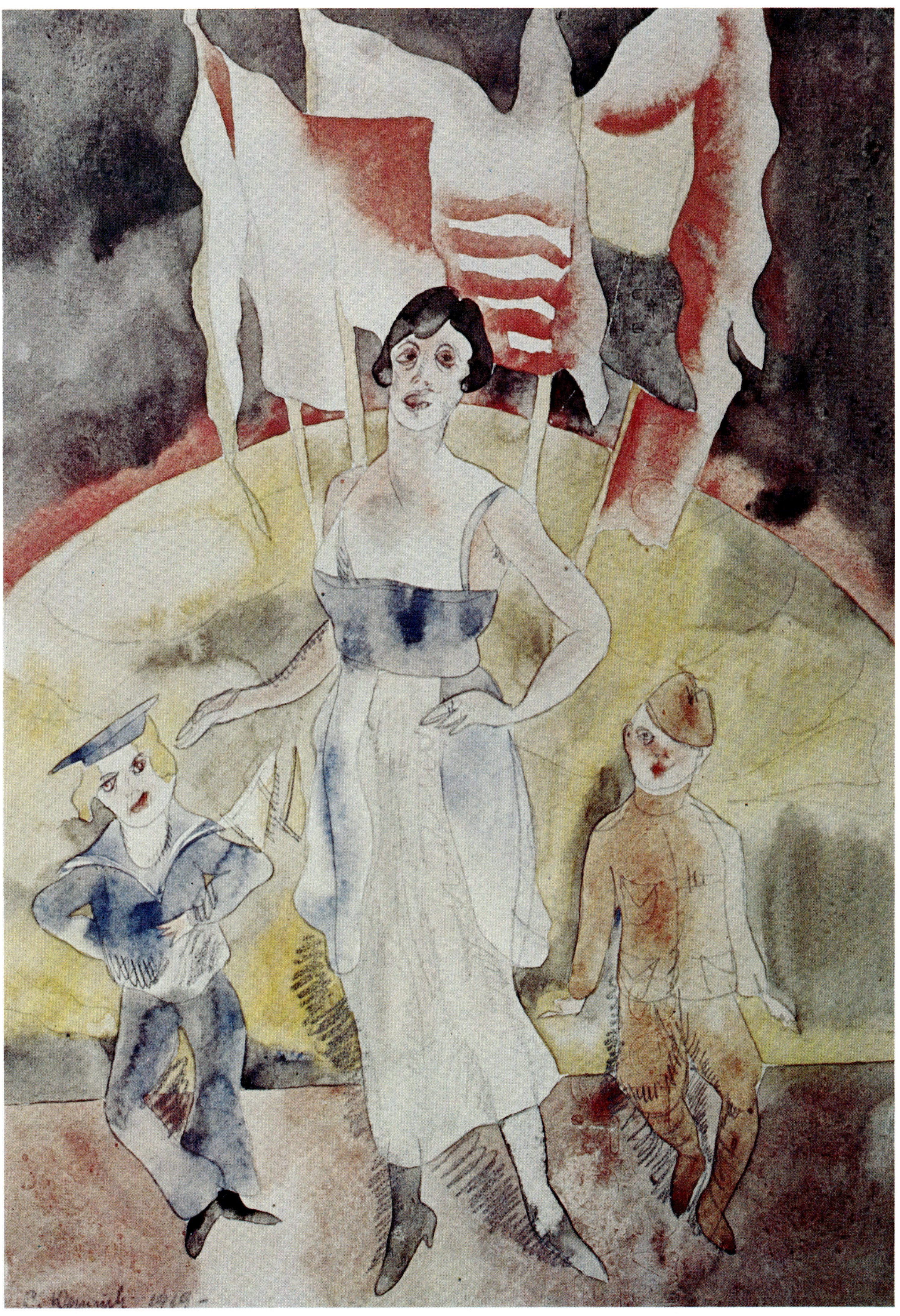

*Charles Demuth*

*Plate 16*
FLOWERS, 1919
*Watercolor, 13 3/4" X 9 11/16"*
*The Columbus Gallery of Fine Arts, Columbus, Ohio*
*Ferdinand Howald Collection*

Demuth's mother was a great gardener, but he made his own garden. His flowers are as different from Georgia O'Keeffe's as Taos is distant from Lancaster. His flowers are vaguely sinister, but still, they exemplify his sureness and delicacy of touch. Everyone who knew Demuth, talks about his elegance, which you see in these flowers; the best his people can achieve is a kind of dapper desperation. There's a lot of beauty in Demuth's world, but his people are a rum and crummy lot.

This is Demuth's Lancaster life—prim and proper—as opposed to prowling around Provincetown and Paris. At least he could recover his health in Lancaster, what there was of it. Demuth had a real predilection for murky situations, the kind that can lead to real trouble.

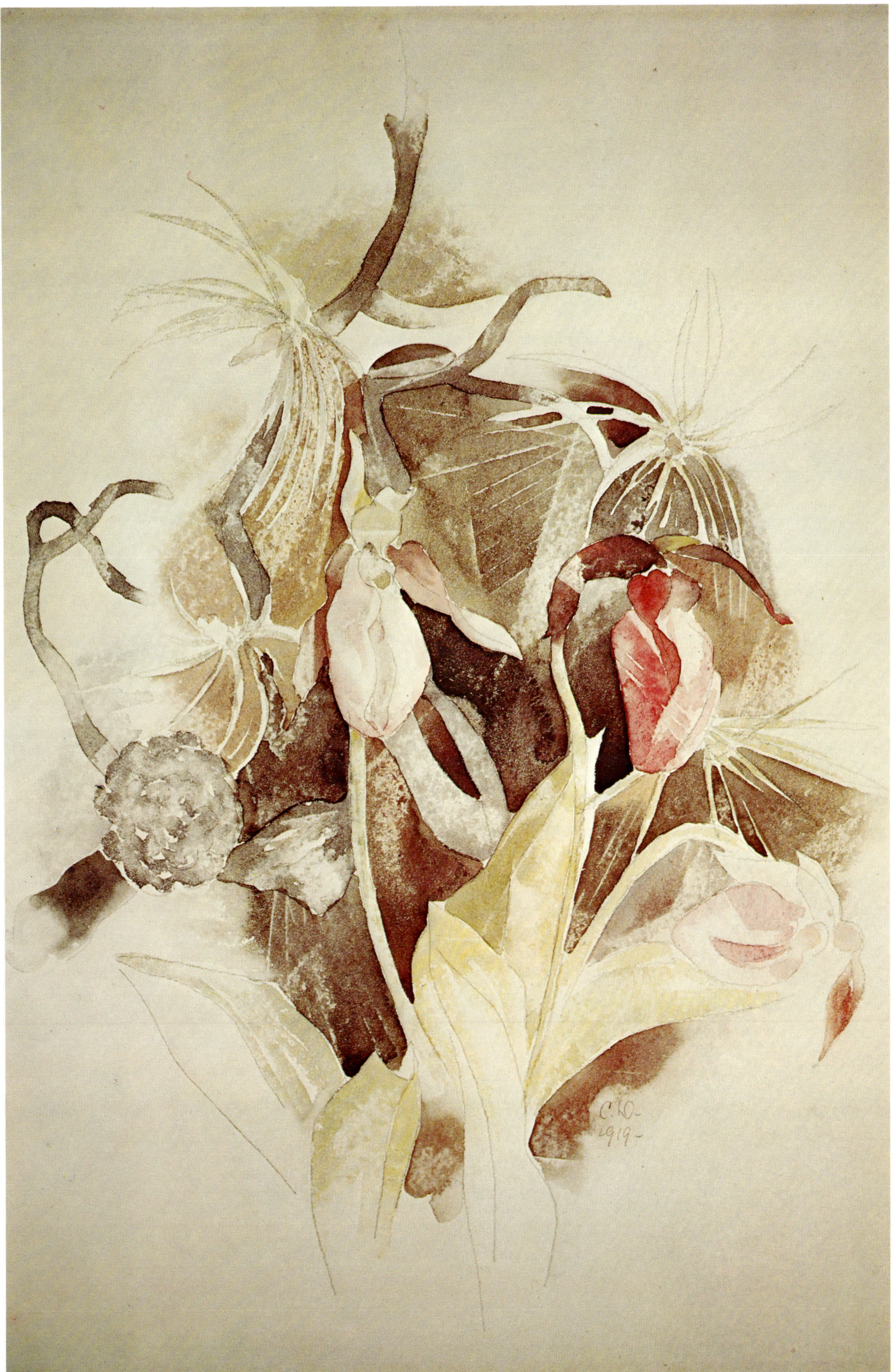
C.D.
1919

*Charles Demuth*

*Plate 17*
THE TOWER, 1920
*Tempera on pasteboard, 23″ X 19 7/16″*
*The Columbus Gallery of Fine Arts, Columbus, Ohio*
*Ferdinand Howald Collection*

This is the kind of picture on which Demuth's fame now rests. Hartley speaks of "the quaint and typical house" in which Demuth lived, and "the so typical church that forms one of the best of his subjects in his larger paintings." Demuth was fascinated by the buildings of Lancaster, which is a handsome city with wide streets, brick houses, and white churches. His architectural paintings have a solidity and order that is lacking in his boneless figures. Here he found simplicity, and flat surfaces that he could push around. Buildings have a pleasing lack of psychological twists. His architecture soars, which is more than can be said for his people. And the buildings gave him a chance to play with planes, angles, and flatnesses.

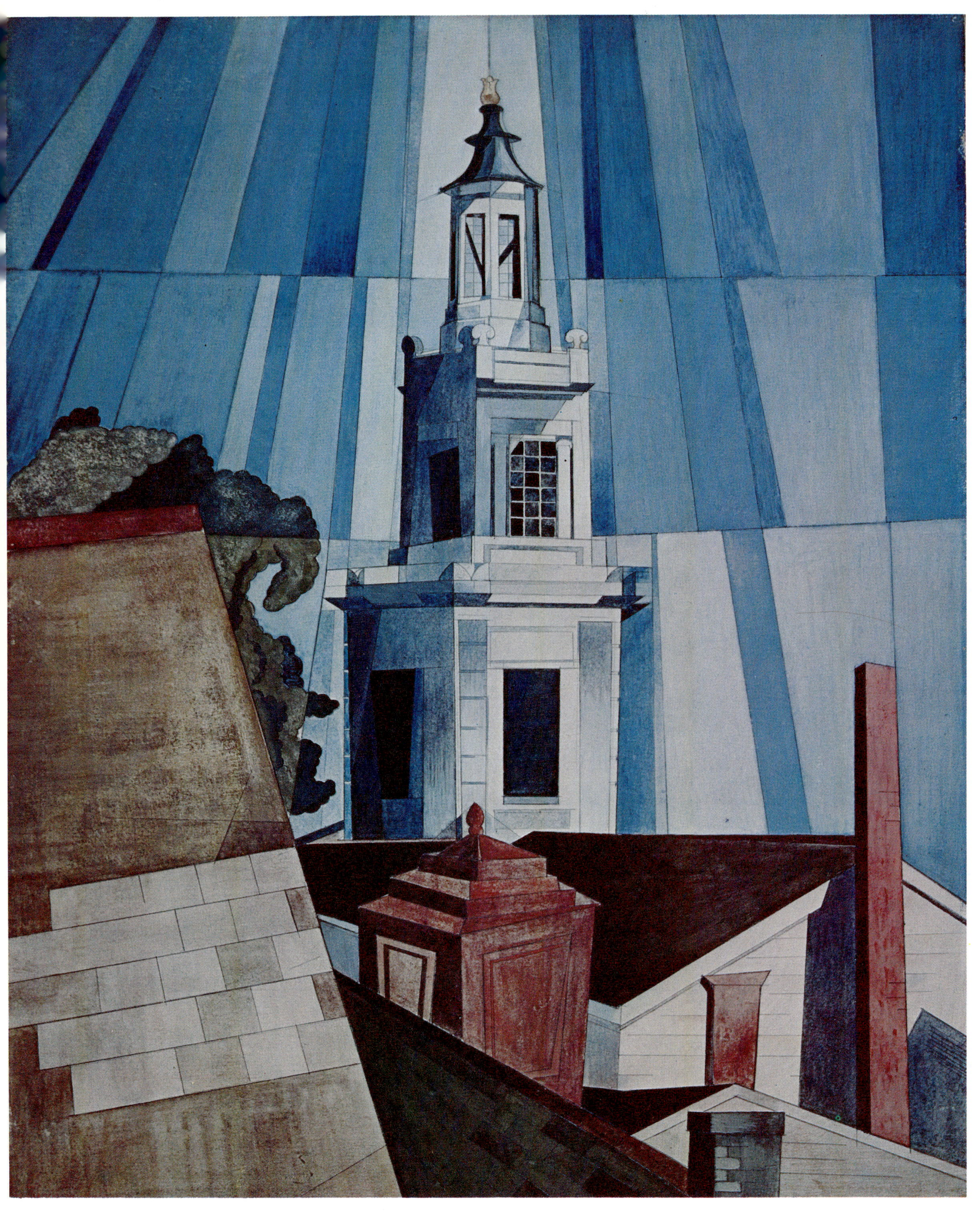

***Charles Demuth***

*Plate 18*
AUCASSIN AND NICOLETTE, 1921
*Oil on Canvas, 23 9/16" X 19 1/2"*
*The Columbus Gallery of Fine Arts, Columbus, Ohio*
*Ferdinand Howald Collection*

Demuth was a pioneer in industrial archeology, though the term hadn't yet been invented. He could make a lot out of a ladder and a pair of old smokestacks. In those days old factories weren't considered picturesque, but Demuth could see their good points from a compositional point of view. His extended lines don't add much to the picture, but they were important to him, and certainly they made the picture seem modern; the Stieglitz painters liked to remind you that they were well up front.

Demuth came straight out of the nineties into modern art. He was an esthete, and villanelles, ballades, and the medievel romance *Aucassin and Nicolette* were his meat. He made the transition very well, but his heart was closer to Proust than to Picasso. Considering how foreign these smokestacks were to him, he did remarkably well with this painting, perhaps because he could see it as something completely outside himself.

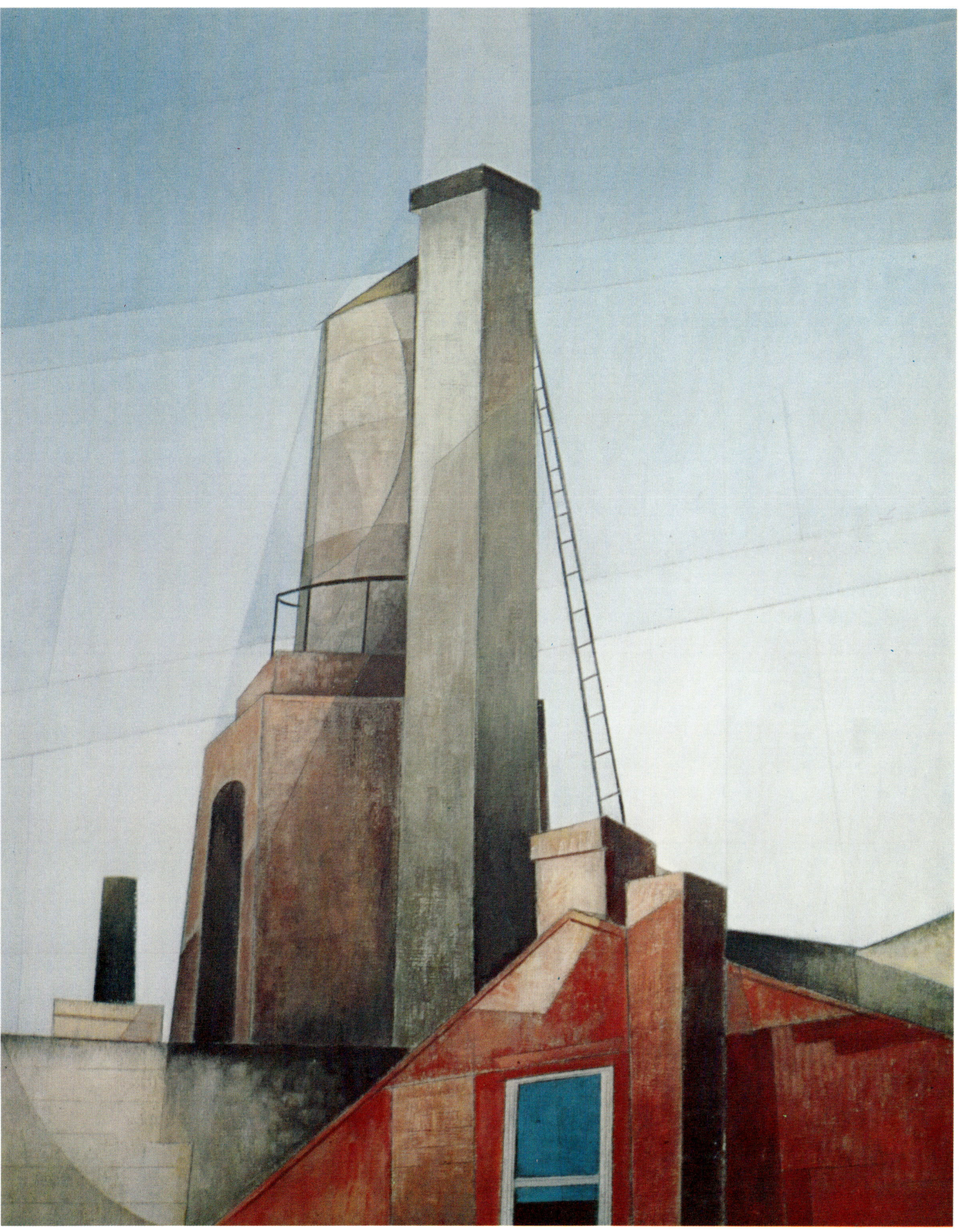

*Charles Demuth*

*Plate 19*
INCENSE OF A NEW CHURCH, 1921
*Oil on Canvas, 25 1/2" X 19 13/16"*
*The Columbus Gallery of Fine Arts, Columbus, Ohio*
*Ferdinand Howald Collection*

Demuth was never a firm believer in the new church of heavy industry, and he wasn't genuinely fascinated by the enormous bulk and power of factories. Even his fellow Precisionist, Charles Sheeler, painted them mainly on commission, while his heart was in Shaker furniture and a Bucks County barn.

Lancaster isn't a heavy industry town, but Demuth didn't have trouble finding smokestacks in Pennsylvania. In the good old days they really had pollution. This is Demuth's darkest and most depressing picture, though he put some wry wit in the title. The contrast between the upright smokestacks and the curving forms in front is only partly convincing. Demuth paid tribute to the iron age, but he didn't like it. Hartley felt that Demuth's special personal tone had been formed by the ultra-sophisticated post-1890 period. His heart was in the old church of pale beauty.

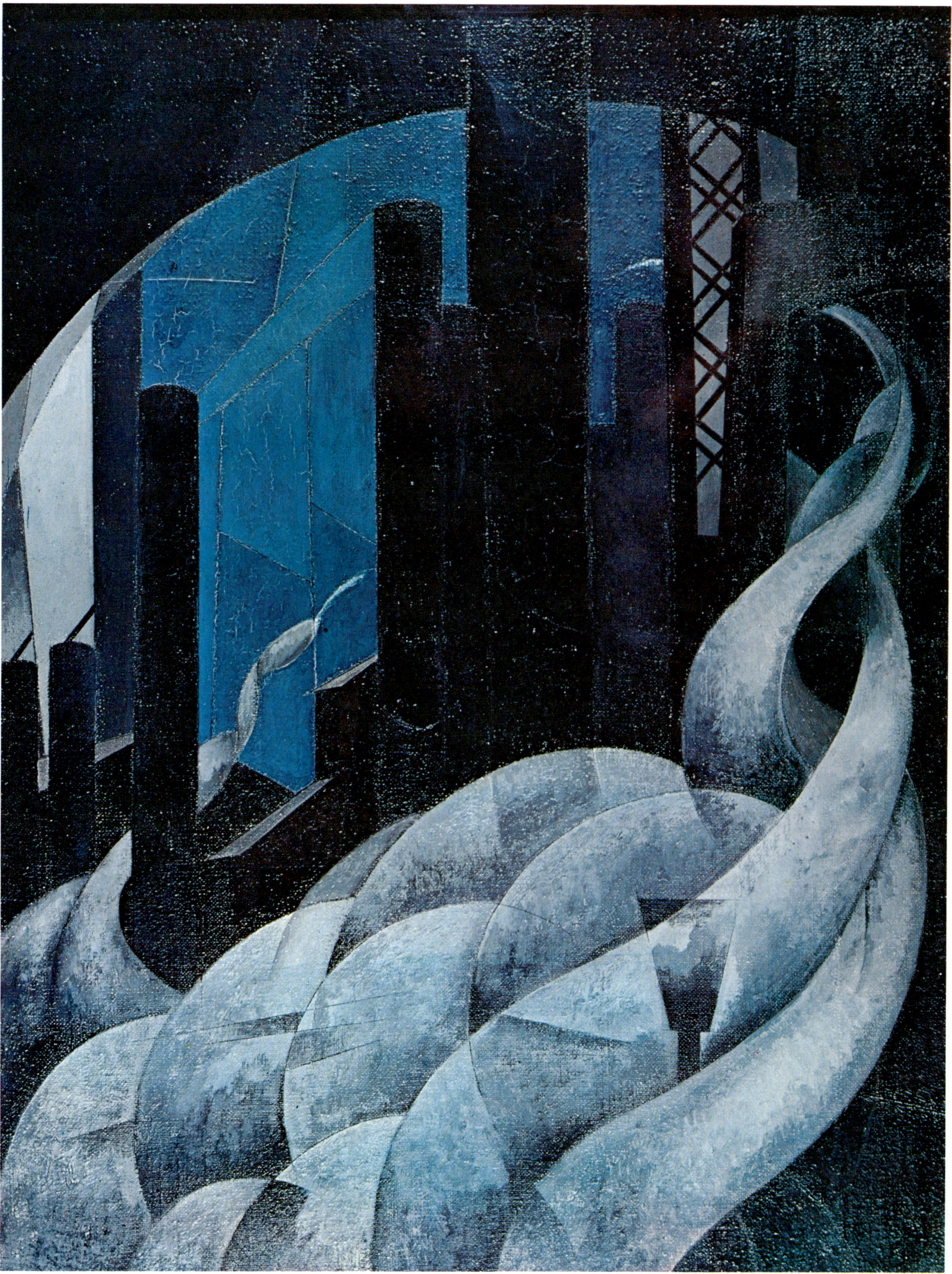

*Charles Demuth*

*Plate 20*
MODERN CONVENIENCES, 1921
*Oil on Canvas, 25 7/16" X 20 15/16"*
*The Columbus Gallery of Fine Arts, Columbus, Ohio*

Like the other Stieglitz artists, Demuth liked a tricky title, but what fascinated him here was the angle, for a stairway makes Cubism come true. You can call this Cubist realism if you want to.

Demuth had a wonderful view from his hotel room in Paris, but he had the good sense not to paint the rooftops of Paris; they've been done. He got many of his best subjects by just looking out the window in Lancaster, for what he saw had never been painted, although artists had been living in Colonial towns since Colonial days. These Lancaster subjects are the best things Demuth ever did, and they justify his reputation.

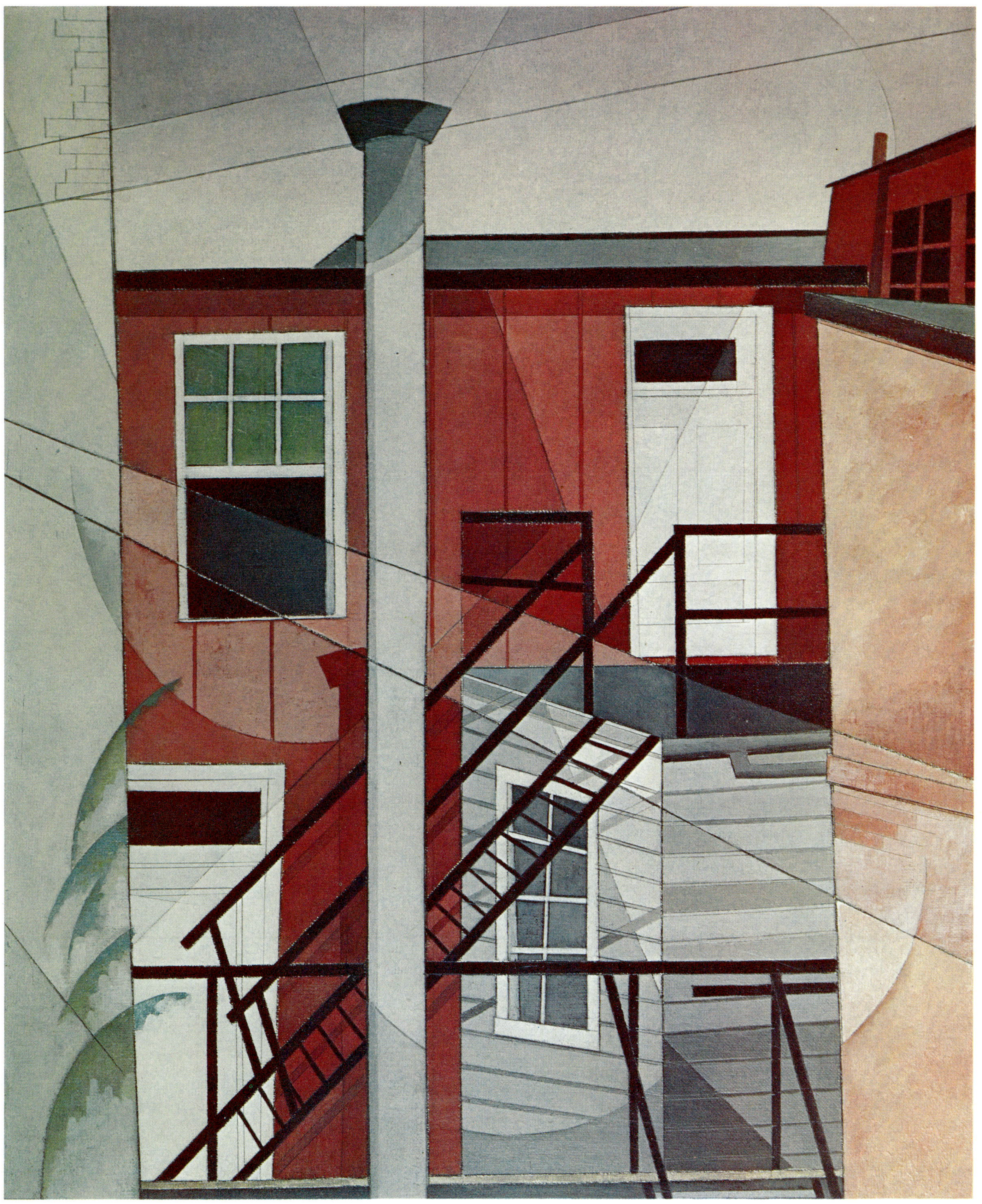

*Charles Demuth*

*Plate 21*
PAQUEBOT PARIS, 1921
*Oil on Canvas, 24 1/2" X 19 7/16"*
*The Columbus Gallery of Fine Arts, Columbus, Ohio*
*Ferdinand Howald Collection*

For Demuth's generation, transatlantic liners were fascinating. They were a world in themselves, with their own special shapes. Demuth enjoyed the giant smokestacks and the ventilators upon the boat deck; the whole ship was a monster of power and speed.

Demuth couldn't ship his Lancaster lens very far, but he shipped it to the steamer. He spent a lot of time in France but he had the good sense to keep it out of his art. Most of Stieglitz's artists started out in Paris, but he helped push them in a native direction. There was a nationalistic flavor about An American Place that wasn't altogether pleasing. Demuth's pleasure in Paris was very real, but the group that hung around the Dôme and the Rotonde had nothing to do with France. Paris was the finest city in America.

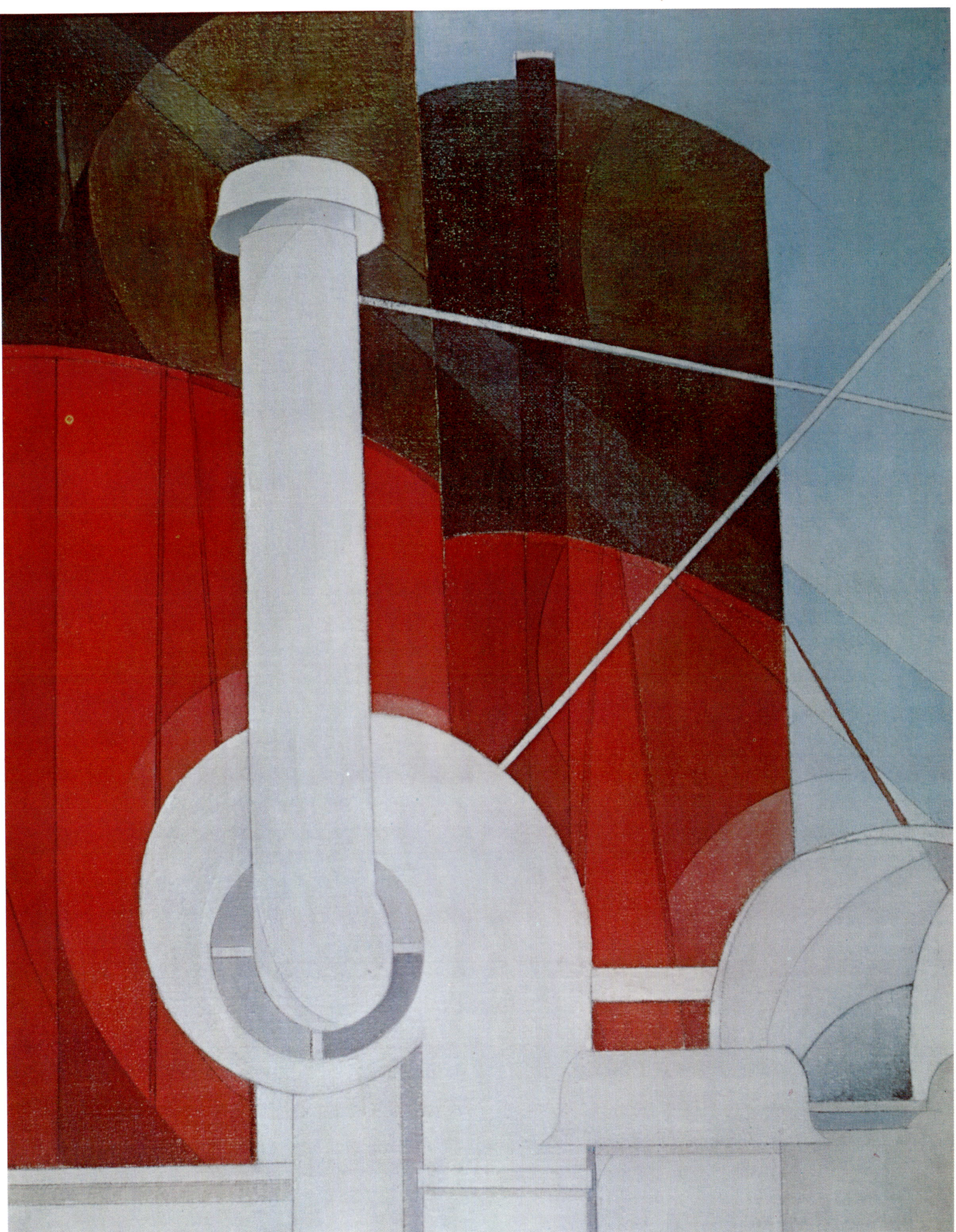

***Charles Demuth***

*Plate 22*
STILL LIFE NO. 1, ca. 1922
*Watercolor, 11 3/4" X 17 3/4"*
*The Columbus Gallery of Fine Arts, Columbus, Ohio*
*Ferdinand Howald Collection*

A lot of Demuth's watercolors are really tinted drawings. A natural draftsman, he drew as though he enjoyed it. This still life has a special kind of elegance. But then, Charles Demuth was an elegant man, always dressed in the best of English taste, and as Marsden Hartley said, his works of art have a perhaps too concrete insistence upon the elements of refinement and grace. In his later years Demuth painted still life because that was all he could handle. There's something self-contained about still life that artists like.

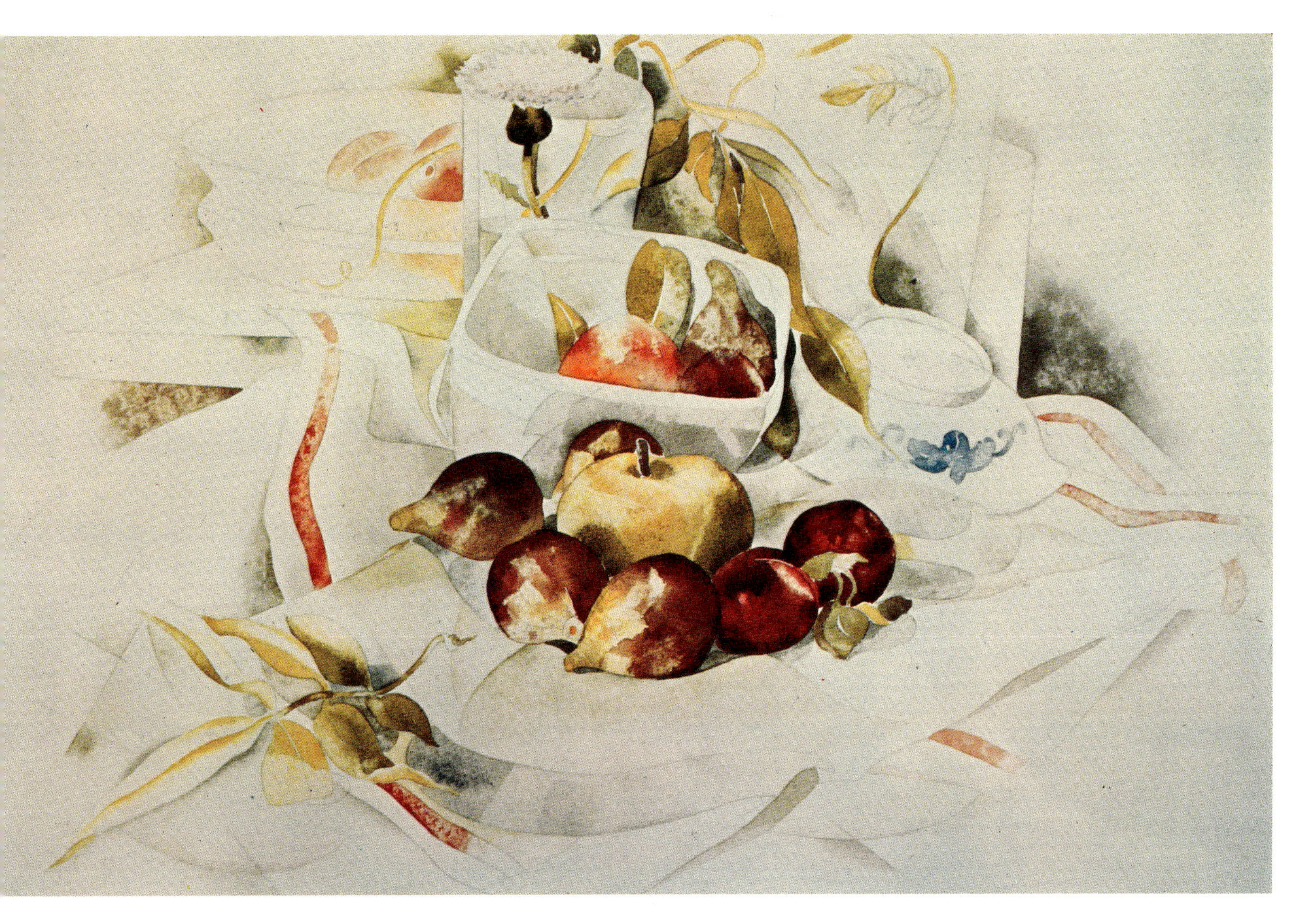

***Marsden Hartley***

*Plate 23*
THE MOUNTAINS, 1909
*Oil on Canvas, 30" X 30 1/8"*
*The Columbus Gallery of Fine Arts, Columbus, Ohio*
*Ferdinand Howald Collection*

This is an early Hartley, the kind of painting he showed to William Glackens, John Sloan, and Arthur B. Davies in New York, before Stieglitz took him on. His inspiration came from Segantini, the Italian painter who loved the Alps and lived in Switzerland. Maine meant just as much to Hartley as it did to Marin, but he wasn't a shore bird, poking around the rocks. He painted the whole state, including Thoreau's woods. Hartley had wonderful glowing color, as rich as an american autumn, but his solid clouds looked like tinted buckwheat cakes to Sloan.

The high horizons in these early mountainscapes are appealing, giving you a sense of the mountains pushing up against the sky. In Hartley's time, people really appreciated the Eastern mountains—the Adirondacks, Catskills, White, and Green. To us they're just hills. Hartley had a good wide range of subject matter, which is more than you could say of Demuth, or of Marin. He has a strong, hearty quality that's lacking in most of the school, even though his pictures are never large.

You can see why artists thought well of Hartley from the beginning, for he was probably the best *oil painter* of the Stieglitz bunch, and he did some of his best work right at the start. His work was always remarkably rich and vivid, with a real feeling for the medium, which is tricky and messy to begin with. There's nothing attractive about oil paint; you have to put it there, and Hartley could do it.

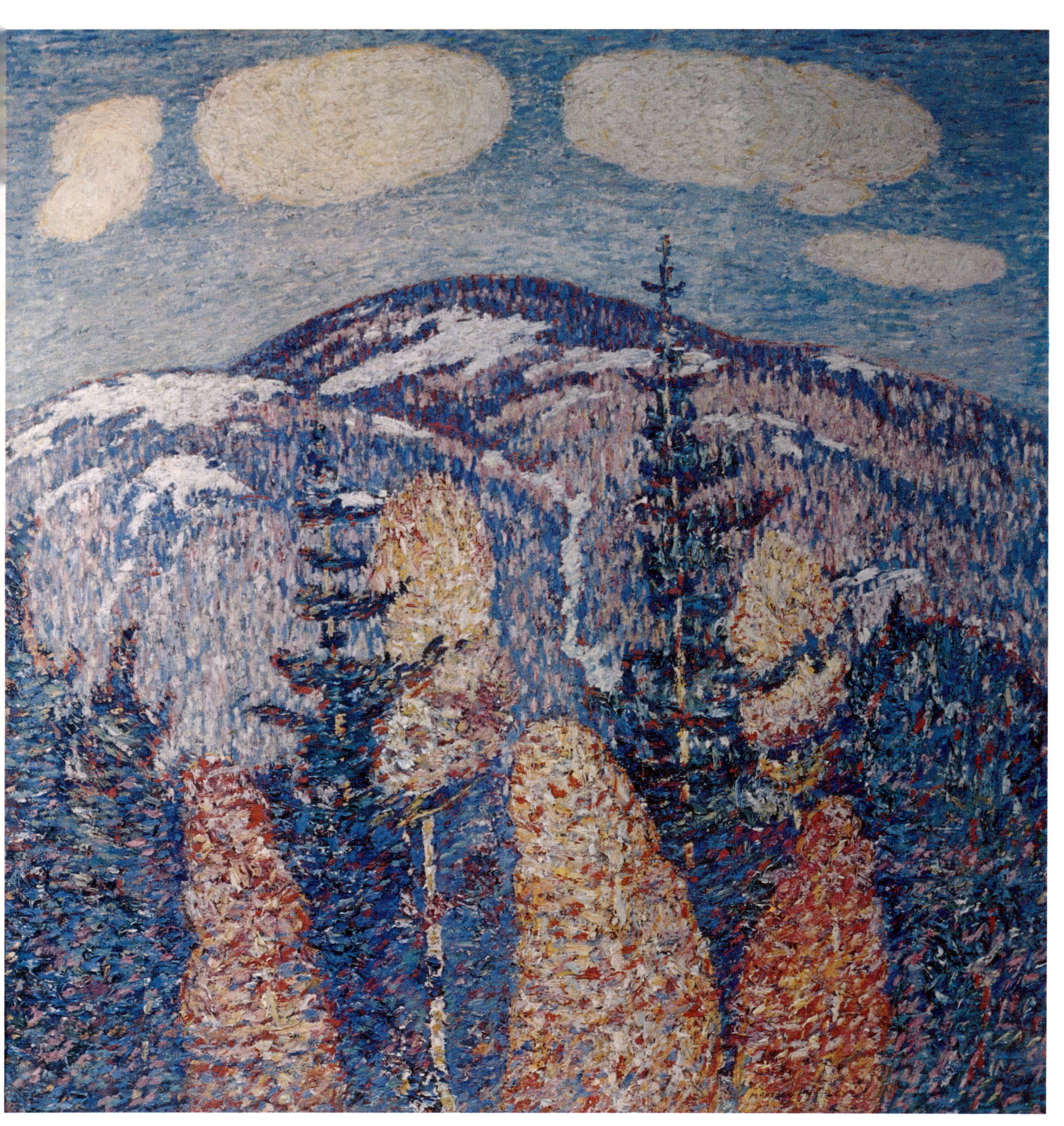

*Marsden Hartley*

*Plate 24*
THE MOUNTAIN, AUTUMN, 1911
*Oil on wood panel, 12 1/4" X 12 1/4"*
*The Columbus Gallery of Fine Arts, Columbus, Ohio*
*Ferdinand Howald Collection*

This is part of the same series as *The Mountains*, Ferdinand Howald was right to buy both of them. These are the pleasing and original paintings that got Hartley's career started. He had a natural subject in the glories of the American autumn, but the great glow isn't all that easy to paint.

Hartley specialized in deep, rich tones; he wasn't much of a draftsman, and there's very little composition in a picture like this. It's a picture of a New England hillside. Maurice Prendergast would have approved of this picture, and so would Ernest Lawson. It has a texture like an Oriental rug. This is Hartley untouched by modernism. He had looked at a lot of Impressionist pictures and said, "I can do better than that." American Impressionism, following the French example only too closely, ran toward light blue water, light blue sky, and fuzzy ladies in long white summer dresses. Hartley brought in the dark, rich burgundy tones.

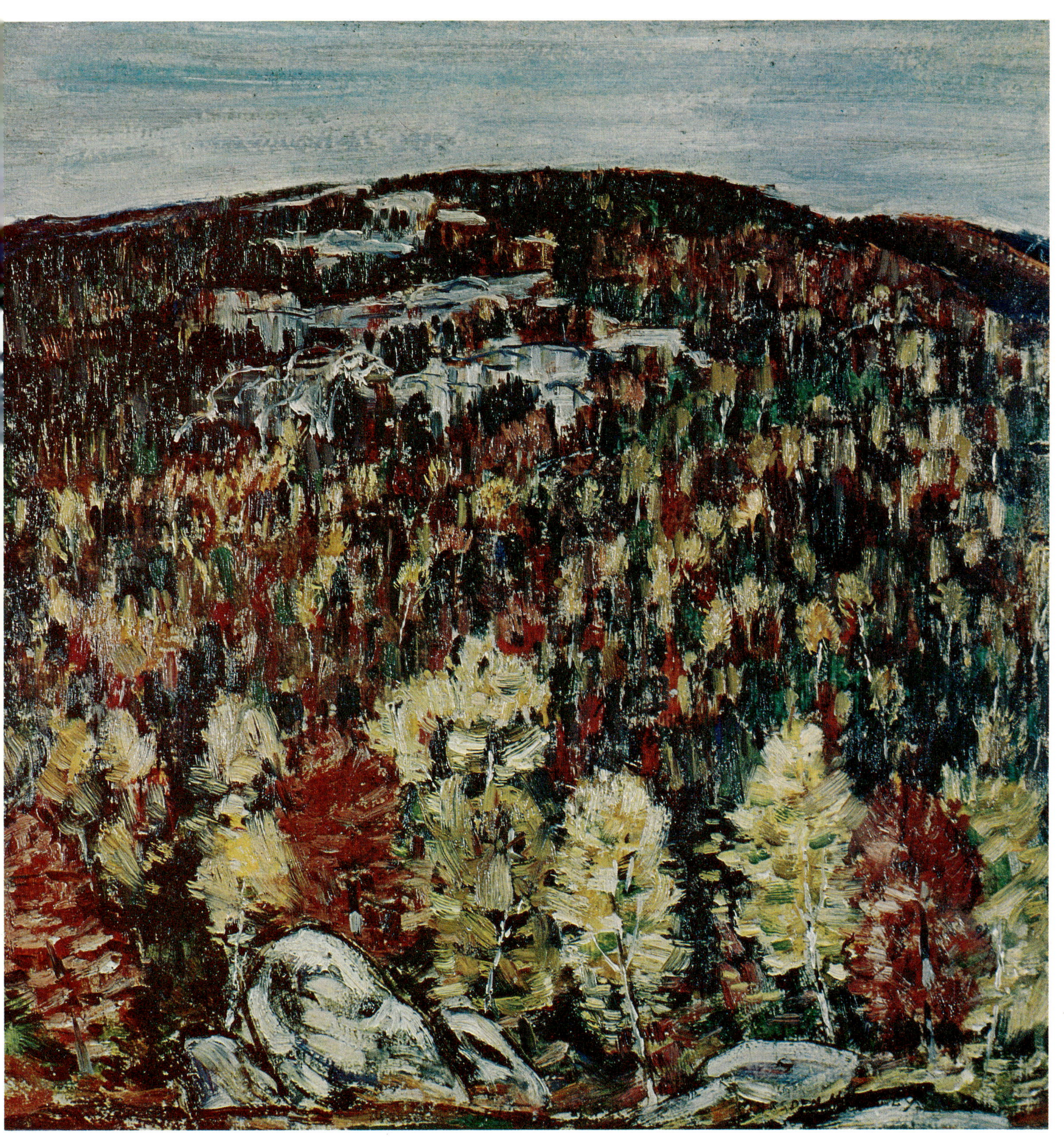

*Marsden Hartley*

*Plate 25*
DESERTION, 1912
*Oil on wood panel, 14" X 22"*
*The Columbus Gallery of Fine Arts, Columbus, Ohio*
*Ferdinand Howald Collection*

Hartley was feeling pretty bad when he painted this one, or maybe he was just struck by the dejected shape of the dead tree. Such an extraordinary composition might have appealed to Hartley, for painters are technicians, too, and it's easy to read too much into their work. He may have seen that tree, and it just caught his painter's eye, nothing more; the desolation may have come afterwards. In Hartley's day teachers talked a lot about triangles in composition, and this is no ordinary equilateral, with the apex in the middle; you hardly ever see a diagonal running from the top right to the lower left. If the drooping forms become symbols of dejection, so much the better; that tree is mighty cast down. The sky is ominous, and the white cloud shapes are reminiscent of his old admiration for Albert Pinkham Ryder. Here's an undeniable case of one painter influencing another.

When he was in the money, Hartley was cheerful enough, but when he was down on his luck, he was sorry for himself and for the world. His robust forms collapsed and, as the old Dunker hymn says, "it's awful, awful, awful."

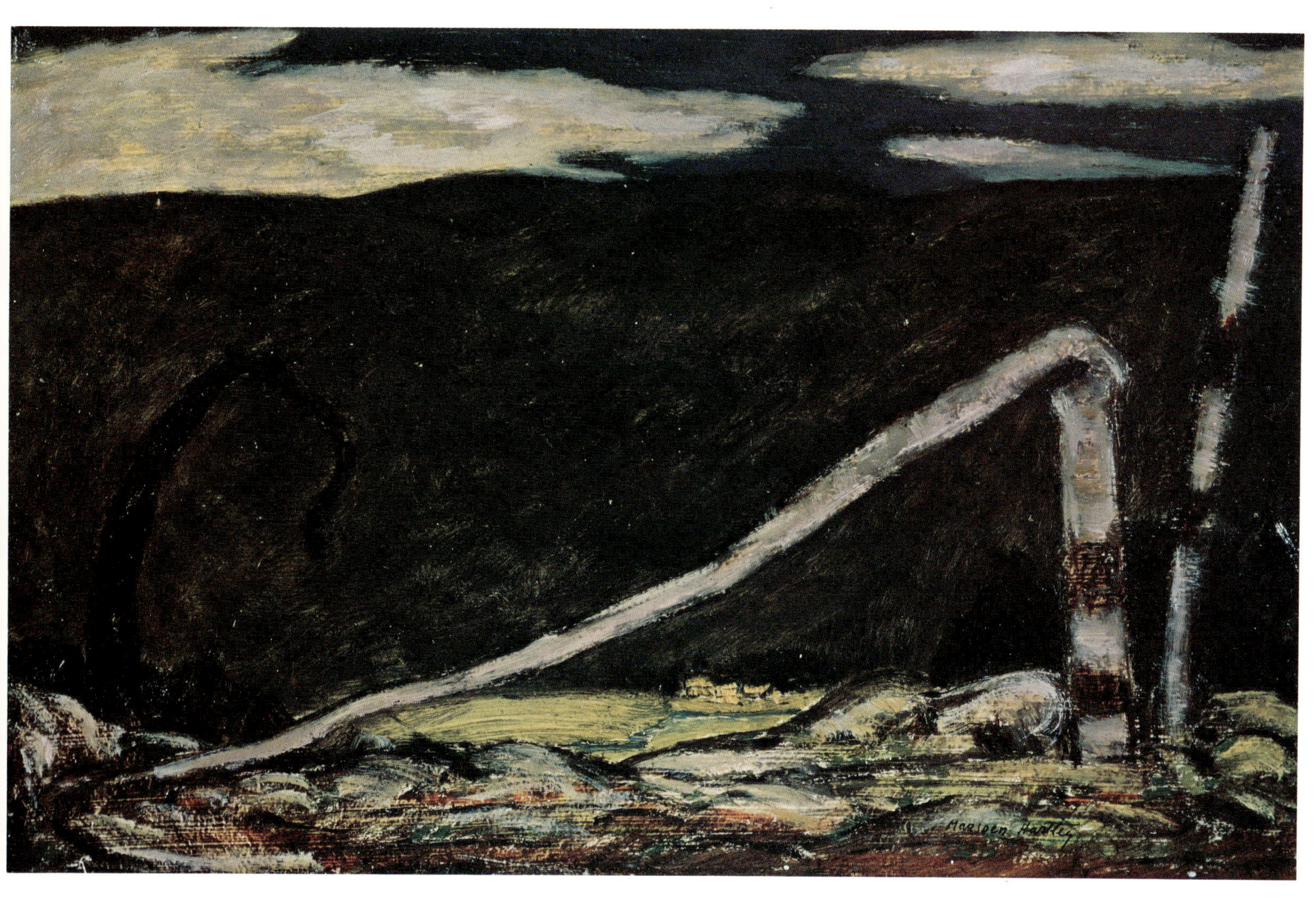
Marsden Hartley

***Marsden Hartley***

*Plate 26*
STILL LIFE NO. 1, 1913
*Oil on Canvas, 31 1/2" X 25 5/8"*
*The Columbus Gallery of Fine Arts, Columbus, Ohio*
*Ferdinand Howald Collection*

Hartley could take ordinary studio props—curtains, a bowl of fruit, a box, and bric-a-brac—and make a picture out of them. Hartley's debt to Cézanne is clear but he didn't take up where Cézanne left off, as he liked to believed; in late Cézanne there's not much left but pale bones, while Hartley used full color. However Hartley did use Cézanne's little jug and his piece of cloth.

Still life is much more unusual than we make it out to be. After all, why should anyone paint bananas? For the artist, that's part of the charm; he wants to prove that he can make a picture out of anything. Hartley used color and richness; he had a very good sense of what he could paint, and he got everything out of it he could, without pushing the boundaries of comprehension. For a thoughtful and theoretical man, Hartley was a very practical painter.

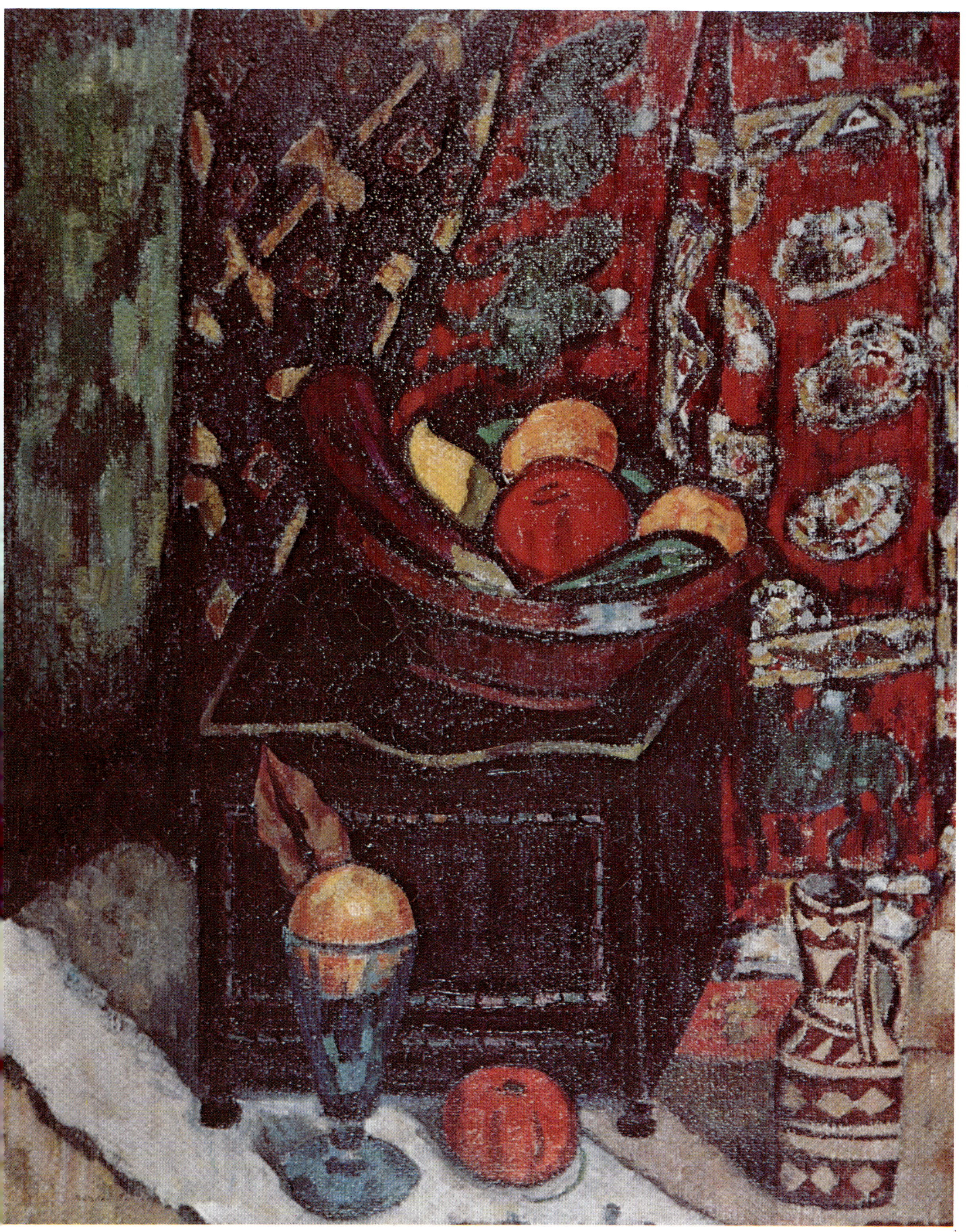

***Marsden Hartley***

*Plate 27*
COMPOSITION, 1914
*Oil on Canvas, 39 1/2" X 31 1/8"*
*The Columbus Gallery of Fine Arts, Columbus, Ohio*
*Ferdinand Howald Collection*

Hartley went pretty far toward abstraction, but he brought his bold composition and full color along with him. In this picture, it's hard to tell what he started with; that may be the sun up there on the horizon, but the swastika is not clear. Hartley's German Expressionist friends influenced his firm outlines and strong colors.

So here's what Germany did for the boy from Maine; whatever happened to Ryder and romance? Hartley made a lot of his attachment to dear old Maine, but Germany was a real home, the way his own home never had been, and he would have stayed in Germany if he could. He would have preferred that, and he would have had a happier life. Whether it would have been all that good for his painting, or for his reputation, is another matter. The Germans, for all their welcome, might not have written books about him. But there's no doubt that Germany did something for Hartley. Look at all those rainbows. He was having the time of his life, and it's fireworks all the way. Hartley is the only German Expressionist we've got.

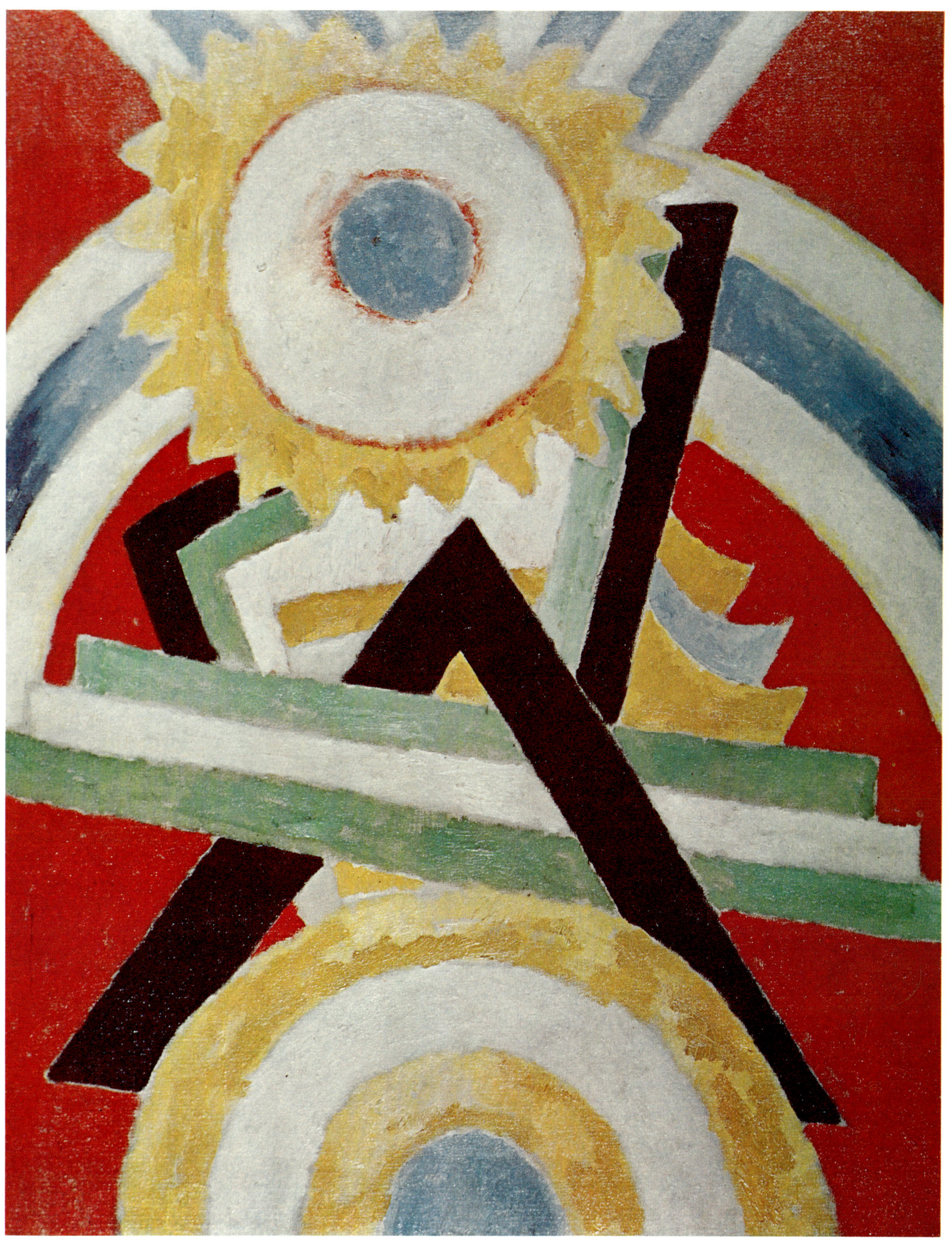

*Marsden Hartley*

*Plate 28*
BERLIN ANTE-WAR, 1915
*Oil on canvas, 39 1/4" X 31 7/8"*
*The Columbus Gallery of Fine Arts, Columbus, Ohio*
*Ferdinand Howald Collection*

Hartley was happy in Berlin, where he stayed a year and a half after the outbreak of World War I. He had lots of friends, the artists liked his work, and he felt completely at home. Pre-war Berlin was full of handsome officers in foolish helmets on prancing horses. There's no profound symbolism here: Hartley put the white horse on top because he wanted to. The whole picture is pure decoration, with peasant houses at the bottom, a setting sun, and a chessboard. It's a lighthearted fantasy, with the white knight galloping off to Valhalla surrounded by a sky full of Iron Crosses. Hartley called these pictures "pre-war pageants."

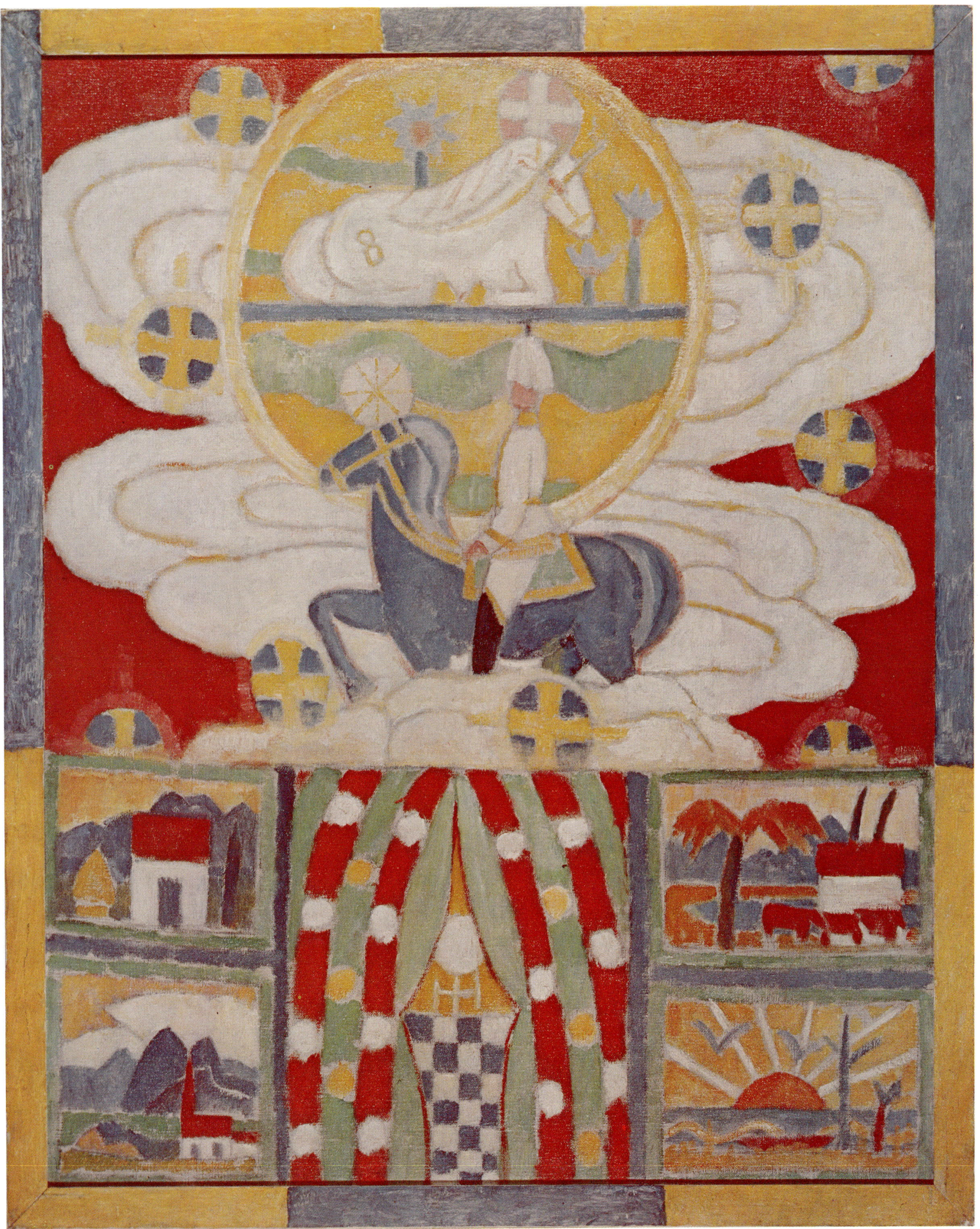

*Marsden Hartley*

*Plate 29*
BOWL WITH FRUIT, 1919
*Oil on canvas, 13 3/4" X 25 3/4"*
*The Columbus Gallery of Fine Arts, Columbus, Ohio*
*Ferdinand Howald Collection*

When he was in his dark mood, Hartley could even turn out a depressed still life. It must have been an effort to paint with so few colors. He was trying to simplify, to get broad, powerful effects. There's a strong resemblance here to Walt Kuhn, who also painted powerful still lifes in a Cézanne-esque manner.

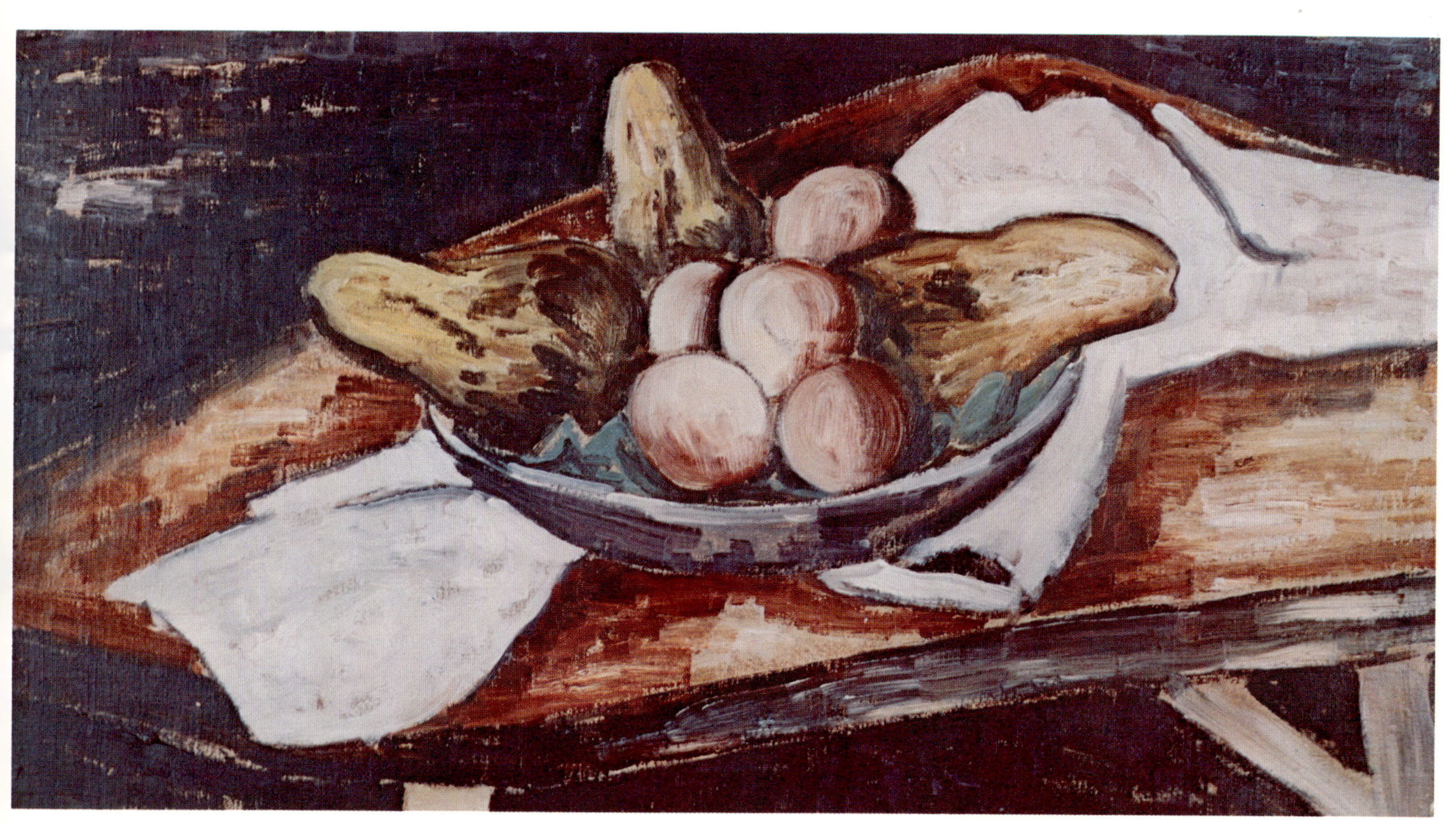

***Marsden Hartley***

*Plate 30*
LILIES IN A VASE, ca. 1920
*Oil on heavy pasteboard, 27″ X 19 1/8″*
*The Columbus Gallery of Fine Arts, Columbus, Ohio*
*Ferdinand Howald Collection*

Hartley had a talent for unusual composition. He easily placed things where they looked best. He could make a striking and original picture out of the most traditional subject matter. Although Hartley was no flower lover like Demuth, he painted flowers to show that he could, the way he painted everything except the female nude—which wasn't exactly one of his obsessions.

This painting isn't in the classic tradition of flower painting, which is a limited art. What interested him was the shape and the upward push of the vase. Hartley doesn't repeat himself much; he says what he has to say in his own way, and then moves on.

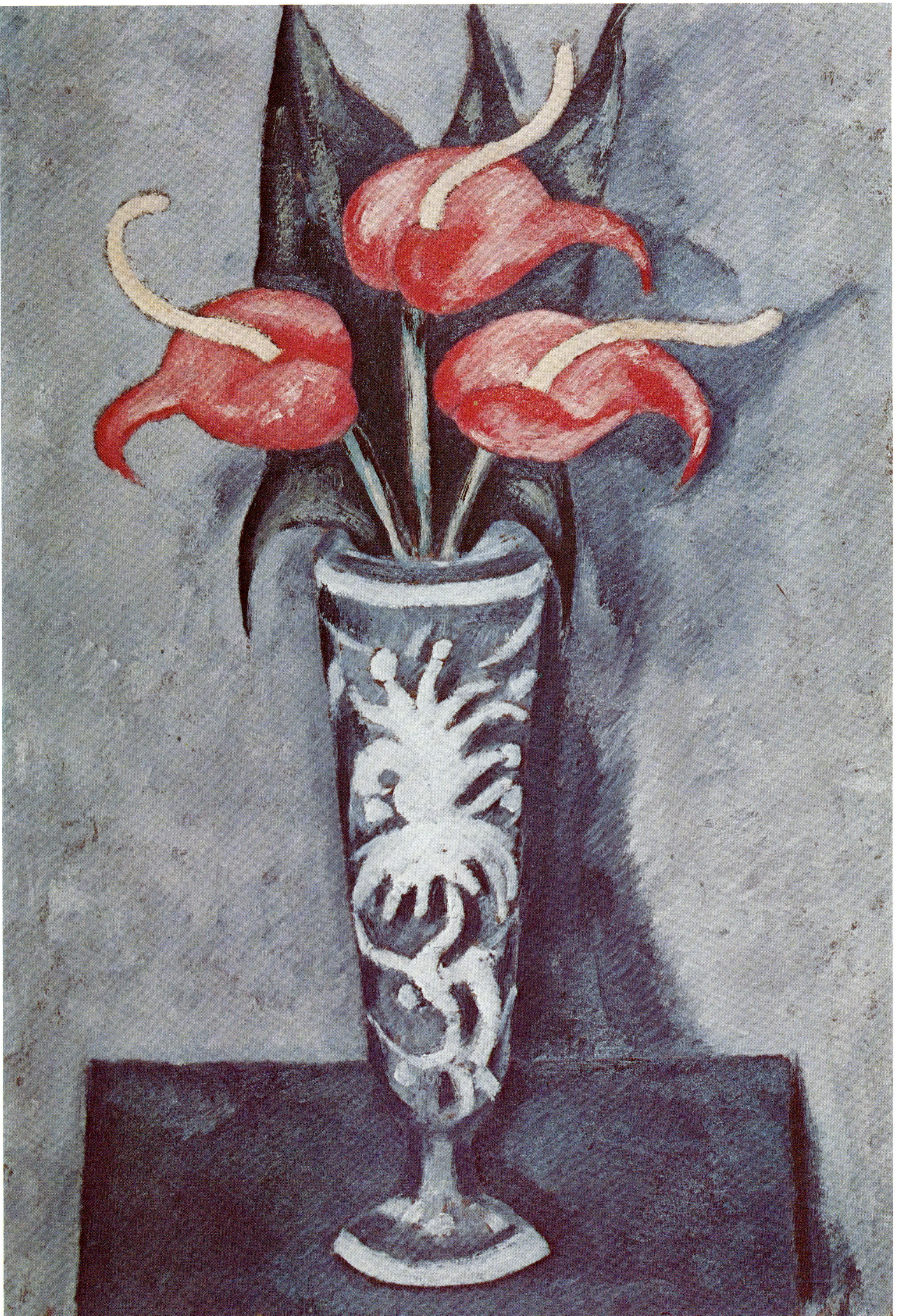

***Marsden Hartley***

*Plate 31*
COLOR ANALOGY, 1921
*Oil on wood panel, 20" X 15 5/8"*
*The Columbus Gallery of Fine Arts, Columbus, Ohio*
*Ferdinand Howald Collection*

During Hartley's second long stay in Europe, which stretched from 1921 to the Crash in 1929, his painting became much more French, for German painting had been pretty much wiped out by the war. He took a fling at cubism, which its founders had moved away from, but he did his best work when he painted his own pictures. Gertrude Stein said that Hartley dealt with his color as Picasso dealt with his forms, which is pretty high praise.

*Color Analogy* isn't an inspiring title, but a painter has to prove he can be just as dull as the next fellow. Actually, the color isn't at all remarkable, and this is not analogy. The shape is more unusual than the colors, and the title was probably an afterthought.

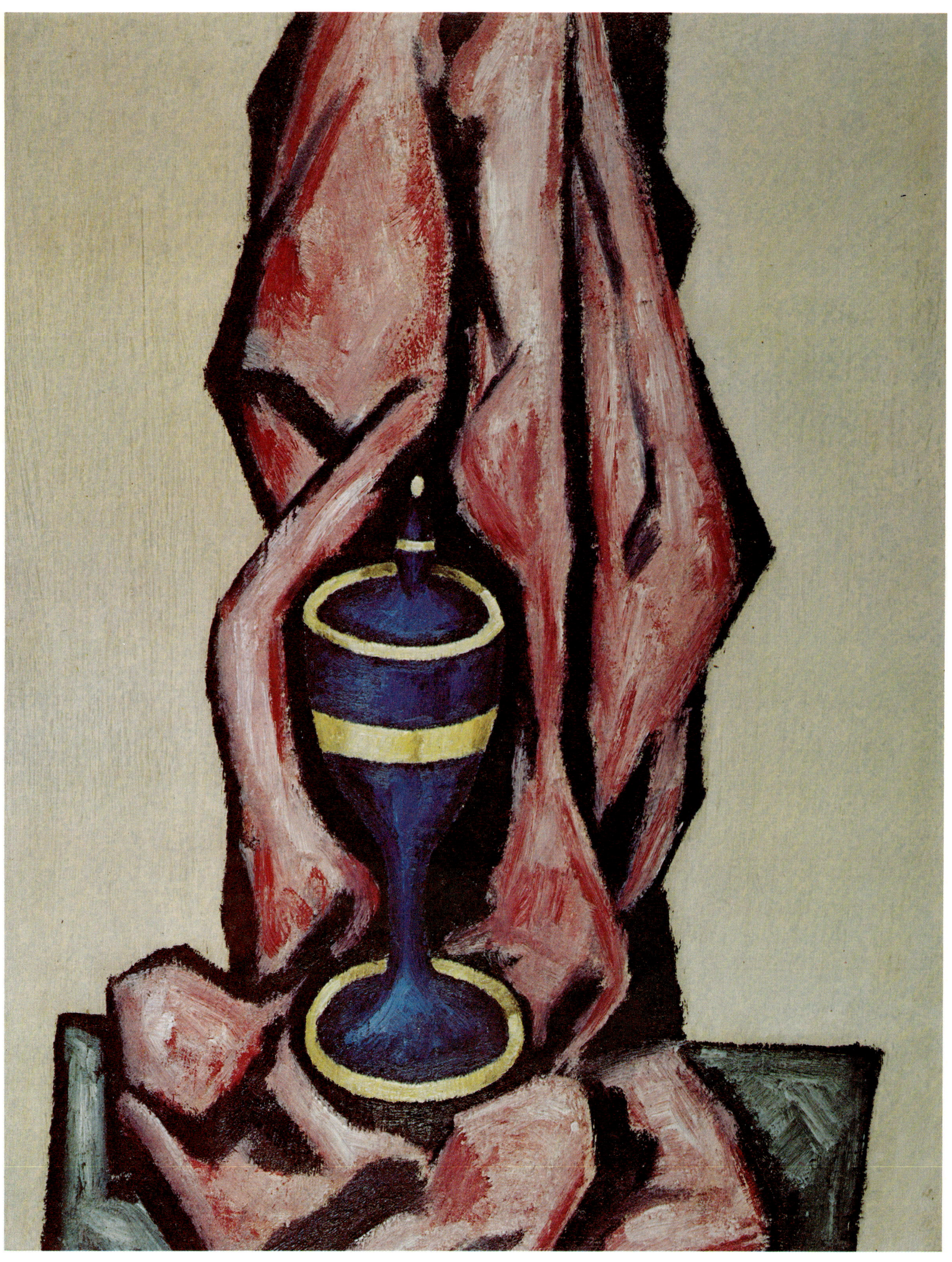

*Marsden Hartley*

*Plate 32*
NEW MEXICO RECOLLECTIONS, 1923
*Oil on canvas, 17 3/4" X 30 7/8"*
*The Columbus Gallery of Fine Arts, Columbus, Ohio*
*Ferdinand Howald Collection*

Like Marin, Hartley had his New Mexico period, for these individualists flew in flocks. Hartley went out to New Mexico in 1918, when he couldn't go to Europe. While there, he was overwhelmed by the landscape, but when he got around to painting his recollections of New Mexico, he picked on the same broken tree that he had painted in 1912. It's the same symbol of desertion, particularly depressing in the enormous landscape of the Southwest. Later in life he said that he needed to escape from intellectualism, and his best work was always close to nature.

Hartley didn't care for the compound life at Taos; he wasn't much of a group man, and he didn't like to be told what to do. He was a loner, he liked to be on his own, and he was a strong personality in his own right. That's why he had trouble with Stieglitz. The Southwest was foreign to him, much more foreign than Europe. It's a different part of the world completely, and while the scenery has a whole new dimension, it had about as much appeal to Hartley as the mountains of the moon. He wasn't used to colonial life; he liked to prowl the city streets.

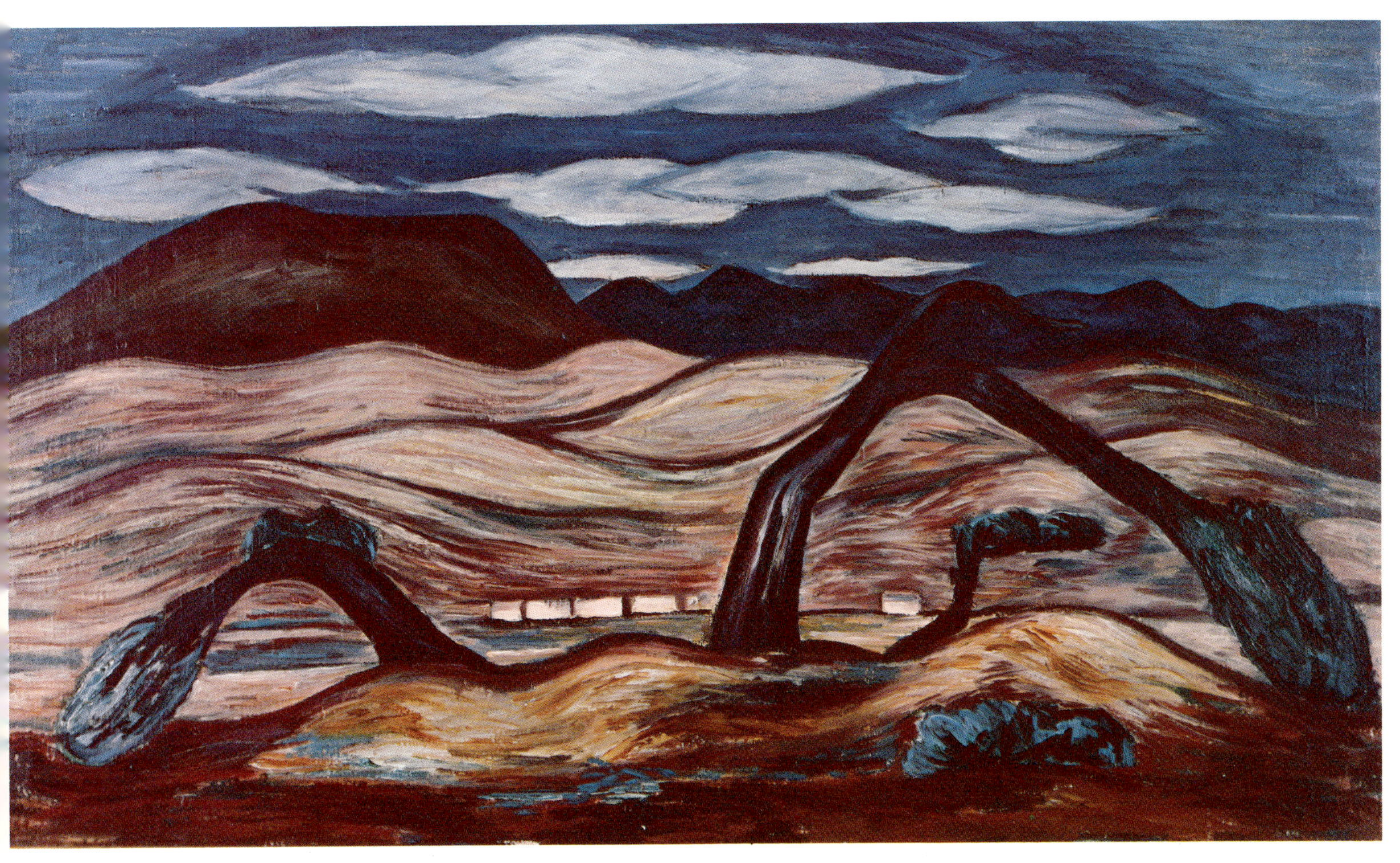

***Marsden Hartley***

*Plate 33*
THE WINDOW, 1928
*Oil on canvas, 35 5/8" X 25 5/8"*
*The Columbus Gallery of Fine Arts, Columbus, Ohio*
*Ferdinand Howald Collection*

Landscape painters are a relatively happy breed because their work takes them outside, like fishermen. The bad time for Hartley was when he was tied up in some studio, with the grime around the windows and nothing to paint. So what do you paint on a rainy day when you haven't got a thought in the world? You paint out the window. These two trees are almost too parallel, and their trunks are not very sensitively drawn. And in front of it goes that old bowl of fruit, and those same old flowers. Hartley bluffed this one out.

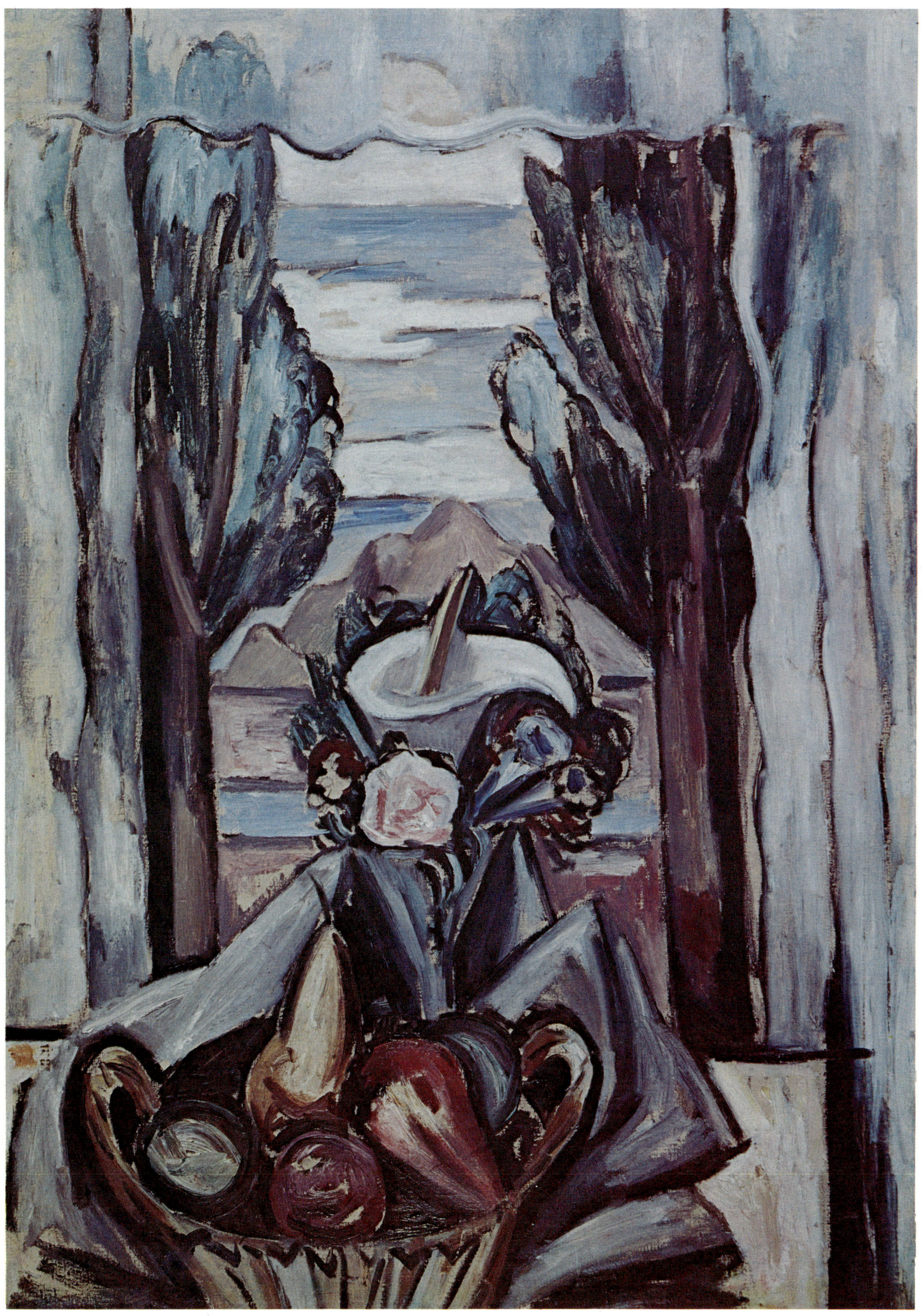

*Arthur G. Dove*

*Plate 34*
MOVEMENT, NO. 1, ca. 1911
*Pastel on canvas, 21 3/8" X 18"*
*The Columbus Gallery of Fine Arts, Columbus, Ohio*
*Ferdinand Howald Collection*

In his early days Dove carried abstraction to the point where it didn't have much meaning. This is a movement all right, but movement of what? Cloud forms, or circles in the sky? In 1911, before the Armory Show, this was very advanced. Nobody but Stieglitz would handle pictures like this and there wasn't much of a market.

Some people maintain that Dove was the first abstract painter in the world, even before Kandinksy, but neither of them was much more abstract than the Cubists. The argument is between the French and the Eastern Europeans; certainly abstract movements in Europe flowed from two different sources. But Dove started no school and he had no followers; he was a solitary figure, not a leader. He didn't particularly influence the other members of the Stieglitz group; they imported their own abstraction.

The questions of how abstract Dove was, and how early, are academic. Like most of what happened to Dove and his painting, abstraction was a personal matter, and had no particular resonance or result. These particular forms look Futuristic rather than Cubistic. The Italians have their own claims to being the founders of abstractionism; certainly they influenced Duchamp and Picabia, whom Dove knew around Stieglitz's gallery, but that was after the Armory Show in 1913.

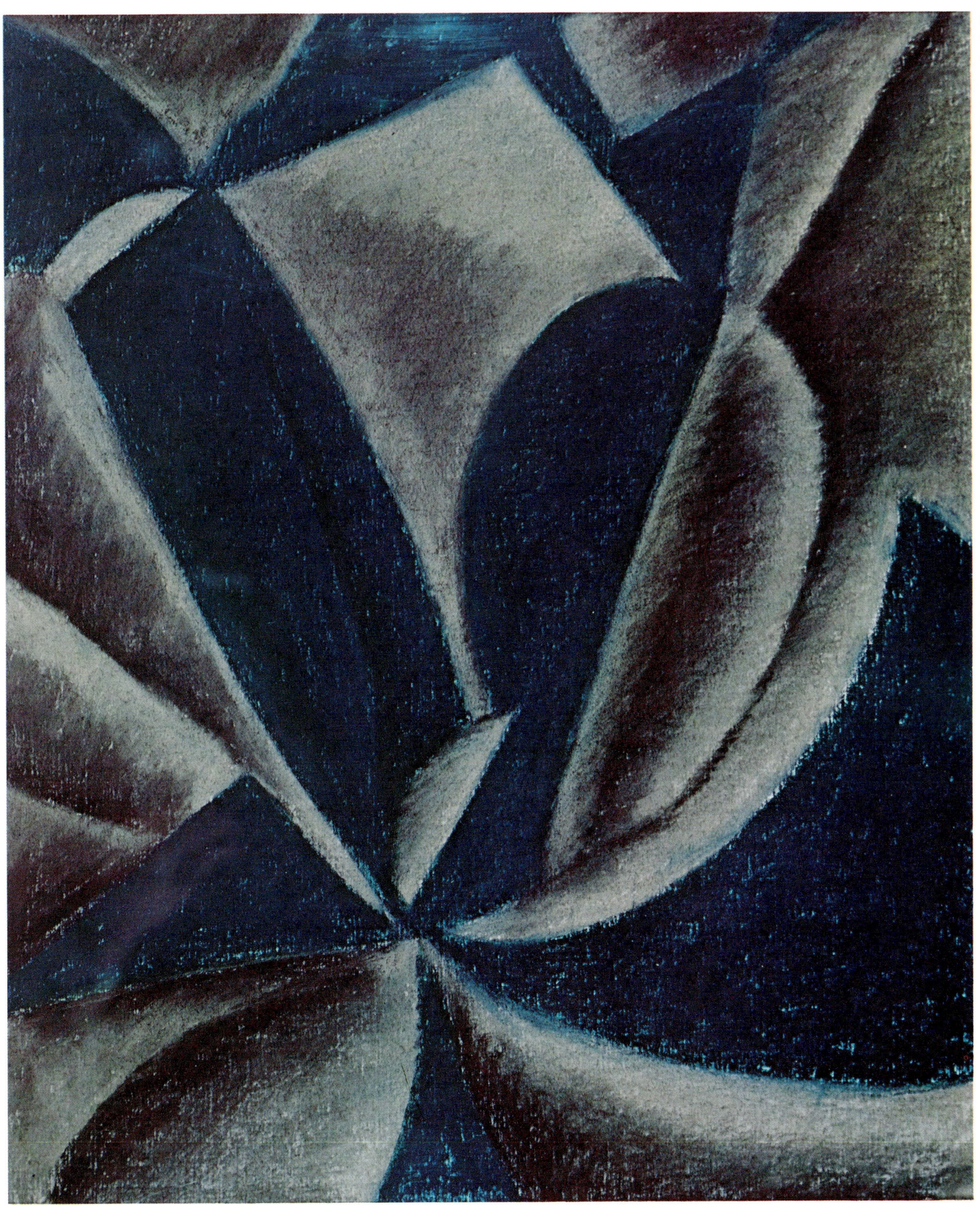

## *Arthur G. Dove*

*Plate 35*
NATURE SYMBOLIZED, 1911
*Oil on canvas, 17 7/8" X 21 1/2"*
*The Art Institute of Chicago, Chicago, Illinois*

This is a good title for a lot of Dove's work, though it is difficult to know what he is symbolizing. In 1912 Stieglitz had a whole exhibition of pictures with this title. Marcia Tucker, who believes that Dove was "perhaps the first painter to produce totally abstract works, antedating Kandinsky's abstractions of 1911 by about a year," says that he was trying to paint "what was for him the 'reality' of nature—reality of forces, colors, and masses rather than specific objects." (Marcia Tucker, *American Paintings in the Ferdinand Howald Collection,* p. 43.)

Stieglitz showed his first Dove in 1910, and in 1912 he showed the "Arthur G. Dove First Exhibition Anywhere." For a moody thinker, which was his self-image, Stieglitz was an excellent showman. He called Dove's pictures a series of abstracts—which is fair enough—and he thought it was perfectly natural that they should be over the heads of the people. The show went on to Chicago afterward, where it caused much more hullabaloo than in New York. Chicagoans remember him, and after the Armory Show brought abstraction to the Middle West in 1913, they called him "John the Baptist."

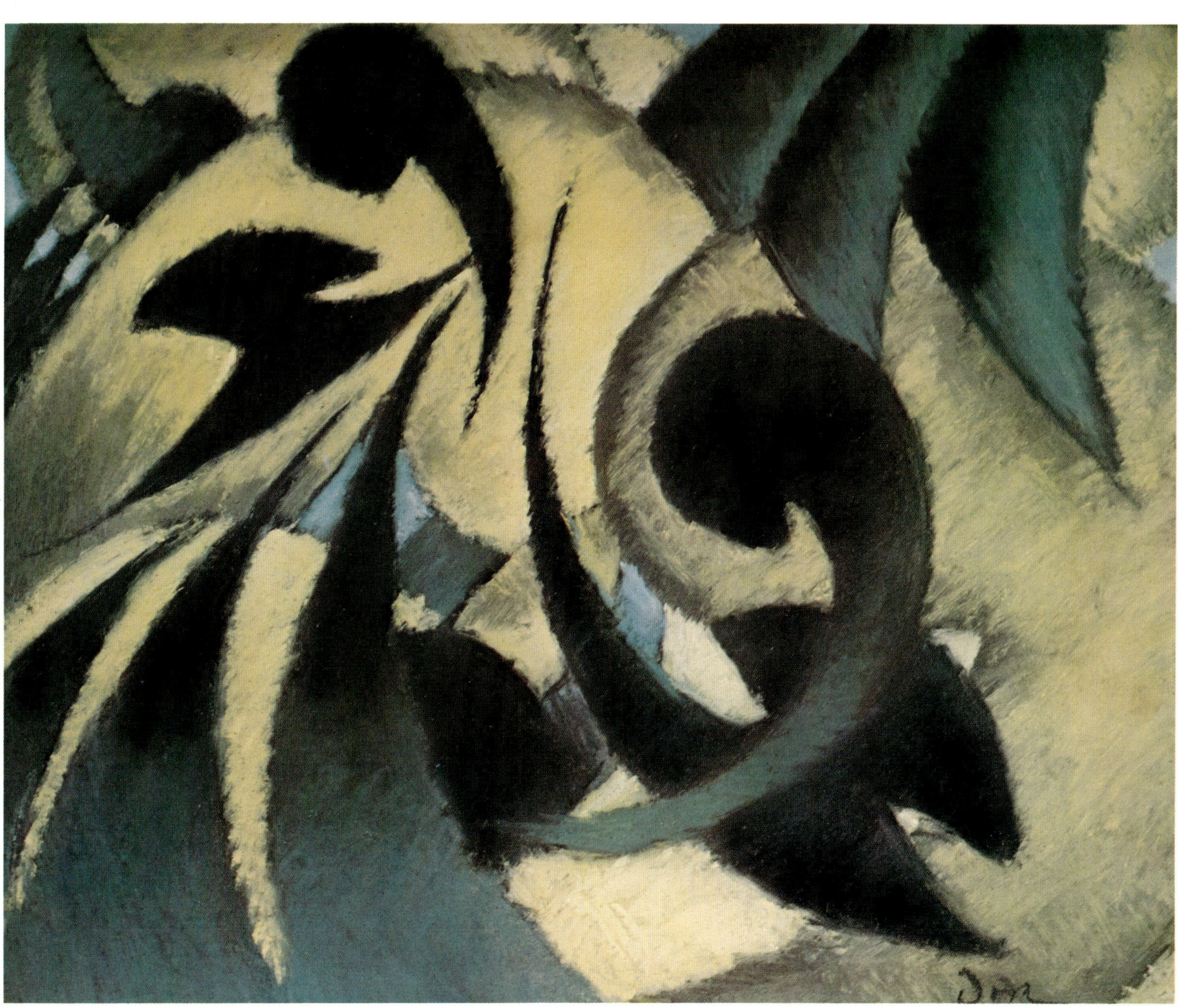

*Arthur G. Dove*

*Plate 36*
PLANT FORMS, 1915
*Pastel on canvas, 17 1/4" X 23 7/8"*
*Whitney Museum of American Art, New York, New York*
*Gift of Mr. and Mrs. Roy R. Neuberger*

In his early years, Dove ran into a good deal of raillery and incomprehension. Dove didn't intend these plant forms to be recognizable, for he was far beyond specifics. As one early critic said: "But Mr. Dove is much to keen/To let a single bird be seen;/To show the pigeons would not do/And so he simply paints the coo." (Bert Leston Taylor, quoted in Frederick S. Wight, *Arthur G. Dove,* p. 28.) This kind of kidding probably didn't hurt Dove and certainly gave him widespread publicity.

Dove was the least successful of the Stieglitz painters, and he never really caught on with collectors and the buying public. At first, because of his high degree of "modernism," he had the advantage of novelty. His later work is less abstract and got passed over. Georgia O'Keeffe, the other abstractionist member of the Stieglitz Stable, thought very highly of his work, more highly than she did of Hartley's.

The early pictures are quite uncompromising, and they looked a lot more barren in those days than they do now, when painting has been reduced to far greater simplicity than this.

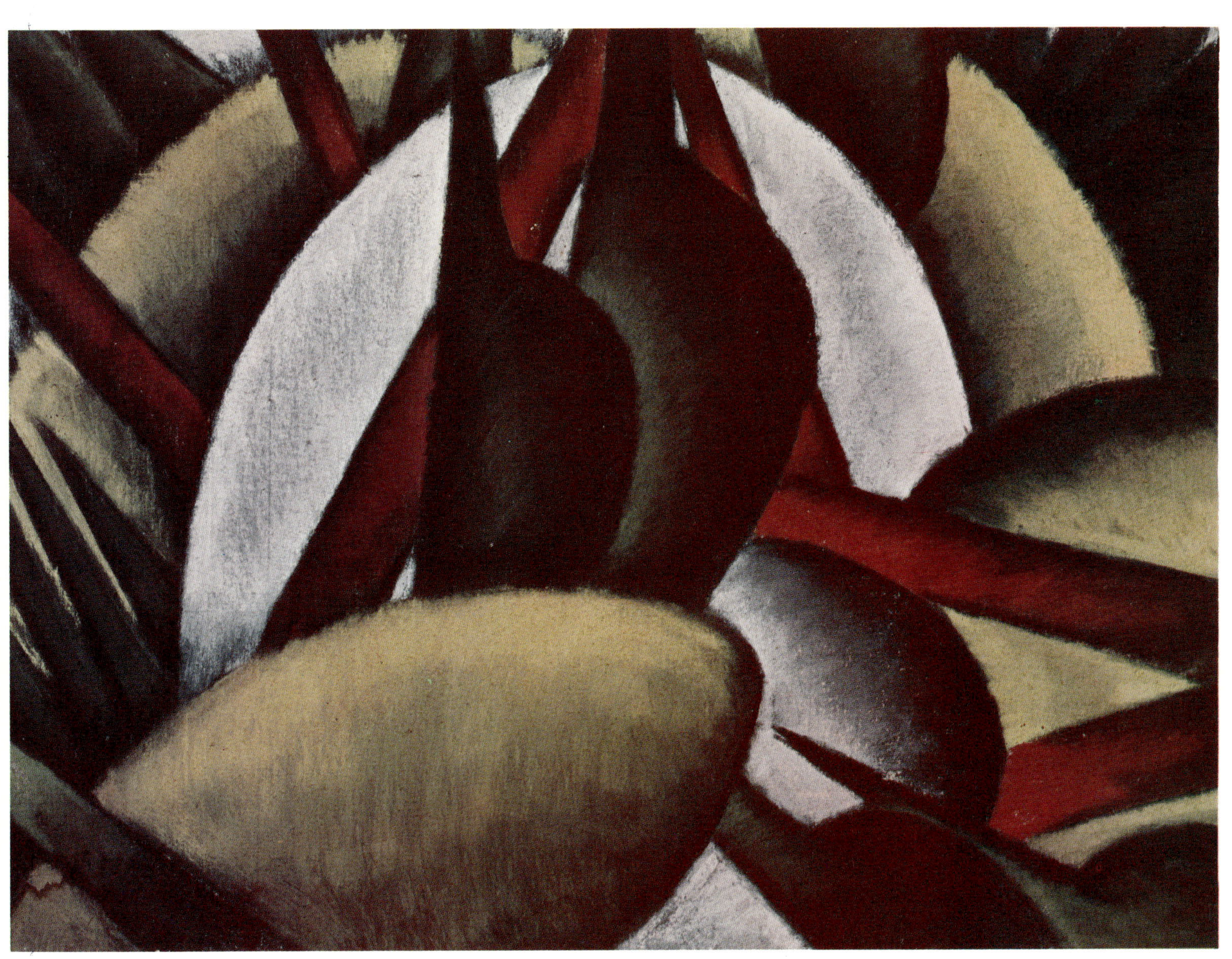

*Arthur G. Dove*

*Plate 37*
THUNDERSTORM, 1921
*Oil on canvas, 21 1/2" X 18 1/8"*
*The Columbus Gallery of Fine Arts, Columbus, Ohio*
*Ferdinand Howald Collection*

The Stieglitz painters were primarily landscape painters. What Stieglitz liked in Dove was the direct feeling for nature; perhaps Stieglitz wasn't interested in people anyway. Dove reduced nature to extremely simple forms. This thunderstorm is dark and menacing enough, but a thunderstorm isn't all that simple. Dove went at nature directly and tried to express its essence, but he had a good sense of pattern, and here he made a diagram of a thunderstorm rather than a picture of it.

Dove wanted to simplify impressionism and he certainly succeeded. His thunderclouds look as though they are made out of steel drums. This is no gentle mist; the rain comes down in solid rods, to make you feel the driving force. Dove wanted to reduce the storm to its simplest form, and he almost lost what he was looking for. He didn't try to make it pretty; his early work is stark and bare, and people weren't ready for it.

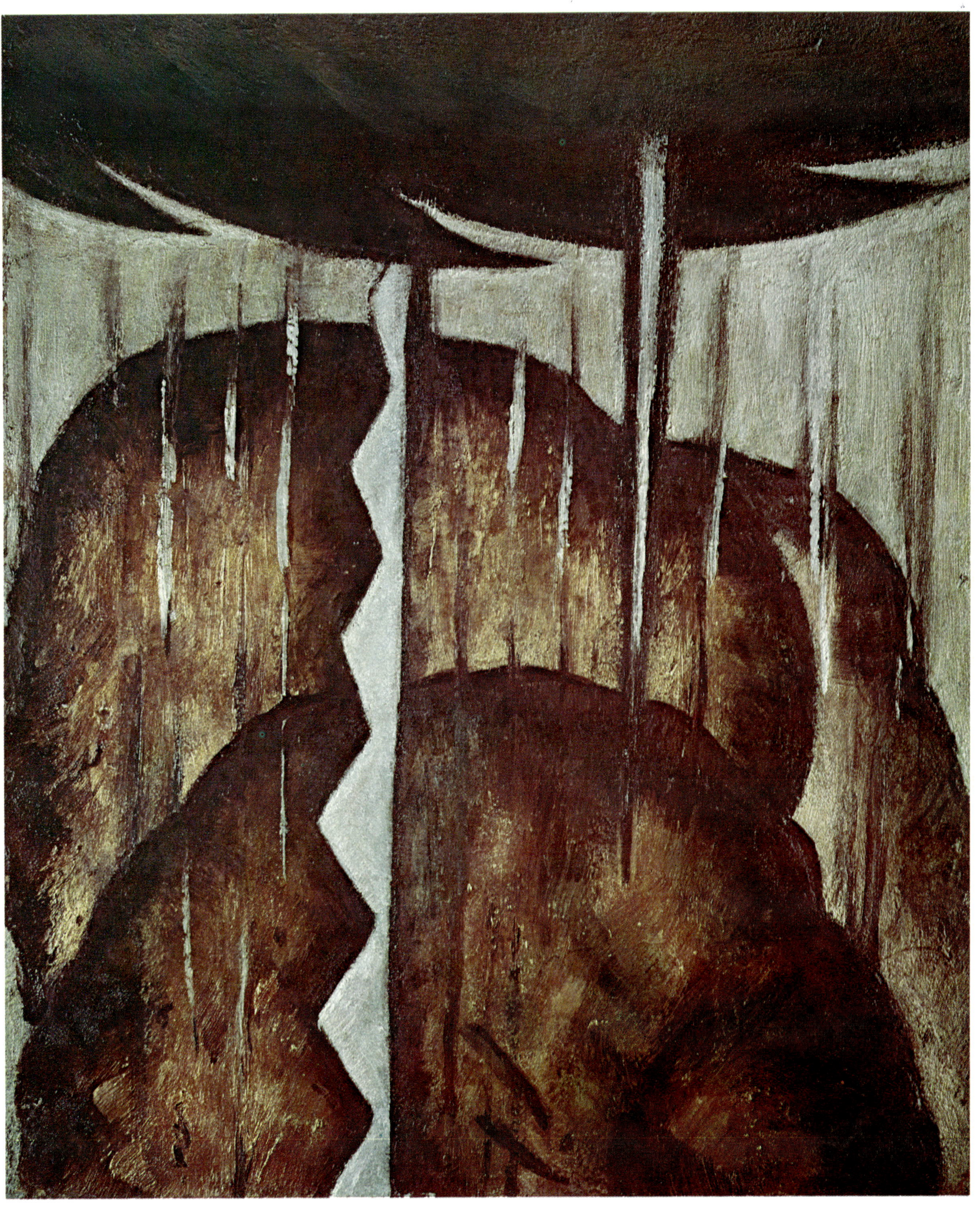

*Arthur G. Dove*

*Plate 38*
WATERFALL, 1925
*Oil on canvas, 10" X 8"*
*The Phillips Collection, Washington, D.C.*

Dove said that Duncan Phillips saved his life, since Phillips was his later mentor, after Stieglitz. Dove, a harshly independent man, was forced to lean on people, and he was almost embarrassingly grateful for the support Stieglitz and Phillips gave him. Dove told Phillips that he took to Stieglitz some paintings which he considered had something new in them. Stieglitz walked right up to them and picked out the new. Dove told Phillips that he was glad to have been allowed to live during their lifetimes; it was a great privilege.

Dove said that he didn't like titles for his pictures, which should tell their own story. Certainly this waterfall is clear enough.

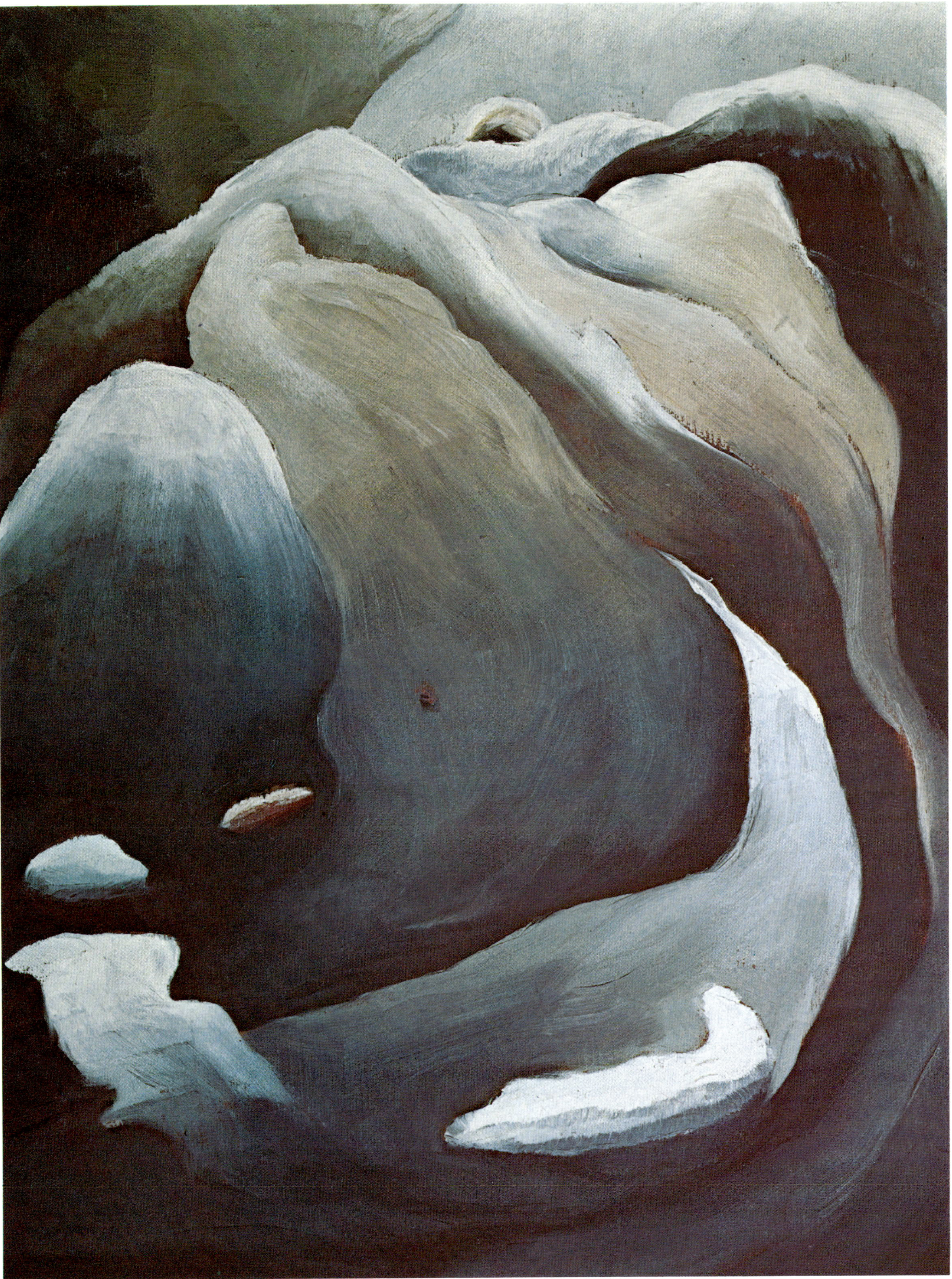

*Arthur G. Dove*

*Plate 39*
FOG HORNS, 1929
*Oil on canvas, 18" X 26"*
*The Colorado Springs Fine Arts Center,*
*Colorado Springs, Colorado*
*Gift of Oliver B. James*

Frederick Wight felt this was one of Dove's best. "Images of the solemn hoot and blast swell out of their own caverns, as smoke rings out of canvas, the sounds rolling over the heavy waves, and an answering sound coming from the horizon." (Wight, p. 56.)

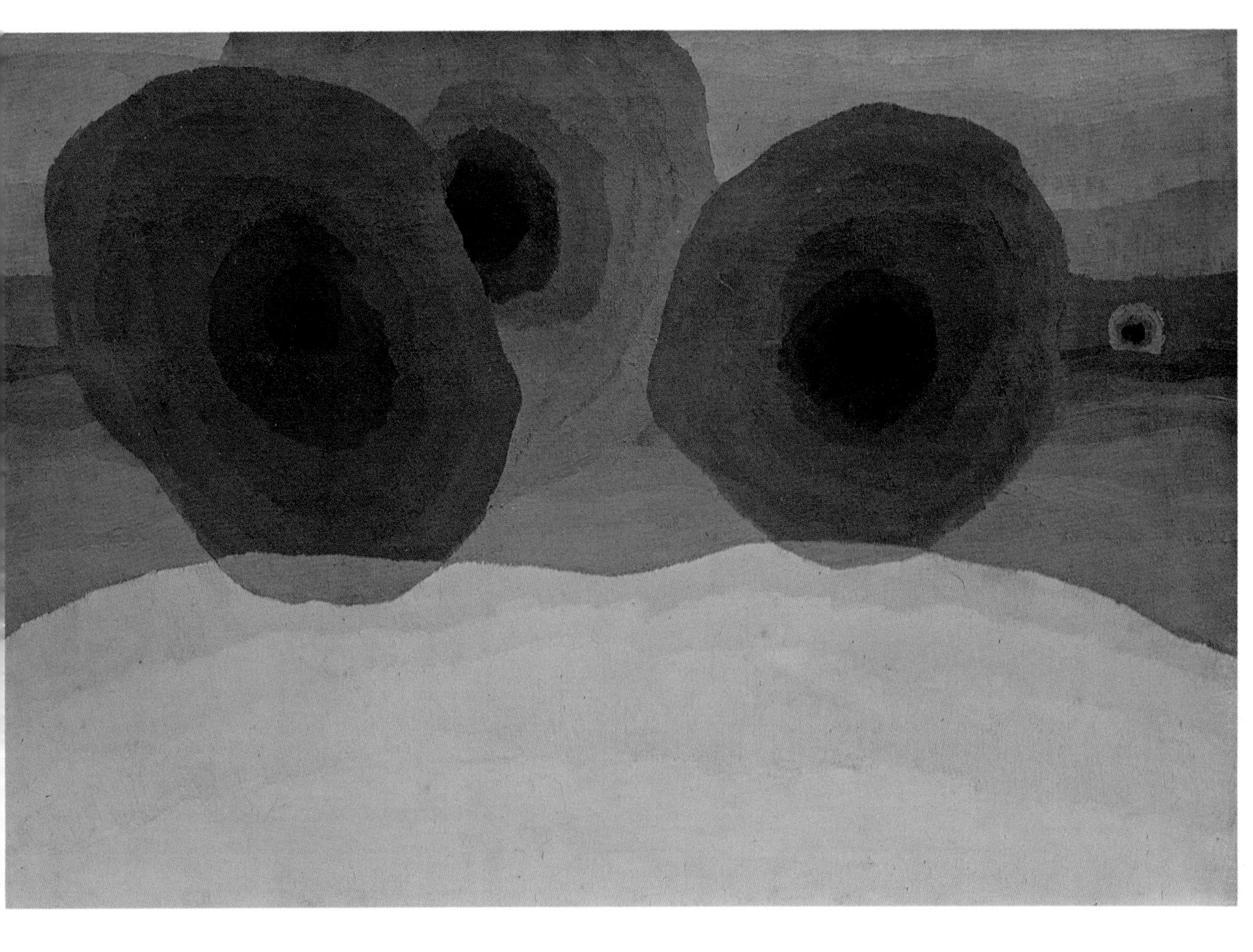

*Arthur G. Dove*

*Plate 40*
OIL DRUMS, 1930
*Oil on canvas, 22 1/4" X 27 1/4"*
*Museum of Art, Carnegie Institute,*
*Pittsburgh, Pennsylvania*

Dove was one of what Stieglitz called the "A-1 men" (in which he included O'Keeffe), and Stieglitz fought for him manfully. Stieglitz complained that he was always in the position of money-grubbing, yet that he never made a penny from the grubbing, which was probably true. He felt that it would have been better for Demuth, Marin, Dove, and O'Keeffe if they had been Frenchmen—then they would have become rich like the French artists so highly supported by art-loving Americans. He had a point: when Alfred Barr bought Dove's *Grandma* for the Museum of Modern Art, all Dove got was $700, and that, according to Stieglitz, was like pulling teeth.

Elizabeth McCausland called Dove the most abstract and theoretical of the Stieglitz group, but he drew away from that position. In the beginning, he was trying to simplify, to go toward an art of pure form and color dissassociated from representation. Later on, he got amazingly close to his two subjects, the water and the land. And it was no longer pure form and color he was trying to convey, but old-fashioned meaning and symbolism. This was his life, messing about in boats and fighting the land.

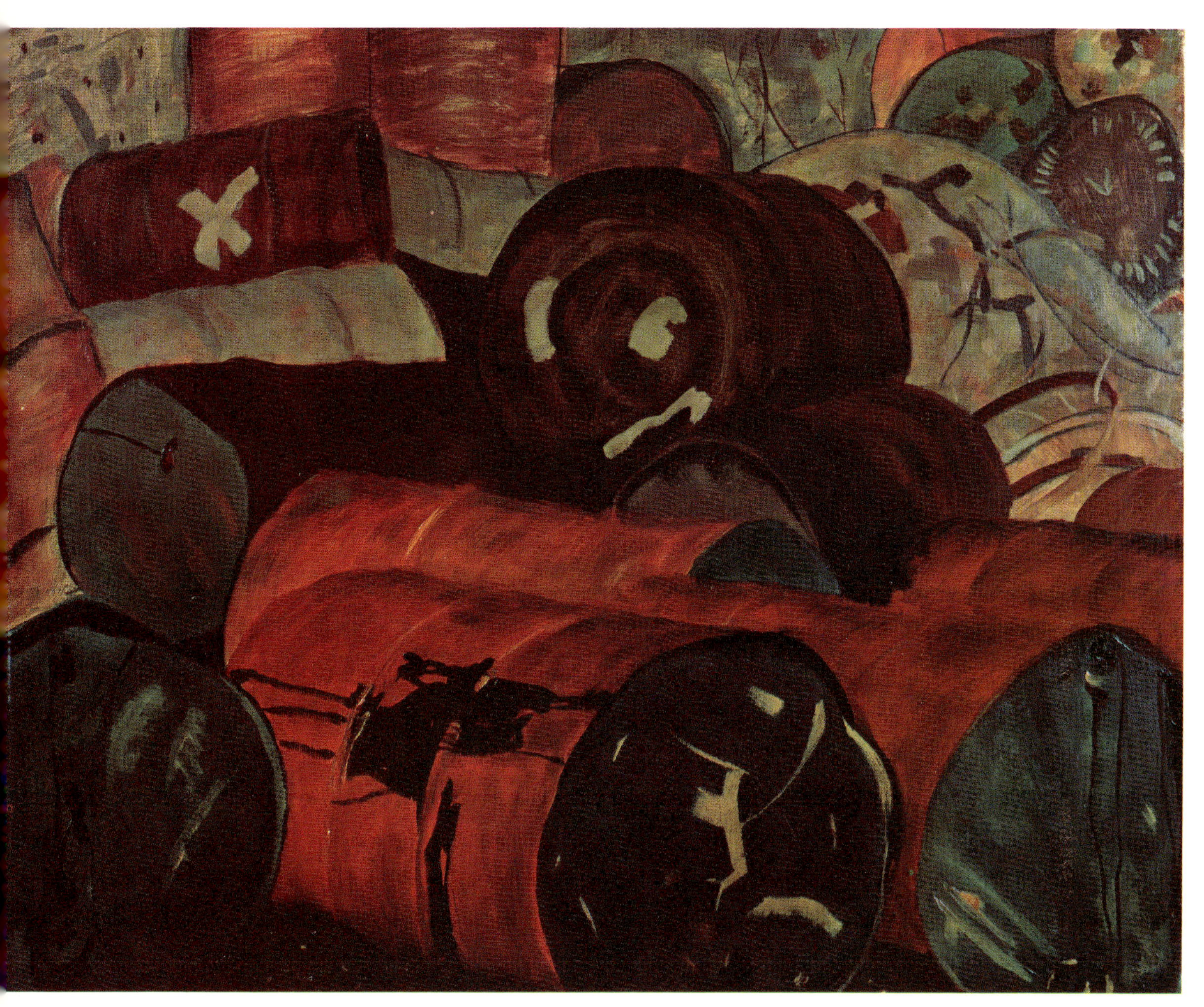

*Arthur G. Dove*

*Plate 41*
SAND BARGE, 1930
*Oil on canvas, 30" X 40"*
*The Phillips Collection, Washington, D.C.*

Duncan Phillips, Dove's best patron, worked his way through the realists to the moderns. When he liked a man's work, he kept right on buying. He took a rather possessive attitude toward his artists, although he didn't like everything they did. He paid Dove a regular income and ended up with a splendid batch of paintings by what he called this "uncompromising abstractionist."

Dove really only had two supporters, Stieglitz and Duncan Phillips, and an artist needs more than that to make the grade. There was no explosive effect; none of that enthusiasm jumping from person to person, which is the meaning of success. His father didn't help him even when he could, and the Depression—a time when even for successful artists, sales stopped—hit him hard. Yet Dove was never forgotten; one thing you've got to say for Stieglitz, he was loyal, at least he was loyal to Dove. Dove's later work is far more pleasing and colorful than his early abstractions, some of which are woefully awkward. You would think the critics and the public would have been pleased, but Dove's reception in the thirties was no better than in the teens. It's easy now to see what Duncan Phillips liked about *Sand Barge*, but it wasn't easy then.

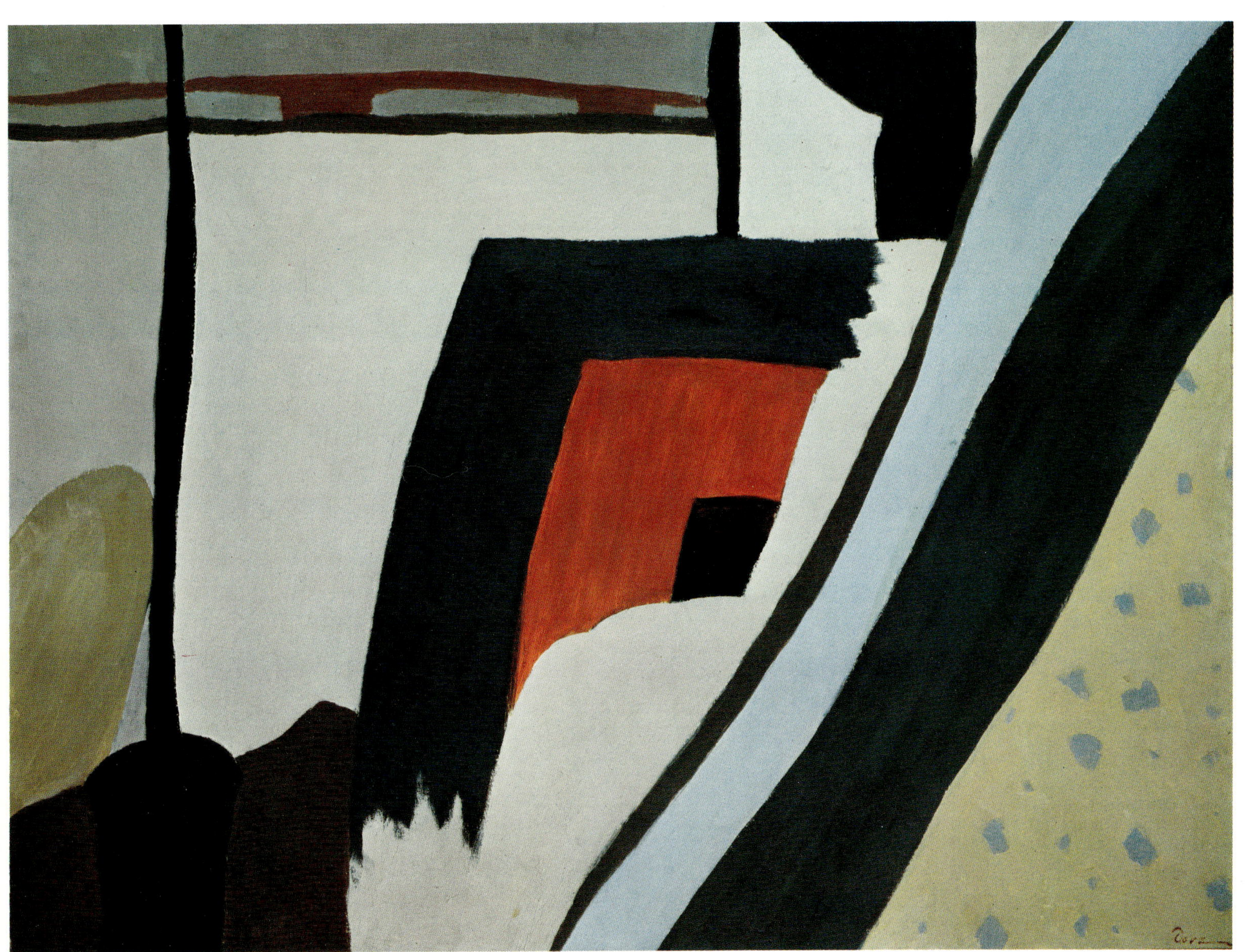

*Arthur G. Dove*

*Plate 42*
FERRY BOAT WRECK, 1931
*Oil on canvas, 18" X 30"*
*Whitney Museum of American Art, New York, New York*
*Gift of Mr. and Mrs. Roy R. Neuberger*

Dove lived on the water long enough to know what it could do, and to realize that the bottom of the smiling Sound was covered with the hulks of boats bigger than his own. A letter to Stieglitz starts out: "It is now 3:45 in the midst of a terrific gale and we are anchored in the middle of Manhattan Bay held by a 3/4 inch line run through a shackle to a mooring. We have been fairly pounding the bottom out of the boat for 24 hours and just hoping that line will have the decency not to cut through. Sheets of rain drive across the cabin roof and we are taking turns at watch and nursing a light fire in our stove until morning on a small pail of charcoal. Life has seemed this way for the last month. So full of contrasts that even they become somewhat monotonous." (Wight, p. 48.)

This picture is as close as Dove ever came to drama; it's painted in storm green and storm gray. Dove is good at conveying the ominous note; you can practically smell the fog and feel the rust.

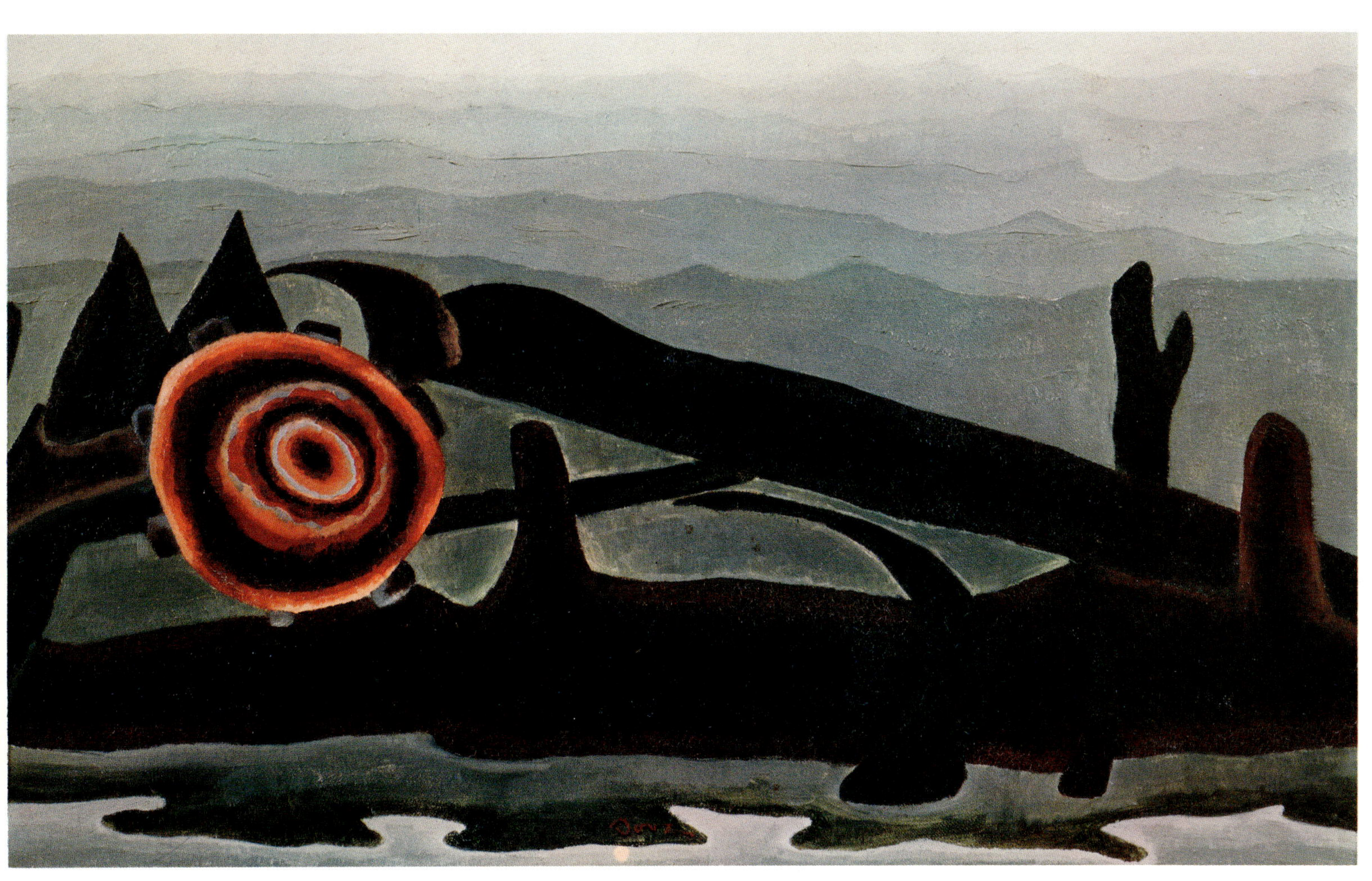

*Arthur G. Dove*

*Plate 43*
FIELD OF GRAIN AS SEEN FROM TRAIN, 1931
*Oil on canvas, 24" X 34"*
*Albright-Knox Art Gallery, Buffalo, New York*

Paul Rosenfield was a sort of drum-beater for the Stieglitz Stable, He wrote: "There is not a pastel or drawing or painting of Dove's that does not communicate some love and direct sensuous feeling for the earth. There is not one that does not bring us with a queer thrill close to some of the gross and earthy substances from which we moderns involuntarily shrink; and lay our hands gently on having animal hides, and rub them over rough stubbly ground, and pass good gritty soil through our fingers." (Paul Rosenfeld, *Port of New York,* p. 168.)

If Dove thought he was going to have an easier time when his father died he was wrong. Farmers in the Middle West couldn't make a living, and neither could Dove in upstate New York. Dove is the only modern American painter who ever tried to make a living as a dirt farmer, and his exasperation shows. In his nature scenes, the forms sometimes get out of control; they become swollen, bulbous, and menacing.

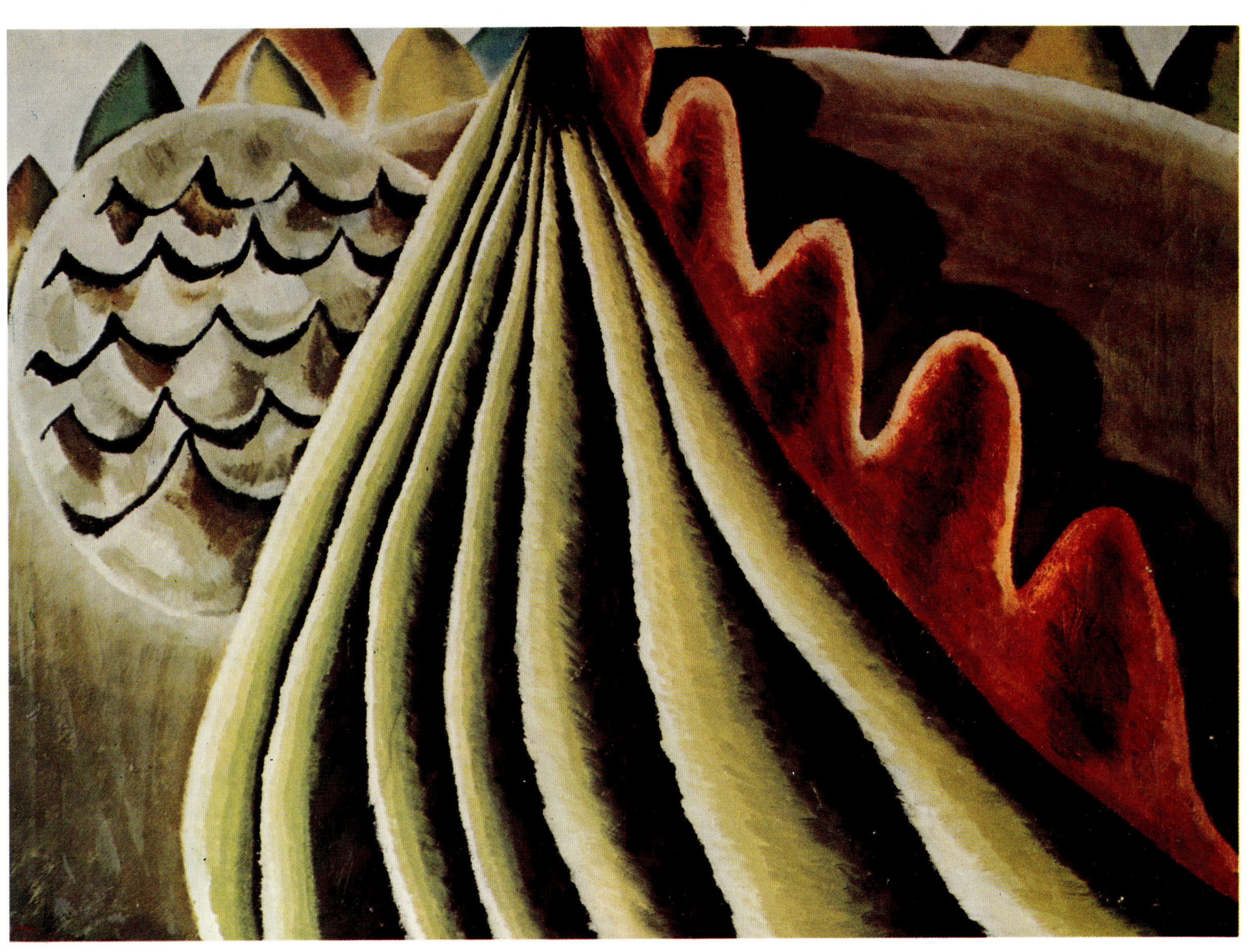

*Arthur G. Dove*

*Plate 44*
COWS IN PASTURE, 1935
*Oil and tempera and wax emulsion on canvas, 20" X 28"*
*The Phillips Collection, Washington, D.C.*

Duncan Phillips said that Dove loved the animals of the pasture and the barn, but he did enough dirt farming to eliminate any undue sentiment. "Even as he dared to be romantic in his abstraction, so also he was among the first to be humorous, sometimes even nonsensical, while never ceasing to be an enchanting painter. In *Cows in Pasture*, the somnolent curves and the absorbent tans and greens and browns are expressive of the subject in its every essence. Black and white and dun-colored cows are huddled in a pasture. Their hindquarters are settled comfortably in mossy, congenial turf. A bull calf has a sleepy eye and there is a bit of clover on his brain. The lazy contours suggest the slow and drowsy rumination. Cows, too, have their stream of consciousness." (Wight, p. 17.)

Dove didn't find the country as idyllic as Duncan Phillips did. When he was on the boat, he probably thought he would be glad to get back to farming, but it didn't work out that way. He had the real farmer's love and hate for nature. These cows may look cute, but the work is heavy, dirty, and never-ending.

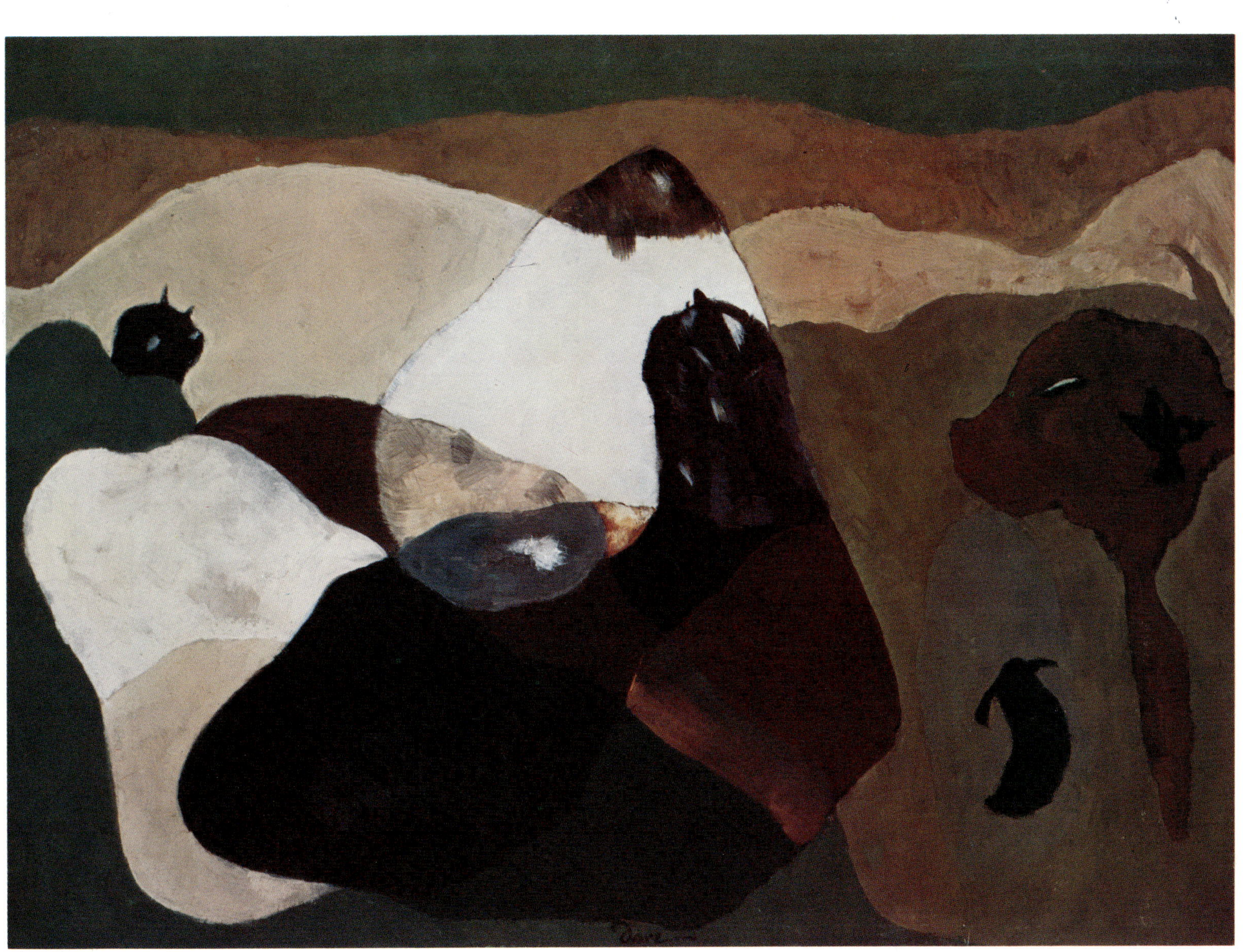

## *Arthur G. Dove*

*Plate 45*
HIGH NOON, 1944
*Oil and wax emulsion on composition board, 18" X 27"*
*Wichita Art Museum, Wichita, Kansas*
*Roland P. Murdock Collection*

Dove was fascinated by the sun, and he tried to paint it directly. "In spite of a discouraging and even tragic life during the 1930's, Dove's painting continued to celebrate the beauty of nature and life. At his best he was a genuine poet of nature—abstract but not at all dry, emotionally convincing and formally satisfying. These qualities are summed up in the relatively late "High Noon, 1944." (Samuel M. Green, *American Art,* p. 534.)

Dove looked at the sun too long. This sun is monstrous. Dove had heart trouble and he knew he was going to die. He has gone far beyond pure form and color; this is a primitive, religious sun and it's going to kill him.

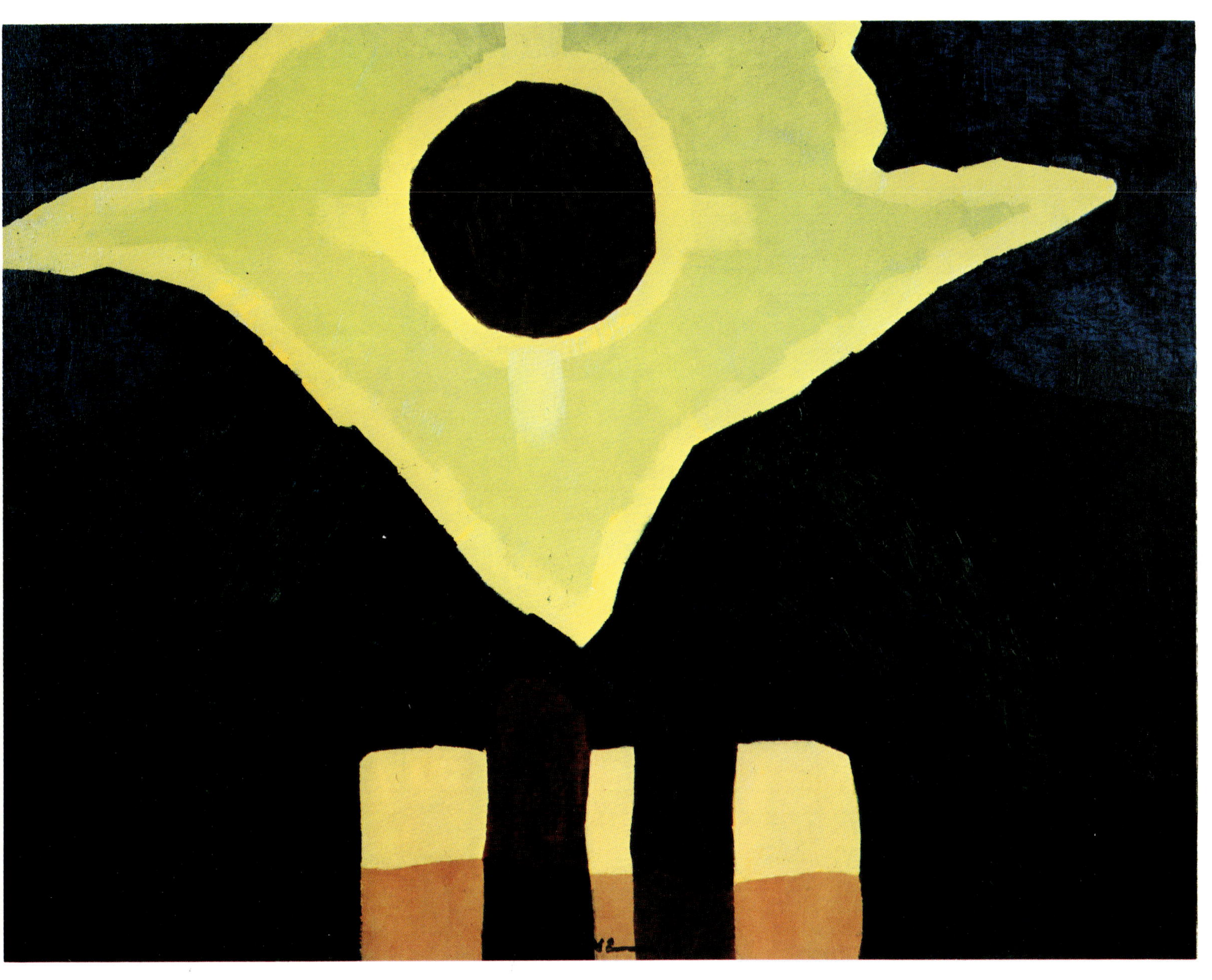

*Alfred Maurer*

*Plate 46*
SELF-PORTRAIT WITH HAT, 1927
*Oil on board, 39″ X 23 7/8″*
*Walker Art Center, Minneapolis, Minnesota*

Maurer and Weber brought modernism to Stieglitz; he didn't bring it to them. For Maurer, modern art was troubling and introspective. Abstraction made a soul-searcher out of a carefree man. Then as now, nobody saw abstractly; they *thought* abstractly and painted what they thought. Maurer found the process painful. You see a lot of what happened to Maurer in this picture. He was puzzled by abstractionism, and so were his friends. He had started off so confidently, and it had all gone sour. He is the only one of the group who was ruined by modernism, if that's what did it. Somewhere along the line his spring broke. In Paris he had been the debonair, dancing Alfy, with the world at his feet, and he ended up in New York as poor old Alfy. We make him into a martyr of modernism, but it's almost too neat.

He had been everybody's friend in Europe, a great pal of Leo Stein's and a close friend of Dove's. Maurer brought artists to Stieglitz, and Stieglitz was glad to have him. But when he came back to New York, after the outbreak of World War I, things were different. He had a personality change, Stieglitz dropped him, and he became the forgotten man. Andrew Dasburg wrote an article in 1923 in which he described the rise and influence of Cubism, discussing Marin, Demuth, Hartley, and Weber, but he didn't mention poor old Alfy.

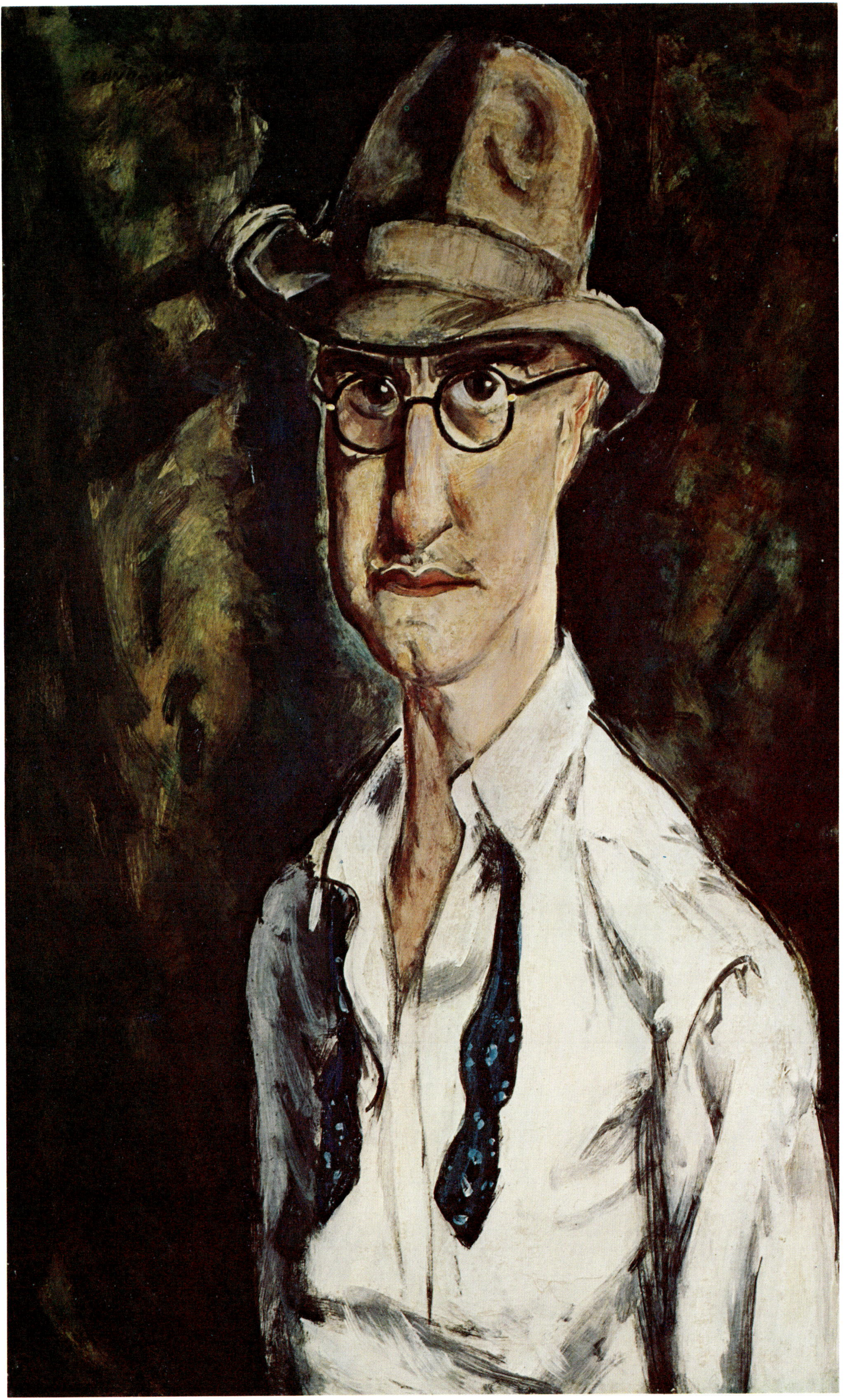

*Alfred Maurer*

*Plate 47*
PORTRAIT OF A GIRL WITH GREEN BACKGROUND, 1929
*Oil on gesso panel, 21 3/4" X 17 7/8"*
*The Columbus Gallery of Fine Arts, Columbus, Ohio*
*Gift of Ione and Hudson D. Walker*

Maurer was one of the earliest American moderns, and probably the most important convert the movement ever made. If he had continued on the other track, after winning First Prize at the Carnegie International in 1901, he would rank today with Frieseke and his pictures would be hung in group shows of American Impressionism. Instead, he changed his style completely and became the martyr of American modernism. During his early days in Paris, until 1914, Maurer was an exceptionally cheerful fellow. Something happened in his life, which may not even have had anything to do with his art, and for the rest of his life in New York this pioneering abstractionist was an unhappy recluse.

There's so much sadness in Maurer's work that it must be real. He was important in the early days as a pioneer of abstraction, that's for sure, but his later life was shoals and misery. The whole Stieglitz group had their historical importance early. They brought abstraction to the States, but it didn't stay. Cubism and Futurism got a lot of attention at the Armory Show in 1913, then they went underground for years. Abstraction was by no means the dominant style in American paintinr between the two wars. There were odd men like Stuart Davis, but the National Academy, the Fourteenth Street School, and the Regionalists were much more prominent during the twenties and thirties. When Abstract Expressionism took over in the late forties it didn't stem from Stieglitz.

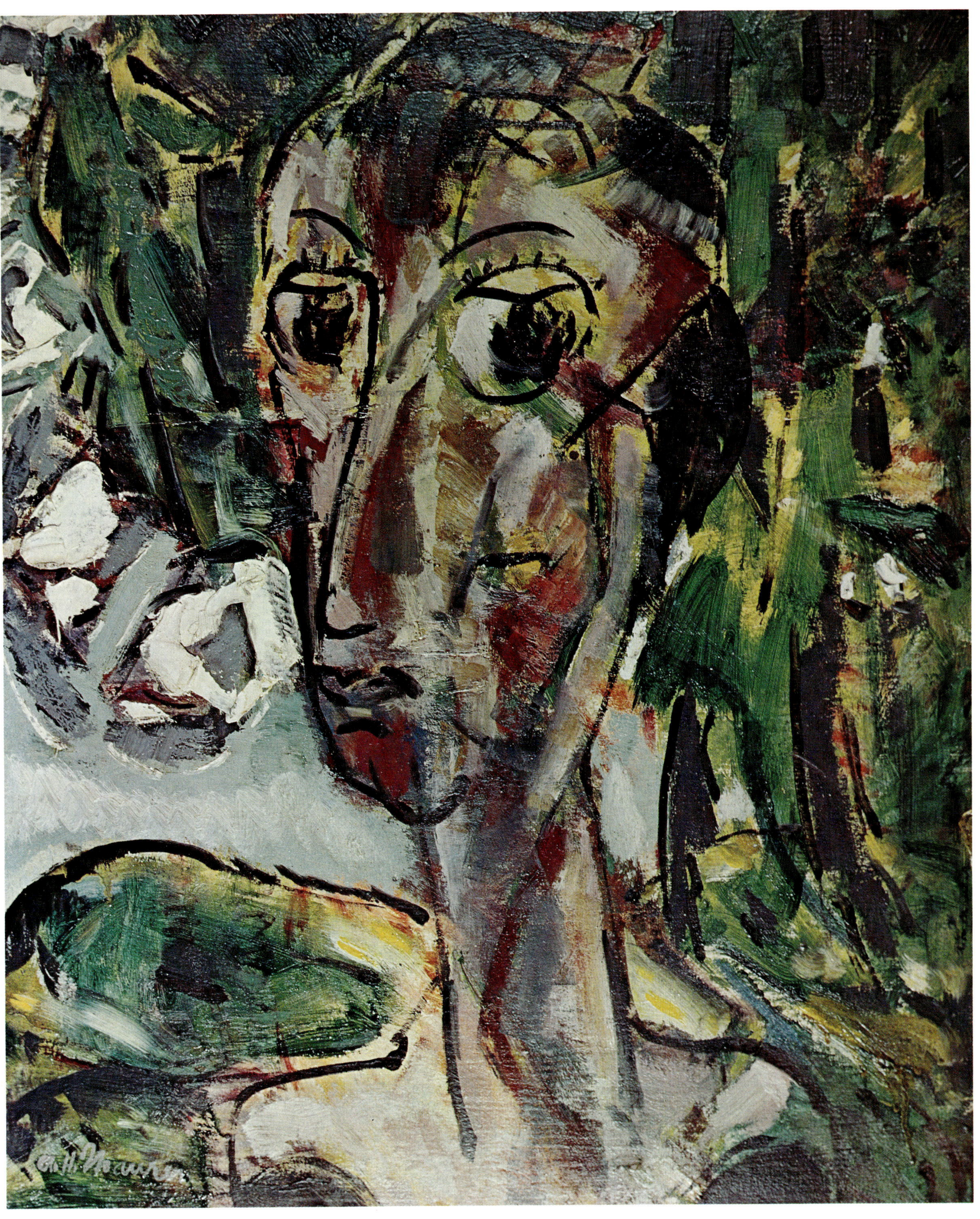

*Alfred Maurer*

*Plate 48*
GEORGE WASHINGTON, 1932
*Oil on board, 39" X 24"*
*Portland Art Museum, Portland, Oregon*

For a man like Maurer, modernism meant giving up form and color, everything that had been pleasant about painting. All that was left was the essential. He tried to get down to the bare bones of reality, and didn't like what he found. We now praise this casualty of modern art for qualities his contemporaries couldn't see.

Maurer made an attempt at a comeback in 1924. Erhard Weyhe, the bookseller and dealer, took him on. Henry McBride wrote appreciatively of Maurer in the *New York Herald*. At Sherwood Anderson's suggestion, Alfy sent the review on to his old friend Gertrude Stein, and told her that if he could be with her, he could talk his head off; his was a story no fountain pen could tell. Anderson went all out for Maurer in an advertisement accompanying the show, telling how Dove introduced him to Maurer. He had long been convinced that Maurer was one of the really great modern painters. "Life twisted, beaten down, perverted often enough, life as it is—in young girls in the back streets of cities, in tired old women—life everywhere having its wonder moments, this poet has caught." (McCausland, *A. H. Maurer*, p. 157.) It looked like success to Alfy: "hope so, at one time I promised myself to strangle success if I ever got hold of it, now I've changed my mind." But it was a flash in the pan, and Alfe went back to obscurity and desperation.

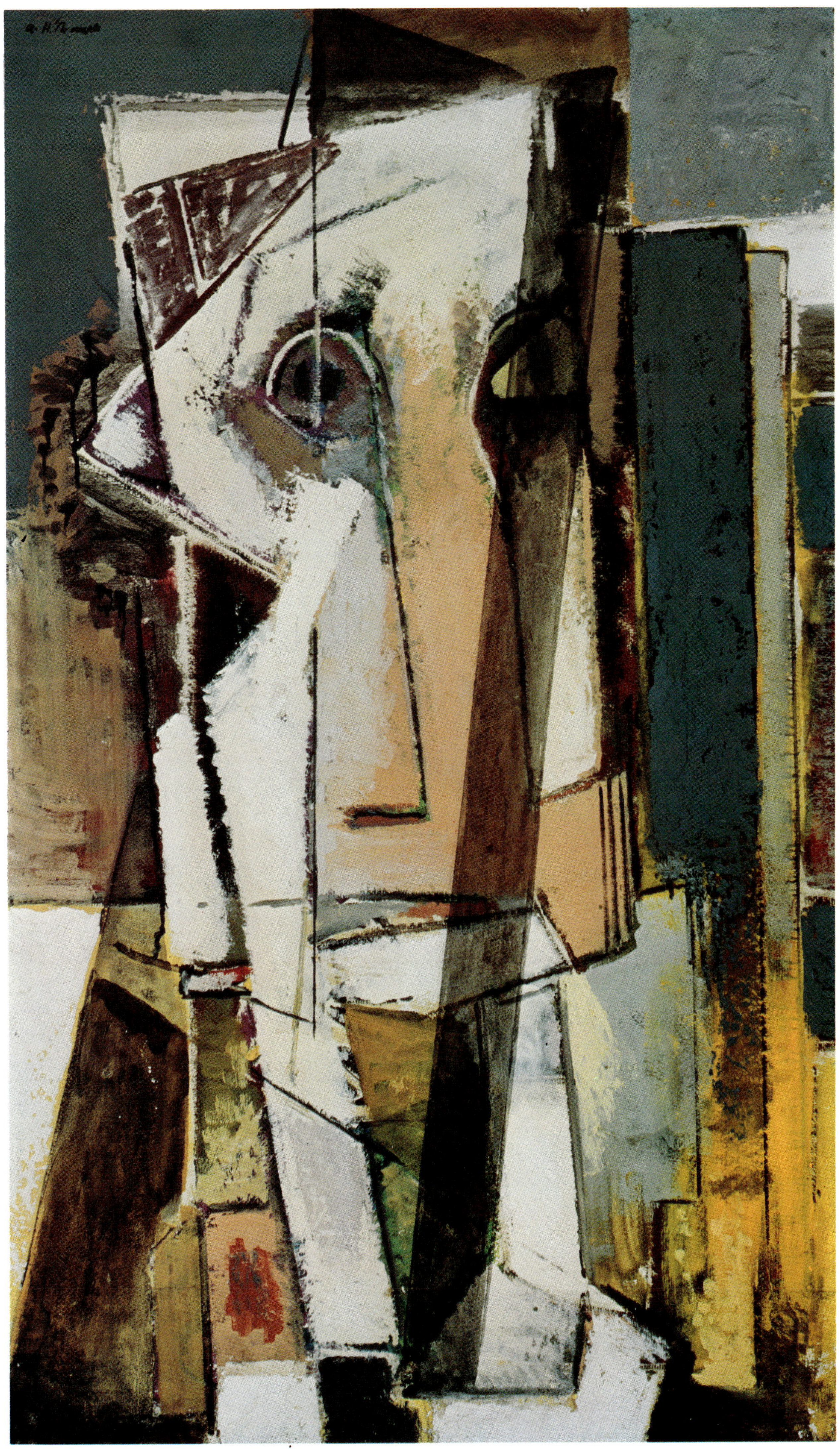

***Max Weber***

*Plate 49*
THE TWO MUSICIANS, 1917
*Oil on canvas, 40 1/8" X 30 1/8"*
*The Museum of Modern Art, New York, New York*
*Richard D. Brixey Bequest*

This is a classic Cubist subject, straight out of Picasso, but Max Weber twisted it around and made it his own. Neither Maurer nor Weber had followers; they were individual painters, not influential teachers.

Weber had a full career as a successful artist. He was always proud of having been Henri Rousseau's friend while in Paris, and a pupil under Henri Mattise, but he didn't rest on his laurels, and he didn't seem to yearn backwards to the good old days when modern art was young. He went right on—a lively, chipper little man, active on juries, busy on projects, very much the artist, a little bit the master. Although full of stories about the past, he didn't waste time on it; he was too busy. Like Maurer, he was a friend of the Steins, and like Maurer he educated Stieglitz in modern art. But that's the end of the resemblance. Compared to Maurer, he had an easy time in this life, and he drifted away from the intense little stieglitz circle into the main stream of American art.

As much as anybody, Weber brought Cubism to America, but he never attained the bare-bones quality of Picasso and Braque, with their Puritan grays and browns. Weber had sparkle and wit, qualities not always present in modern art.

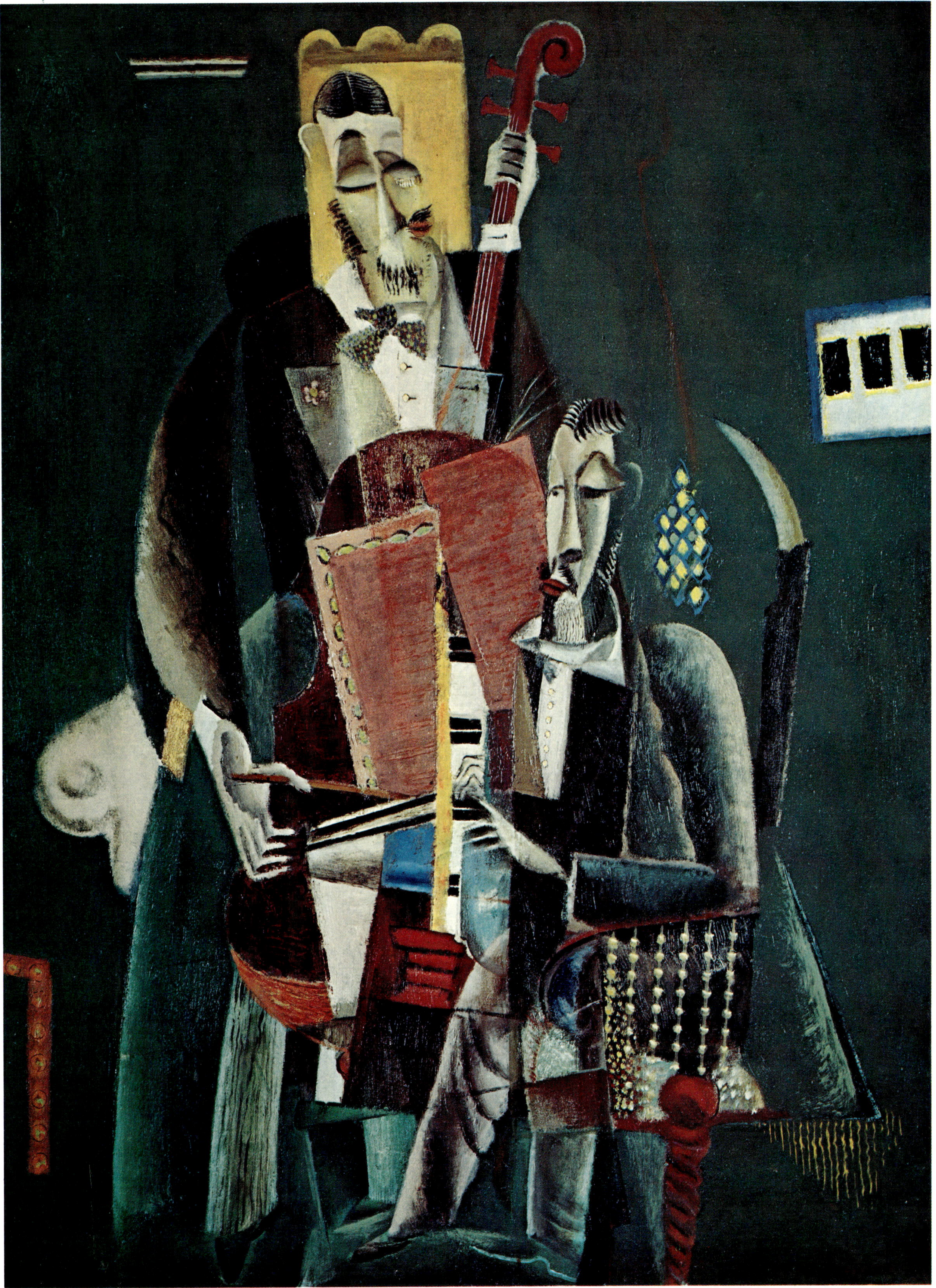

***Max Weber***

*Plate 50*
STILL LIFE, 1921
*Oil on canvas, 15 1/8" X 21 1/8"*
*The Columbus Gallery of Fine Arts, Columbus, Ohio*
*Ferdinand Howald Collection*

The style change came easily for Max Weber. Unlike Maurer, he had never been committed to the old. Weber took to Cézanne and Cubism with the greatest of ease. He was naturally cosmopolitan, and he had a continental accent from the beginning. When he came back to the States, he taught Stieglitz a lot about abstraction.

Like Marin, Weber was sent to Stieglitz by Steichen; Steichen doesn't get the credit he should for bringing the word to the heathen. When Weber was broke, Stieglitz let him sleep in the rooms next to 291, which was a signal mark of favor, for Stieglitz kept a certain distance between himself and his artists. He probably had to; he was the boss.

There doesn't seem to be any story about why Weber split off from the group. According to Dorothy Norman, he was always getting his feelings hurt around 291. With Stieglitz, you didn't have to imagine the slights and the rudeness; they were real.

Through Picasso and Braque, Weber was interested in Cubism early, and in Negro art. He considered all primitives as his province, called his book of poems *Primitives*, and illustrated it with woodcuts that cover the primitive world.

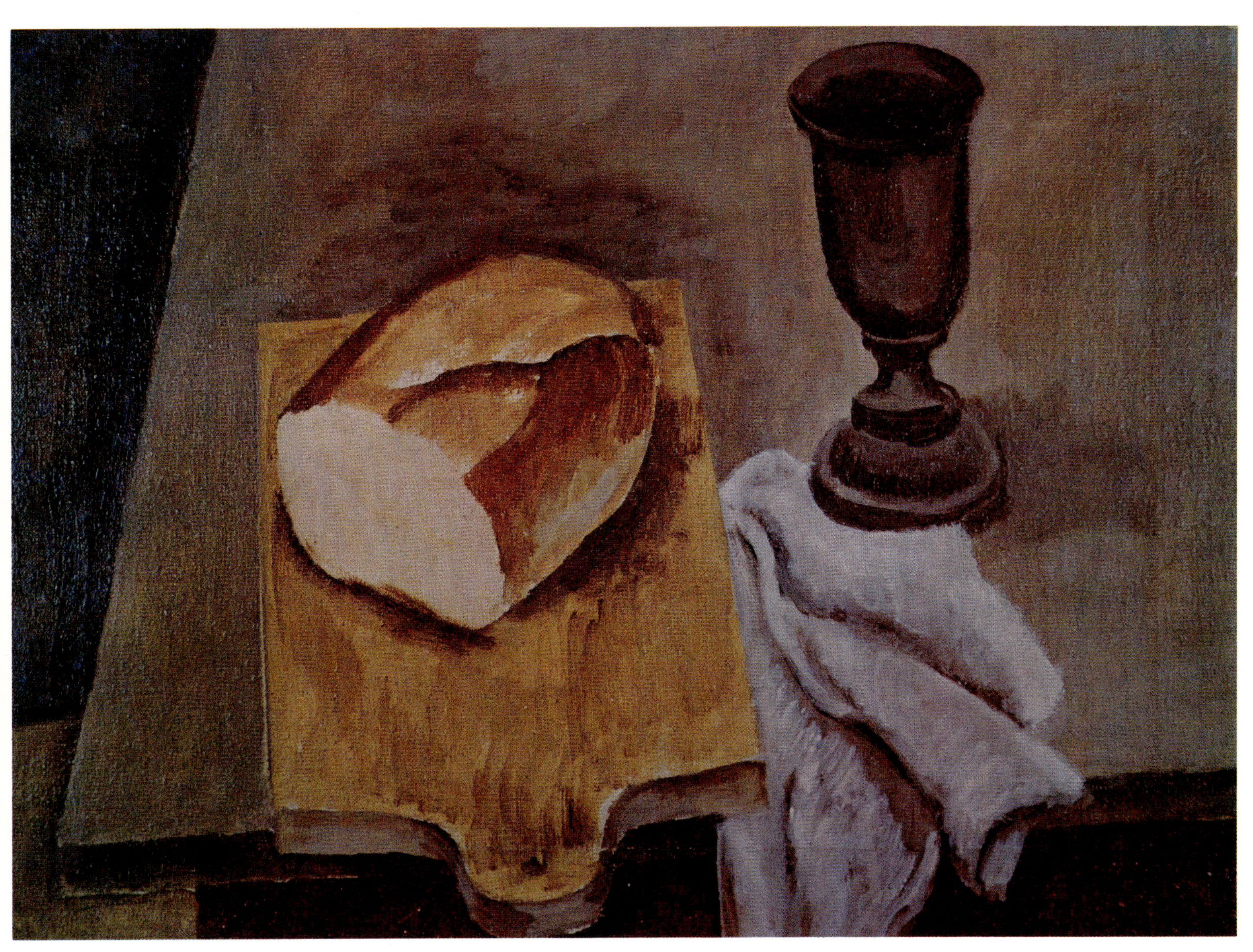

*Max Weber*

*Plate 51*
THE WAYFARERS, 1944
*Oil on canvas, 32 1/4" X 26 1/4"*
*The Columbus Gallery of Fine Arts, Columbus, Ohio*
*Howald Fund*

There was a period in American art when it seemed as though abstraction would go away. Max Weber worked his way through Cubism and came out on the other side, feeling that there wasn't enough there. Under the impact of Hitler, Weber felt a deep sympathy with the Jewish people. He produced hundreds of images of human suffering, tragedy, and hope—a far cry from his abstract youth.

Most of the Stieglitz group moved away from abstraction, and so did Weber; that's also the course that American art took. We're back again in a world of pure form and color, but Weber ended up drenched with emotions. There's a world of sadness and pathos in his later work, but it was the sorrows of the world which bore him down, not his own. He should have been sympathetic to the plight of his old friend Maurer, and probably was. When Weber first arrived in Paris in 1905, Maurer had been pointed out to him as a famous man, a mythical figure.

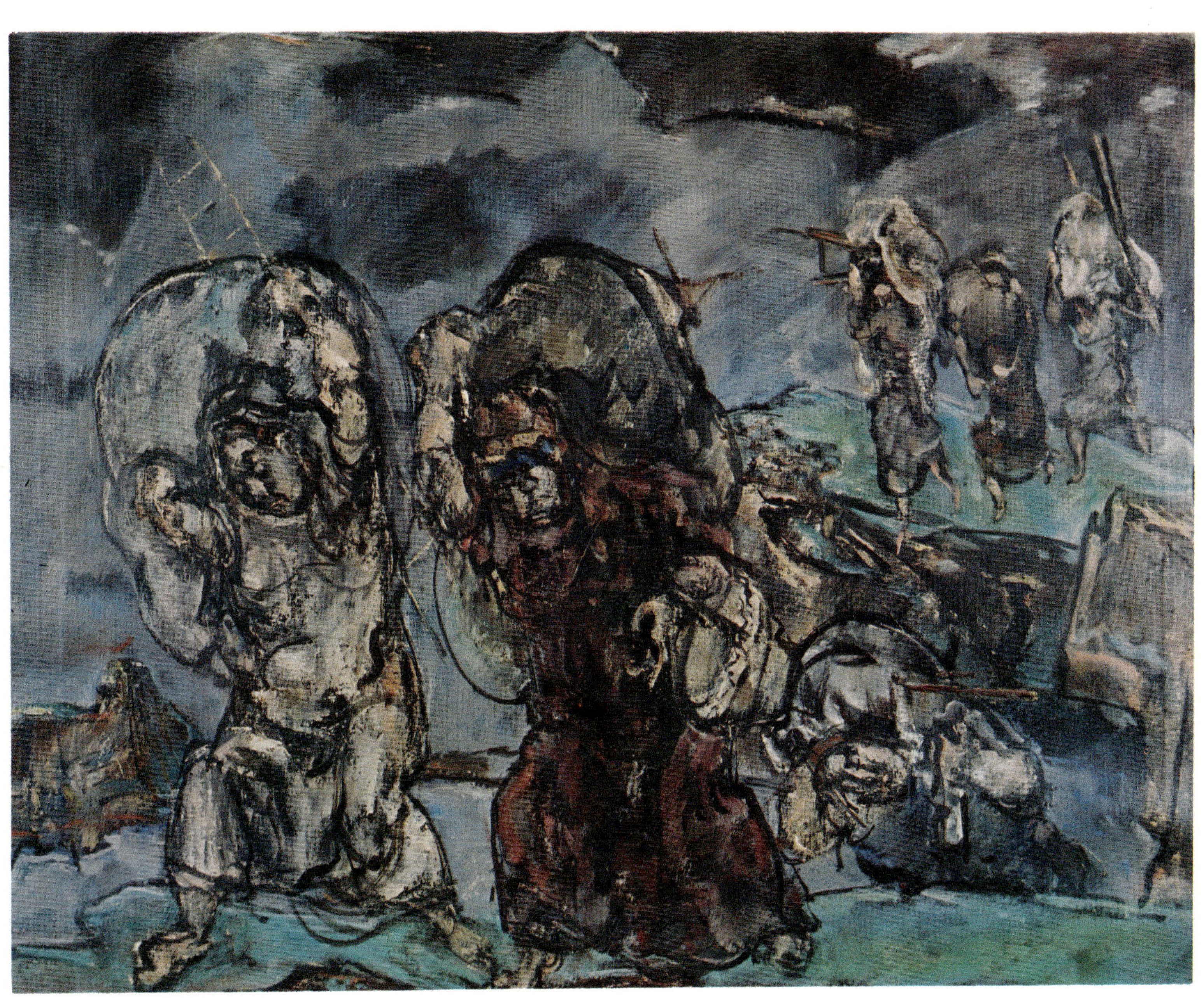

***Abraham Walkowitz***

*Plate 52*
TREES AND FLOWERS, 1917
*Watercolor, 15 1/2" X 29 1/2"*
*The Columbus Gallery of Fine Arts, Columbus, Ohio*
*Ferdinand Howald Collection*

Walkowitz was a nature poet who valued the childlike vision, and prided himself on retaining it. He felt that people were spoiled by cities, and artists by commerce; "El Greco didn't exhibit" was one of his phrases. He didn't push himself, and after he left Stieglitz, nobody pushed him.

These big watercolors of Walkowitz's are among the most personal things he ever did. He thought of them as decorative, and he stressed the compositional elements almost too much in this one, with the trees serving as columns to break up the scene. This summer landscape, with lovers, mothers, and kids, is lyric, if minor, music. It's hard to believe that these cool summer poetries were ever considered advanced or daring, for Walkowitz wasn't all that far from his academic contemporaries.

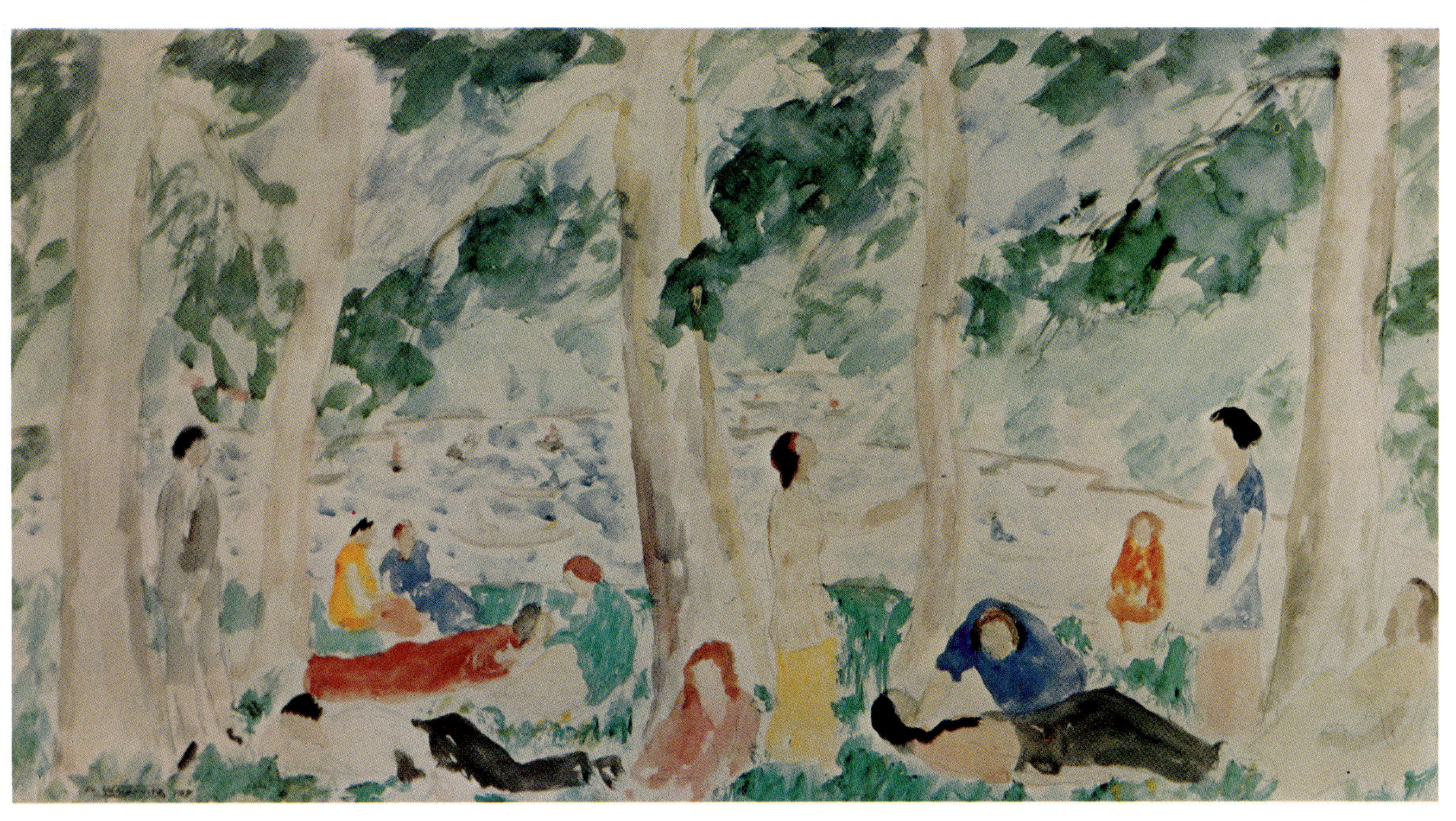

*Abraham Walkowitz*

*Plate 53*
BATHERS, 1919
*Watercolor, 15 7/8" X 29 3/8"*
*The Columbus Gallery of Fine Arts, Columbus, Ohio*
*Ferdinand Howald Collection*

Walkowitz was a great Maine man, where he knew Marin and Hartley and William Zorach. This bathing scene looks a bit like the work of Maurice Prendergast, whom Walkowitz might have known and would have liked, but the resemblance probably stems from their similar artistic backgrounds.

Walkowitz was interested in children's art, and you can see why. He always retained a touching quality of awkward wonder in his work. When he brought Stieglitz a batch of children's pictures from a settlement house with which he was connected, Stieglitz gave them one of his famous "First Shows Anywhere." Stieglitz had a real ability to appreciate things he had never seen before; he said that children's drawings had much of the spirit of modern art.

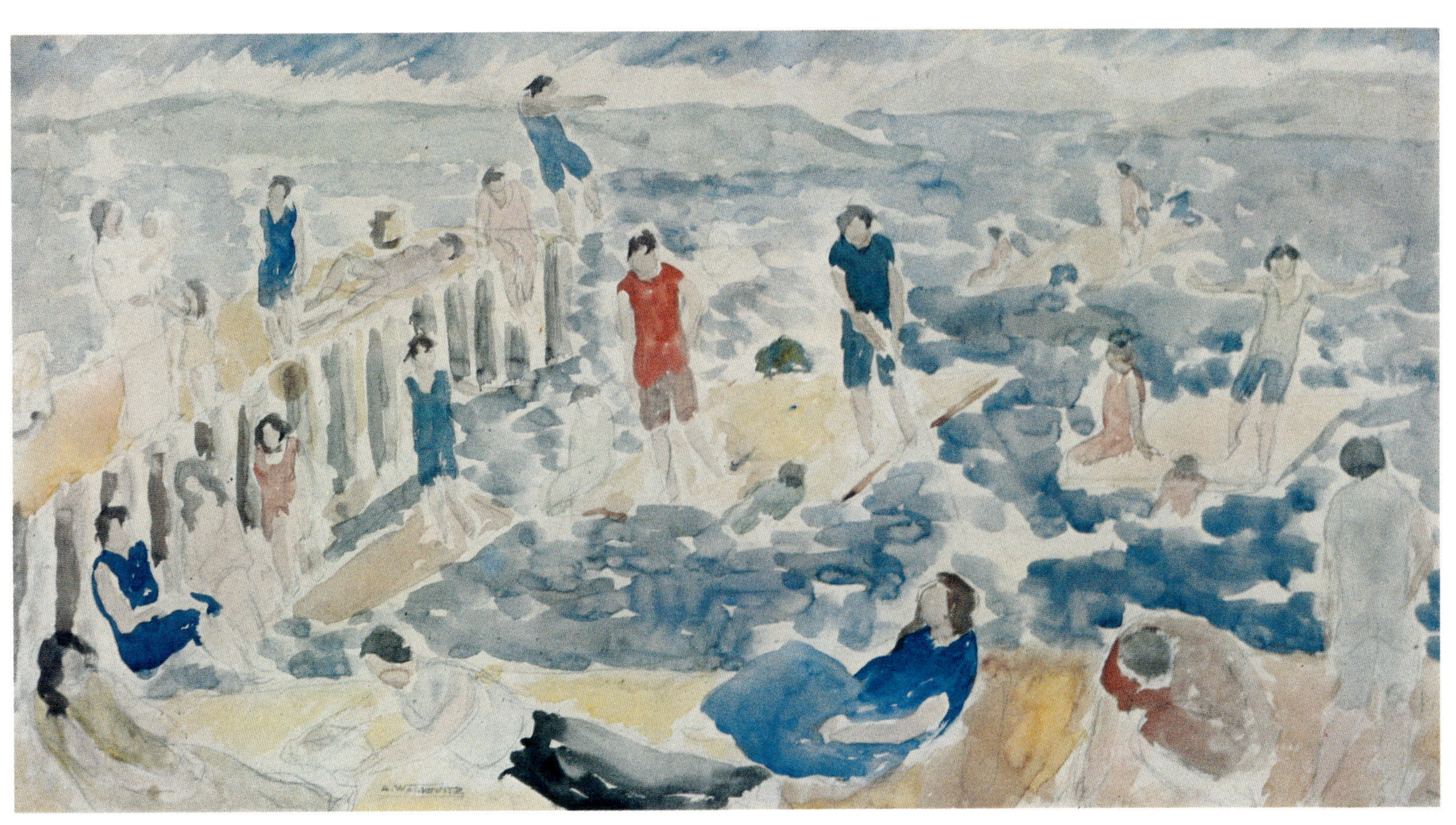

*Abraham Walkowitz*

*Plate 54*
BATHERS RESTING, 1920
*Watercolor, 15 3/8" X 29 3/8"*
*The Columbus Gallery of Fine Arts, Columbus, Ohio*
*Ferdinand Howald Collection*

Walkowitz didn't bring French abstraction to Stieglitz, he learned it from him. He had spent his years in Paris, but modern art didn't mean much to him until he came back to New York. He was a rather docile man, which is probably why Stieglitz gave him four one-man shows in five years. He shared the group's admiration for Stieglitz, but he didn't feel that Stieglitz knew much about "inner things."

It's hard to see how anybody could object to Walkowitz, but one of the early critics said he was as weird as the worst of them, which seems severe. Walkowitz said: "I am seeking to attune my art to what I feel to be the keynote of an experience. If it brings to me a harmonious sensation, I then try to find the concrete elements that are likely to record the sensation in visual forms, in the medium of lines, of color shapes, of space divisions. When the line and color are sensitized, they seem to me alive with the rhythm which I felt in the thing that stimulated my imagination and my expression. If my art is true to its purpose, then it should convey to me in graphic terms the feeling which I received in imaginative terms." (Dorothy Norman, *Alfred Stieglitz: An American Seer,* p. 116.) That seems like a lot of freight for a frail and charming bark.

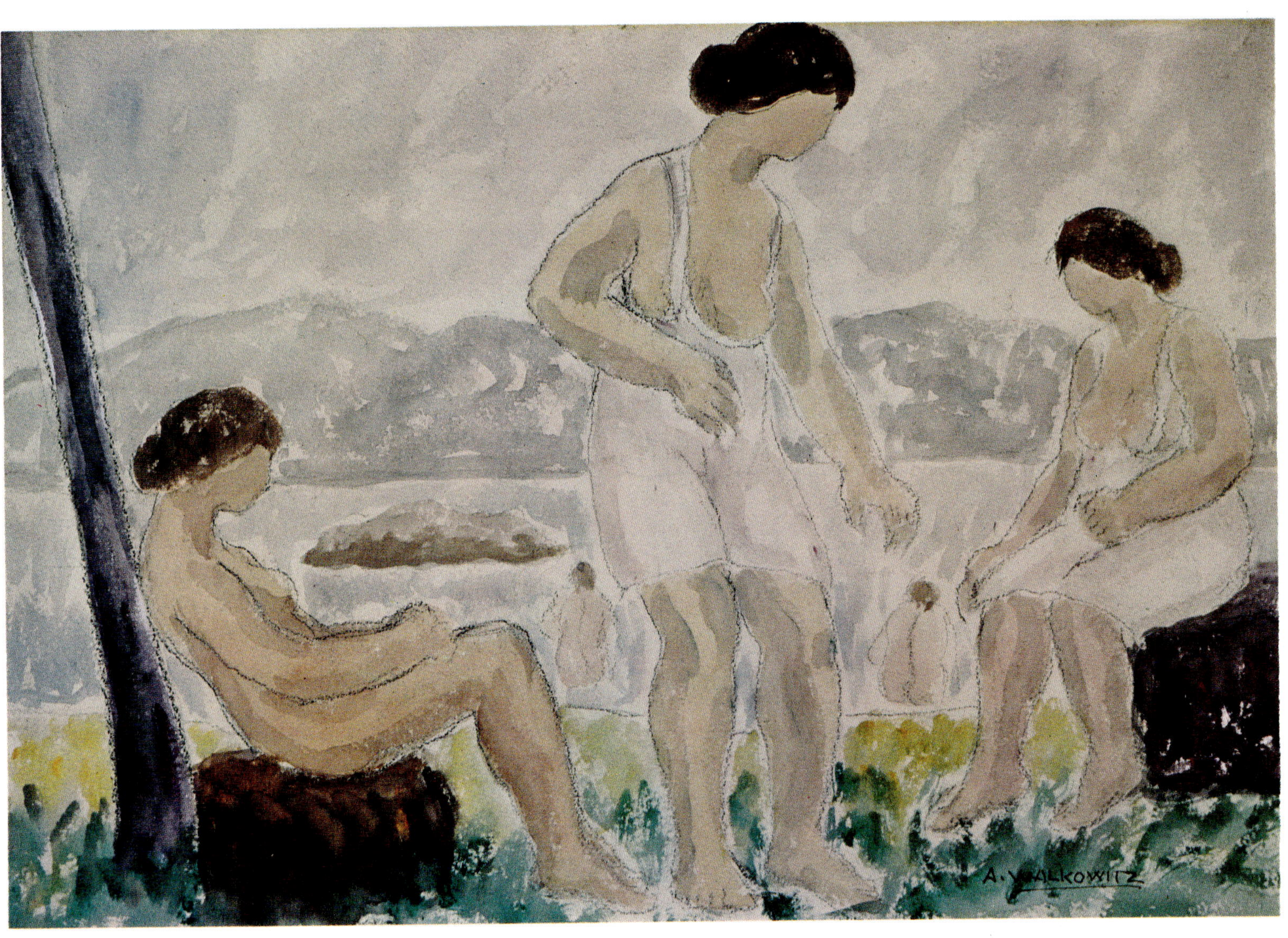
A. WALKOWITZ

*Georgia O'Keeffe*

*Plate 55*
BLUE NO. II, 1916
*Watercolor, 15 7/8" X 10 15/16"*
*The Brooklyn Museum, Brooklyn, New York*
*Bequest of Miss Mary T. Cockcroft*

This is the earliest kind of O'Keeffe painting, done just after the charcoal drawings which were shown by Stieglitz in 1916, and exhibited without her knowledge. They are remarkably abstract; after the Armory Show, there may have been other Texas schoolteachers who painted abstracts, but not many. Stieglitz, with his eye for the new, picked out her work immediately; O'Keeffe was the only one of his artists who didn't come properly recommended.

Stieglitz said that O'Keeffe's early work created a sensation; some people were deeply moved, as if it were a revelation, while others, including many professional artists, were horrified at his showing such work after Matisse, Picasso, Cézanne, Marin, Dove, and Hartley. When O'Keeffe wanted to know who gave him permission to hang them, he told her that she had. He claimed that she had no more right to withhold them than to withhold a child from the world.

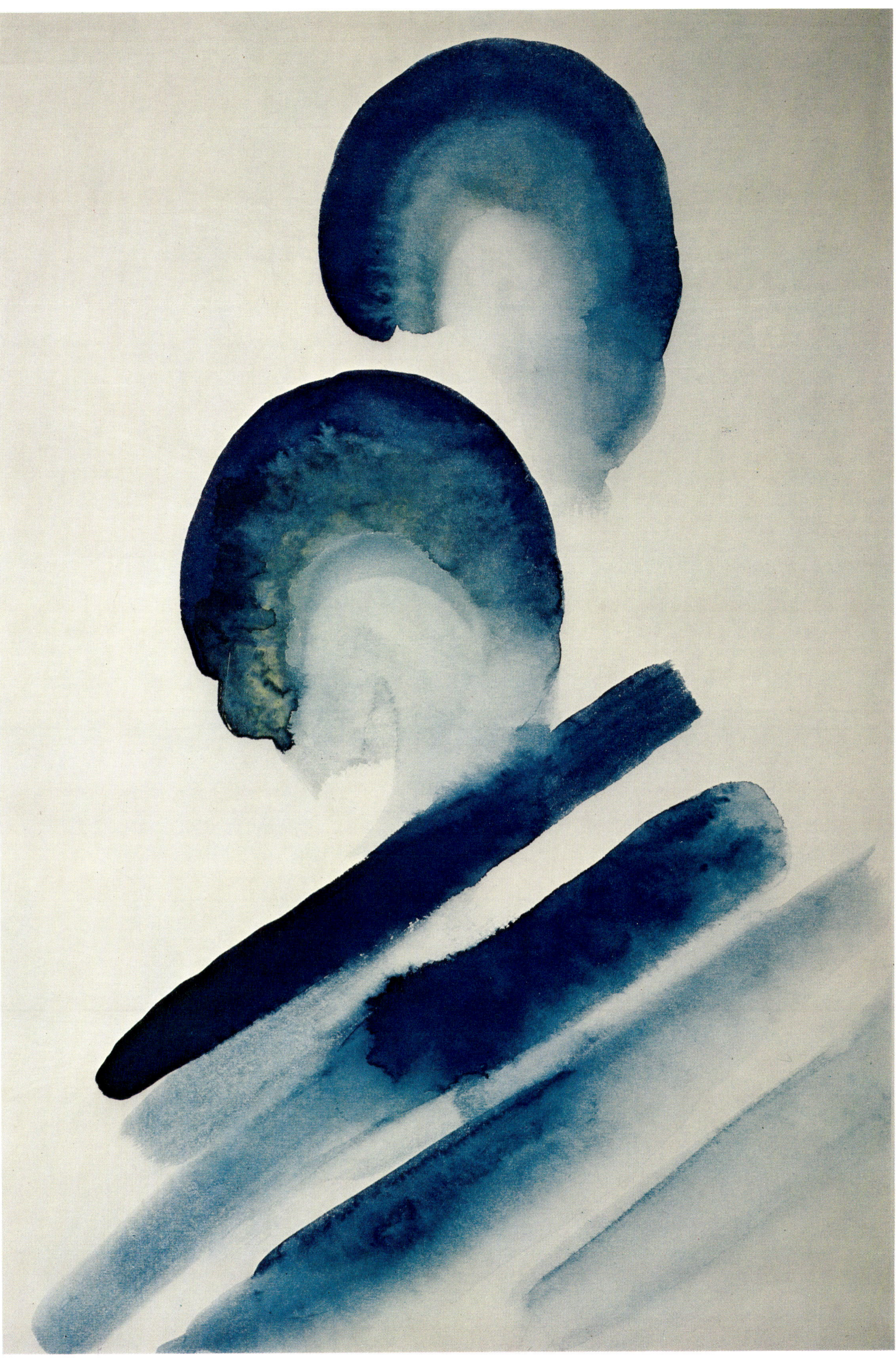

*Plate 56*
LIGHT COMING ON THE PLAINS NO. II, 1917
*Watercolor, 12″ X 9″*
*Amon Carter Museum, Fort Worth, Texas*

In 1916 O'Keeffe decided that her work was too much influenced by her teachers, and struck out on her own. In 1917, the year this watercolor was painted, Stieglitz gave her a one-man show which was, appropriately, the last show in his Gallery at 291 Fifth Avenue. When O'Keeffe came to New York to see the show, it was closed, but Stieglitz rehung it for her.

When Dove saw these early O'Keeffe watercolors, he told Stieglitz that "this girl was doing naturally what many of the fellows were trying to do, and failing." Although she says she doesn't much like pictures, O'Keeffe has a painting of Dove's on her living-room table in New Mexico. She came to abstraction naturally, as she thought Dove did. "It was his way of thinking. Kandinsky was very showy about it, but Dove had an earthy, simple quality that led directly to abstraction. His things are very special. I always wish I'd bought more of them. And all the people Dove influenced, who are better known than he is. The Museum of Modern Art never gave him a really important show—I don't know why. Dove used to paint a lot of small pictures, little landscapes, that didn't look particularly distinguished at first, but in them he would get the feel of a particular place so completely that you'd know you'd been there." (Calvin Tomkins, "Georgia O'Keeffe," *New Yorker,* March 4, 1974.)

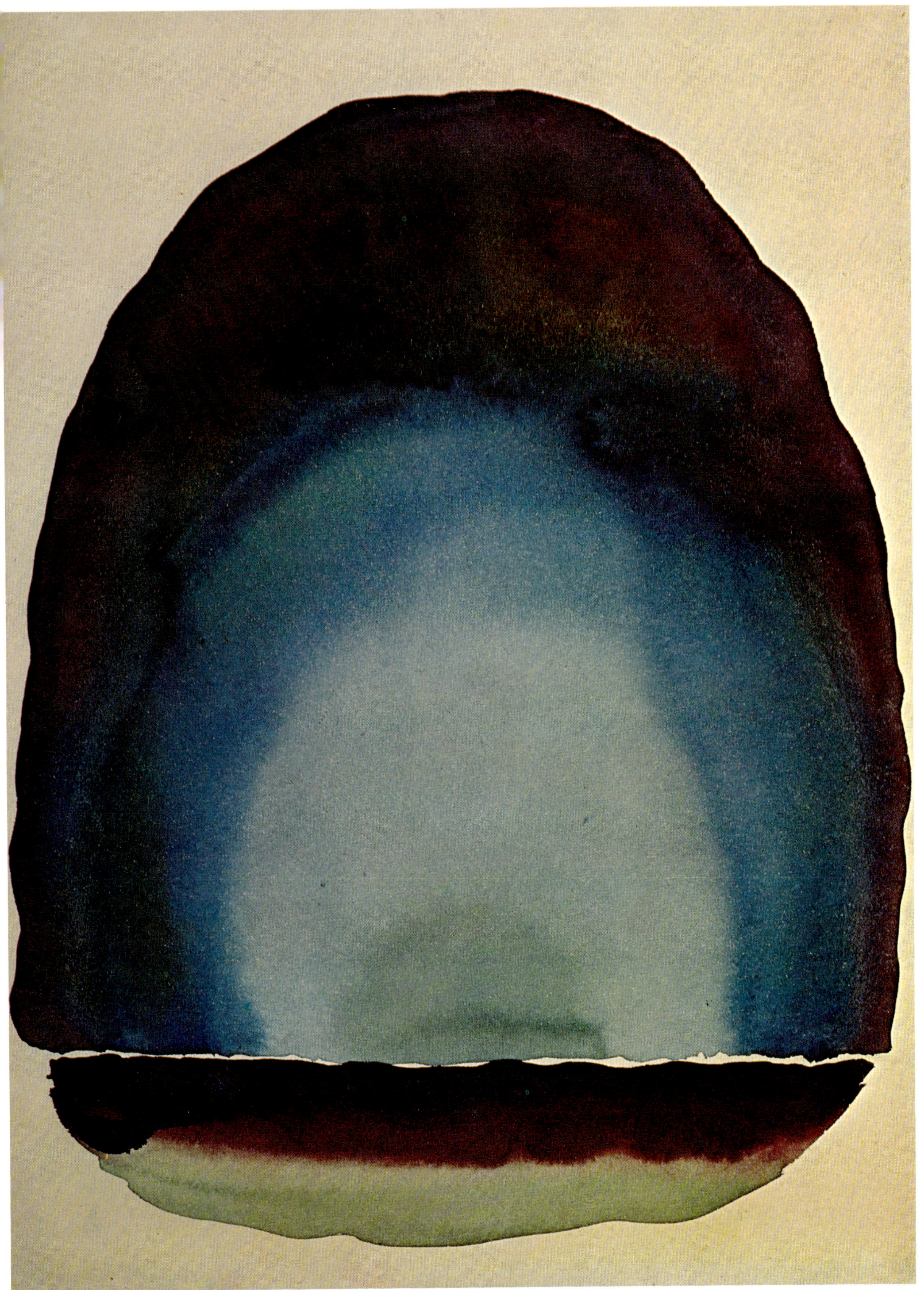

*Plate 57*
BLUE AND GREEN MUSIC, 1919
*Oil on canvas, 23" X 19"*
*The Art Institute of Chicago, Chicago, Illinois*
*The Alfred Stieglitz Collection*

In 1918 Stieglitz offered to back O'Keeffe for a year, so she gave up her Texas job and moved to New York. She gained time to paint and Stieglitz gained a model—he photographed her continually. The vertical lines in this painting may represent skyscrapers; she did quite a few paintings of tall buildings, perhaps under the influence of Stieglitz, who photographed them for years.

Stieglitz was responsible for launching O'Keeffe's great career. At first meeting, she asked him if he thought she was an idiot. He built her up in every way and published an article by William Murrell Fisher about her in his magazine.

"Here are emotional forms quite beyond the reach of conscious design, beyond the grasp of reason—yet strongly appealing to that apparently unanalyzable sensitivity in us through which we feel the grandeur and sublimity of life.

"Quite sensibly, there is an inner law of harmony at work in the composition of these drawings and paintings by Miss O'Keeffe, and they are more truly inspired than any work I have seen . . . Of all things earthy, it is only in music that one finds any analogy to the emotional center of the drawings—to the gigantic, swirling rhythms, and the exquisite tendernesses so powerfully and sensitively rendered—and music is the condition toward which, according to Pater, all art constantly aspires. Well, plastic art, in the hands of O'Keeffe, seems now to have approximated that." (Norman, p. 131.)

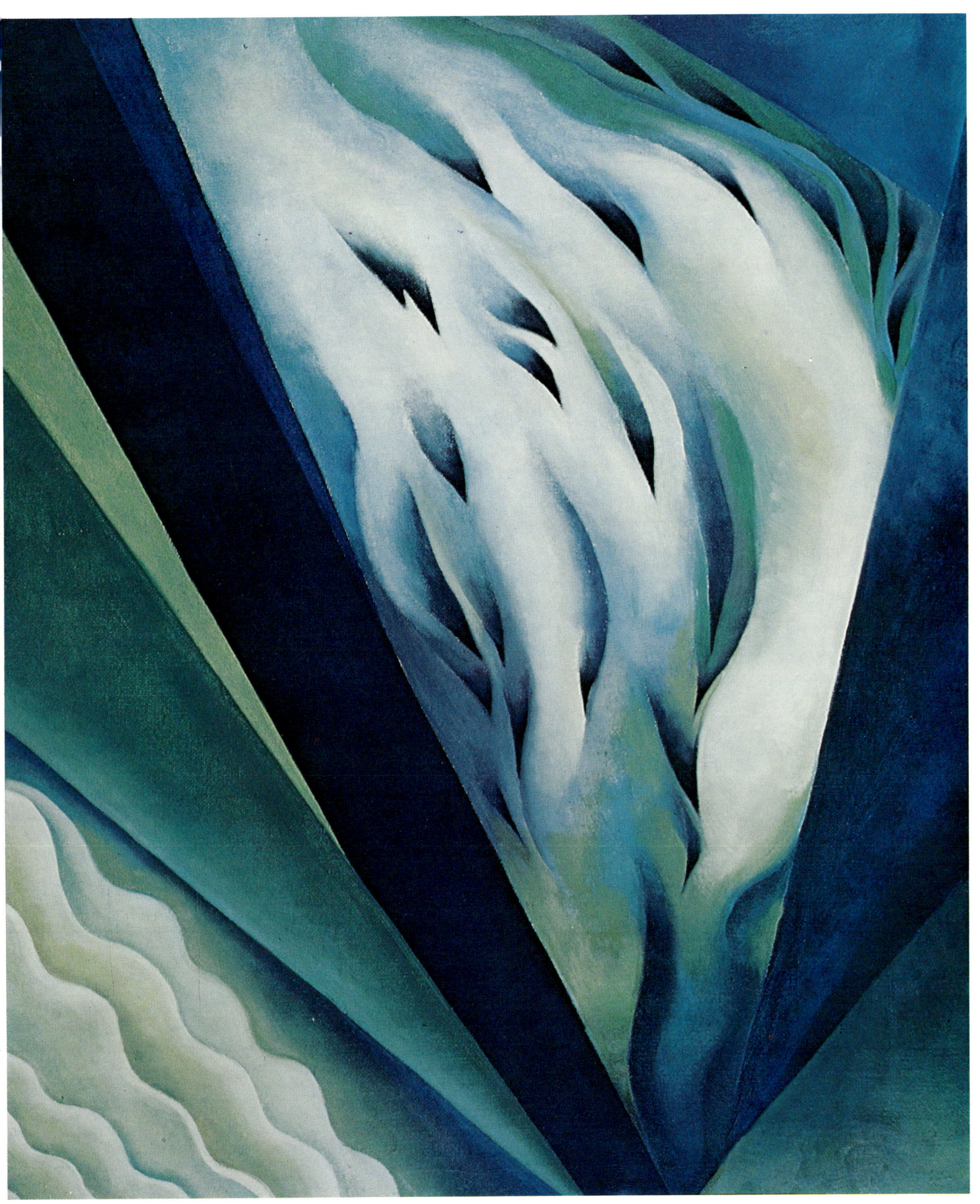

*Georgia O'Keeffe*

*Plate 58*
DARK ABSTRACTION. 1924
*Oil on canvas, 24 7/8" X 20 7/8"*
*The St. Louis Art Museum, St. Louis, Missouri*

During the years when he didn't have a gallery of his own, Stieglitz kept up the good work for O'Keeffe; at the Anderson Galleries in 1923, he put on a show of 100 of her paintings, and he had a joint show of her pictures and his photographs in 1924, the year they were married.

O'Keeffe has alternated between abstraction and super-realism. "Sometimes I know where an image comes from, sometimes not . . . I think Arthur Dove was that way, too. Often, a picture just gets into my head without my having the least idea how it got there. But I'm much more down to earth than people give me credit for. At times, I'm ridiculously realistic." (Tomkins, p. 48.)

She has avoided discussions of symbolism in her work and has particularly rejected any suggestion of sexual imagery.

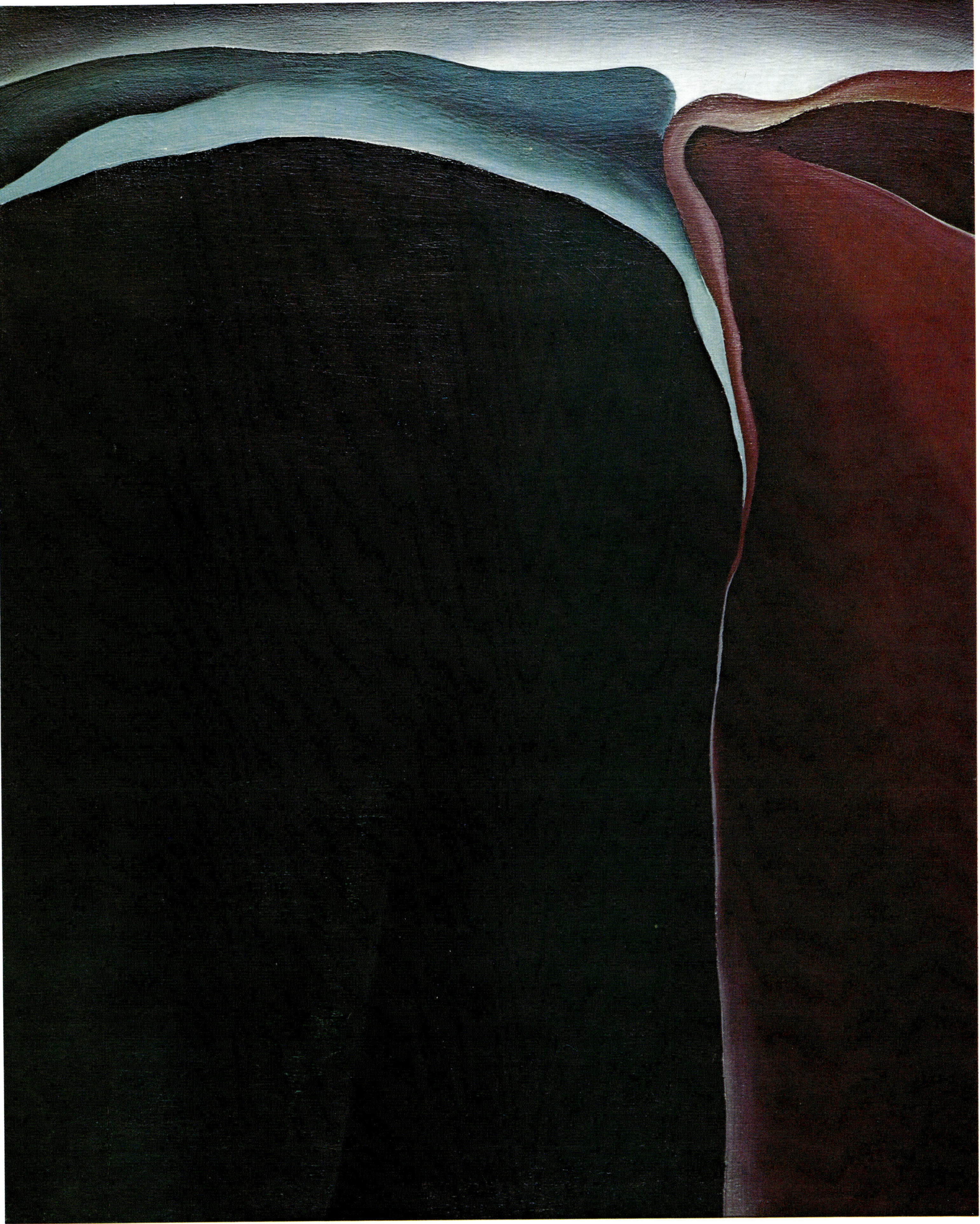

*Plate 59*
ABSTRACTION, 1926
*Oil on canvas, 30″ X 18″*
*Whitney Museum of American Art, New York, New York*

O'Keeffe's art isn't a very homey place. Abstraction was no wrench for her, since her reality is pretty stark, and mankind has never been very welcome at her door.

She is now being hailed as the grandmother of American abstraction; she admires Ellsworth Kelly, but his color field does not stem from hers. Pictures like this are monuments of the past; O'Keeffe was painting pure abstractions in 1926 just as she had been in 1916, but they haven't much connection with today.

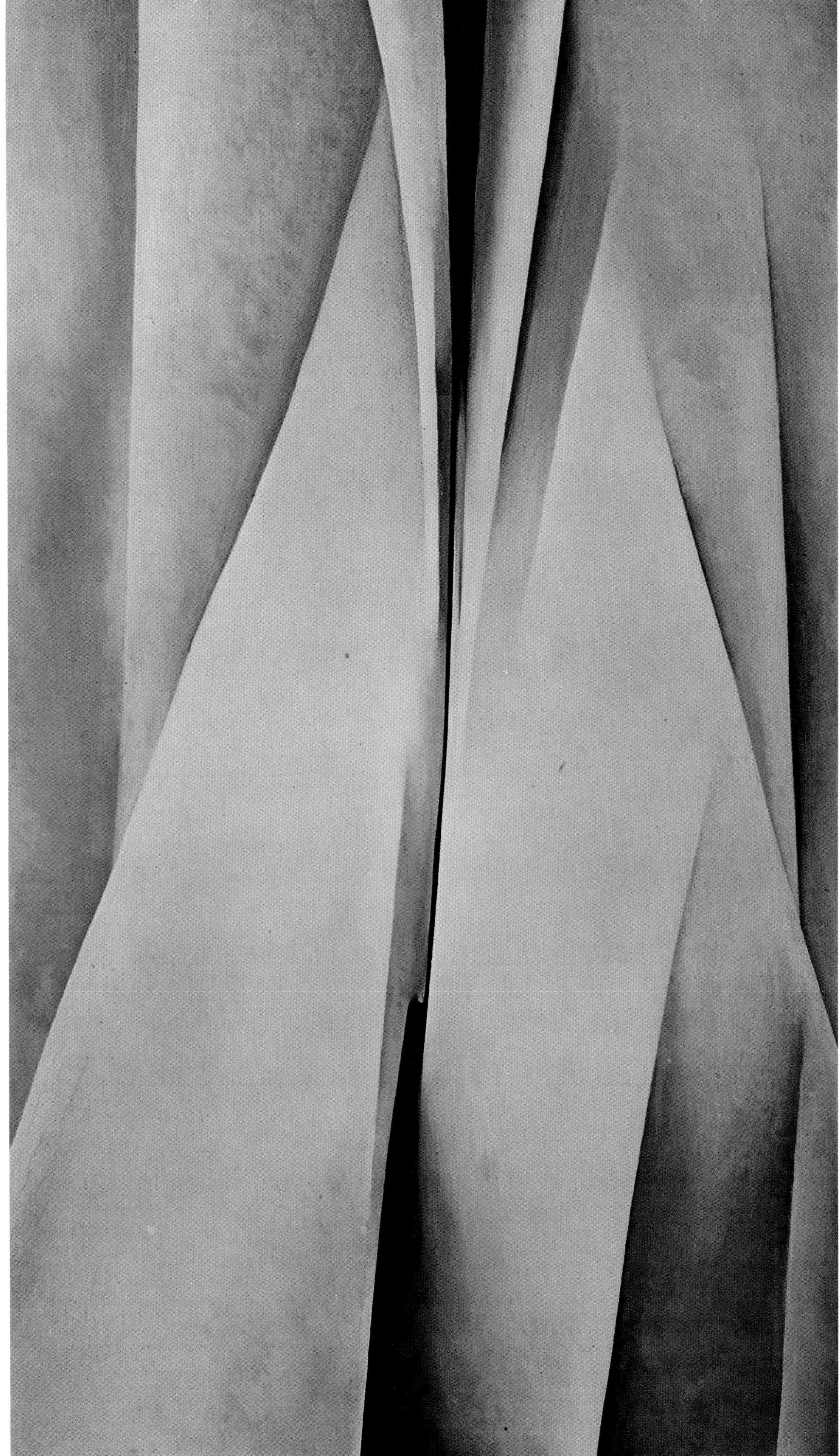

*Plate 60*
BLACK IRIS, 1926
*Oil on canvas, 36" X 30"*
*The Metropolitan Museum of Art, New York, New York*
*The Alfred Stieglitz Collection, 1949*

Curiously female flowers abound in O'Keeffe's work. In the announcement of her exhibition of "One Hundred Pictures, Oils, Watercolors, Pastels, and Drawings," at the Anderson Galleries in 1923, she wrote that "she had found first that, although she was restrained from living where she wanted to, saying what she wanted to, doing what she wanted to, she could at least paint as she wanted to." As she did so, she found she could "say things with color and shapes that I couldn't say in any other way—things that I had no words for." Herbert Seligman felt that "the recurrent intensities of this and the subsequent O'Keeffe exhibition established her as the essential reality which the so-called feminist movement—now particularly at least historic—was groping for and about." (Waldo Frank, *The Rediscovery of America,* pp. 119-120.)

She has quite a following in Women's Lib right now, but she has never been a "movement person." She was a member of the Stieglitz group purely because of Stieglitz; her real need was to be alone.

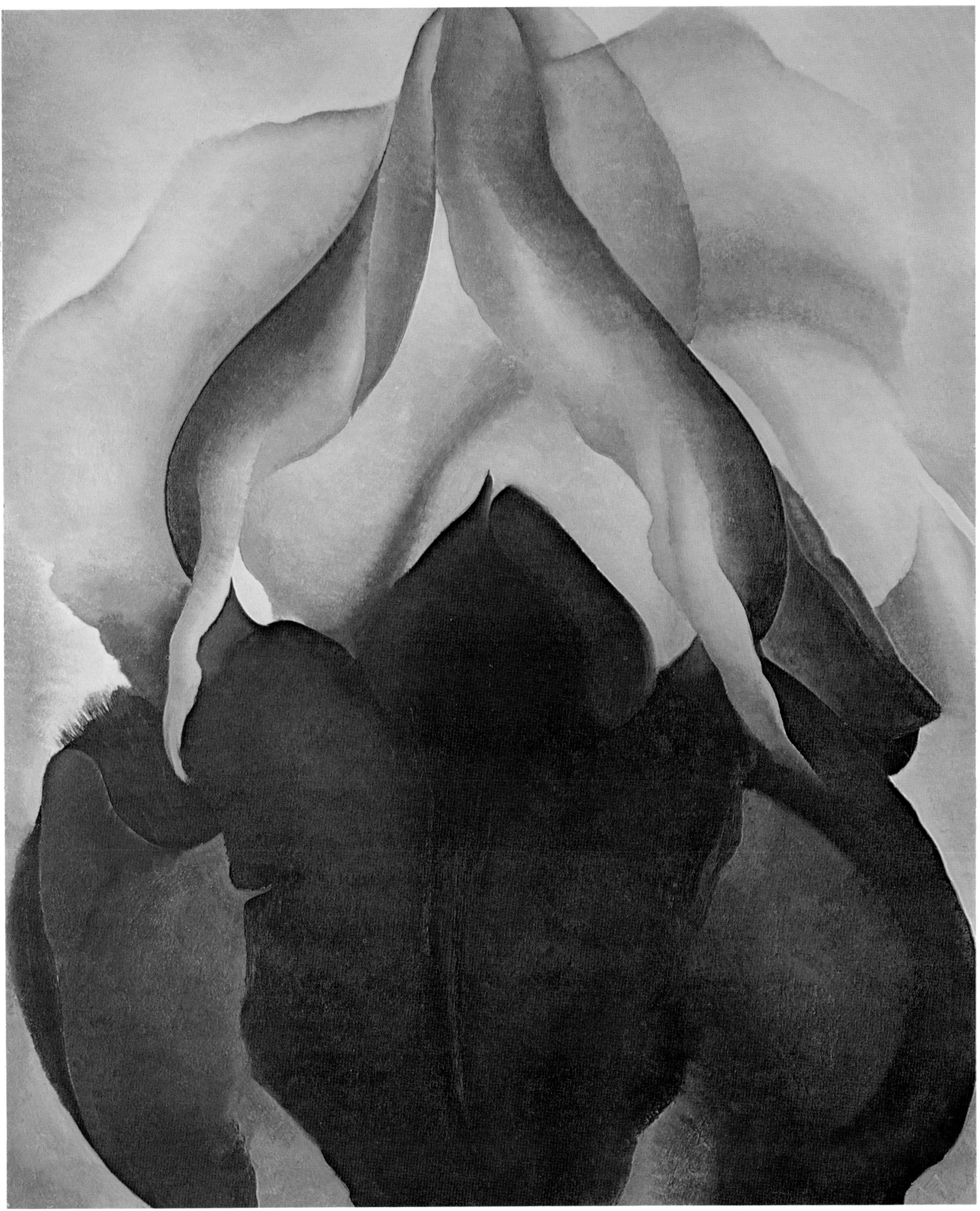

*Plate 61*
BLACK CROSS, NEW MEXICO, 1929
*Oil on canvas, 39" X 30"*
*The Art Institute of Chicago, Chicago, Illinois*

O'Keeffe found her own atmosphere in New Mexico, which she first visited in 1929, staying with Mabel Dodge Luhan in Taos. This was her country, and she became the greatest artist of the Southwest.

The daughter of an unbeliever, she has never had any formal religious belief, but she admits that the Catholic Church has an attraction for her. She is particularly fascinated by the New Mexican form of Catholicism, which isn't exactly a cheerful brand. But then, no one ever accused Georgia O'Keeffe of not being serious; the dark, violent underside of life appeals to her. There is a great deal of death in her work.

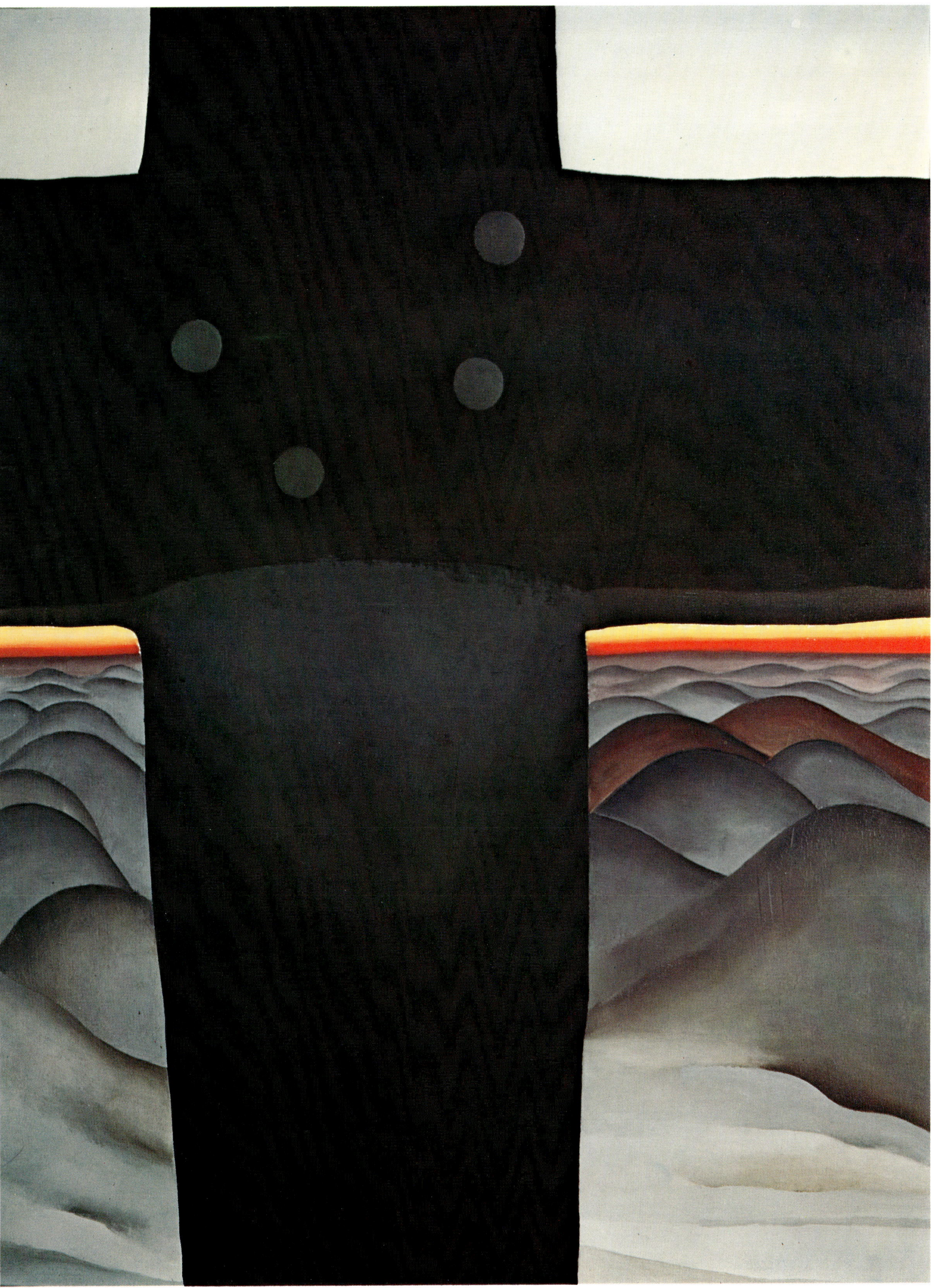

*Plate 62*
LAKE GEORGE WINDOW, 1929
*Oil on canvas, 40″ X 30″*
*The Museum of Modern Art, New York, New York*
*Richard D. Brixey Bequest*

Stieglitz and O'Keeffe tried Maine, but it didn't satisfy them. They spent the winters in New York City and the summers at Lake George, which Stieglitz loved. To judge from this picture, O'Keeffe felt that Lake George was a bit restrictive.

Stieglitz did a great deal of photography at Lake George, but O'Keeffe found it hard to work there. As she has said . . . "I can never bear to have people around me when I'm working, or to let anybody see what I'm doing or say anything about it until it's finished" (Tomkins.) Stieglitz couldn't understand that. The place was full of his family, but it never was a favorite place of hers. Stieglitz kept going there after O'Keeffe started spending the summers in New Mexico.

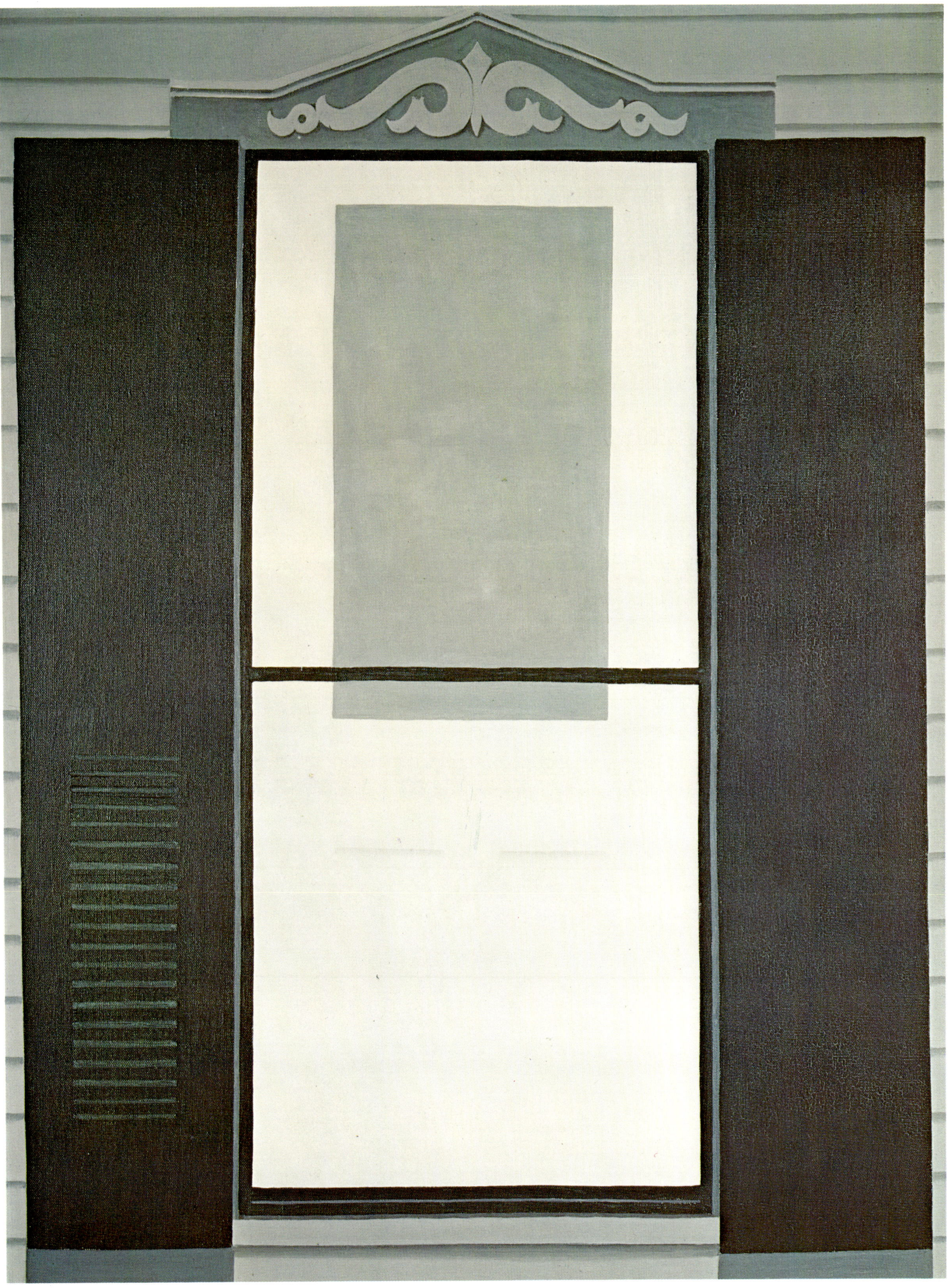

*Plate 63*
COW'S SKULL: RED, WHITE, AND BLUE, 1931
*Oil on canvas, 40" X 36"*
*The Metropolitan Museum of Art, New York, New York*
*The Alfred Stieglitz Collection, 1949*

This is quintessential O'Keeffe. No one else could have painted this picture. In 1939 she wrote, "I have wanted to paint the desert, and I haven't known how. I always think that I cannot stay with it long enough. So I brought home the bleached bones as my symbols of the desert. To me they are as beautiful as anything I know. To me they are strangely more living than the animals walking around—hair, eyes, and all with their tails twitching. The bones seem to cut sharply to the center of something that is keenly alive on the desert even tho' it is vast and empty and untouchable—and knows no kindness with all its beauty." (Lloyd Goodrich and Doris Bry, *Georgia O'Keeffe,* p. 23.)

She'll be remembered more for this painting than for her abstractions. These are the pictures people find meaning in, even though the artist denies it's there. Artists' comments on their own work are often curiously elliptical, and Georgia O'Keeffe is not as simple an artist as she says she is. "I had lived in the cattle country—Amarillo was the crossroads of cattle shipping, and you could see the cattle coming in across the range for days at a time. For goodness sake, I thought, the people who talk about the American scene don't know anything about it. So, in a way, that cow's skull was my joke on the American scene, and it gave me pleasure to make it in red, white and blue." (Tomkins.)

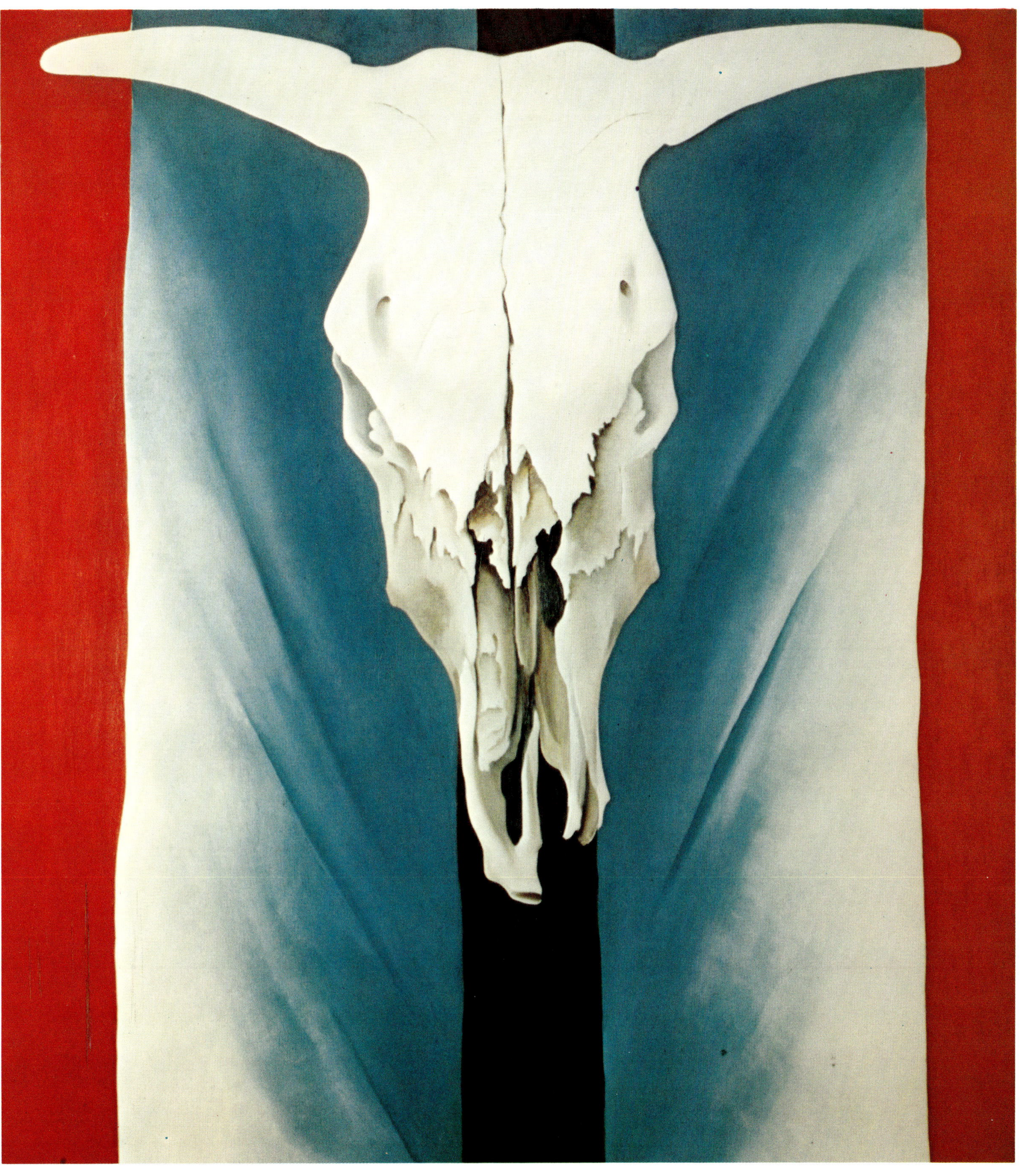

*Plate 64*
FROM THE FARAWAY NEARBY, 1937
*Oil on canvas, 36" X 40 1/8"*
*The Metropolitan Museum of Art, New York, New York*
*The Alfred Stieglitz Collection, 1949*

As Lloyd Goodrich says, "the skull appears outdoors, floating above the desert—an apparition, yet completely tangible." But O'Keeffe's objects weren't always skulls.

"I have picked flowers where I found them—

"Have picked up sea shells and rocks and pieces of wood where there were sea shells and rocks and pieces of wood that I liked.

"When I found the beautiful white bones on the desert I picked them up and took them home too.

"I have used these things to say what is to me the wideness and wonder of the world as I live in it..." (Goodrich and Bry, p. 25.)

O'Keeffe says she has no theories to offer, but with an image as clear as this who needs them? Anybody can read this picture, and it means just what it says.

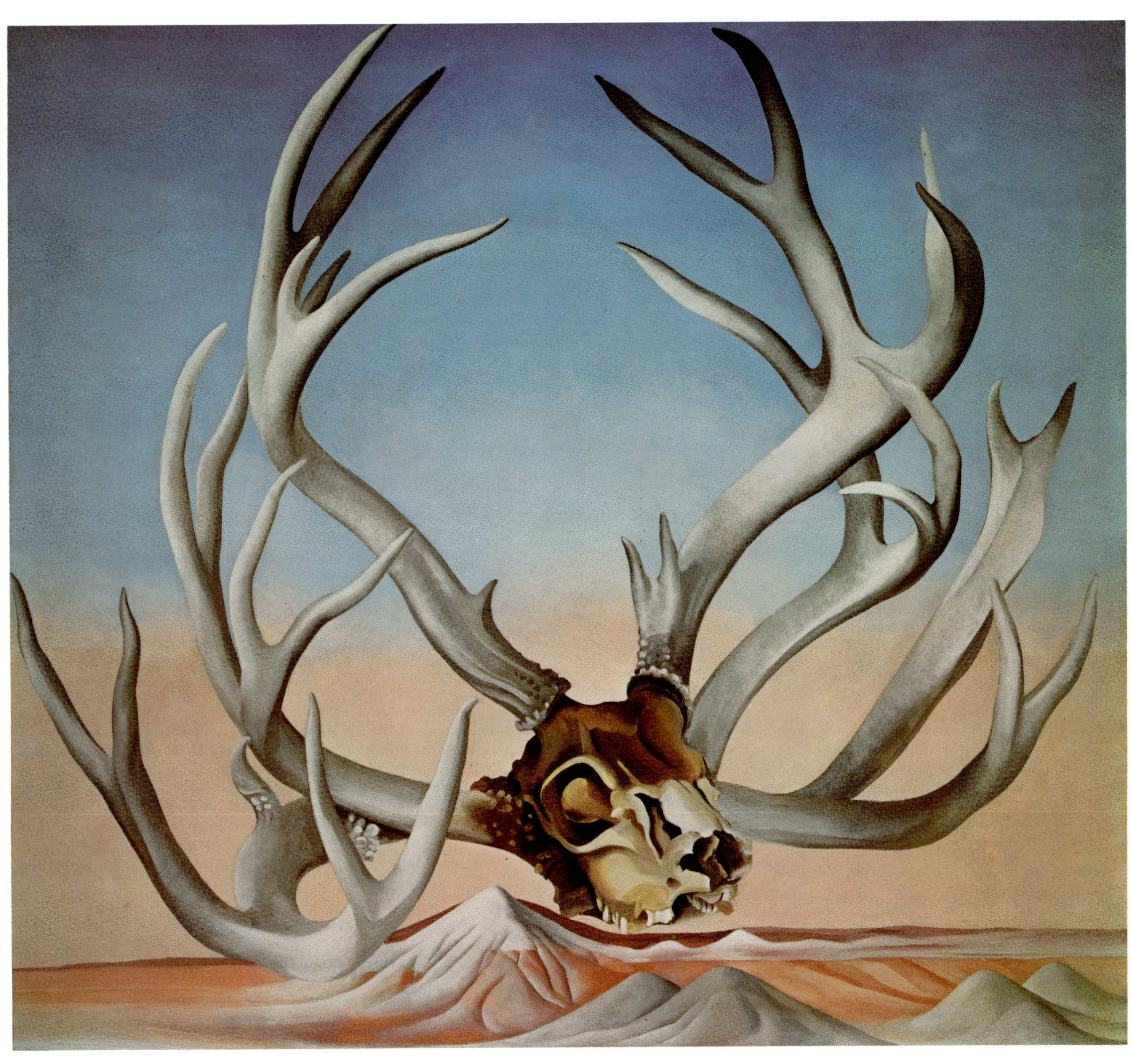

# *Epilogue*

Despite his rage and disappointment, Stieglitz was amazingly successful. A wonderful photographer himself, he put photography on its feet; tiring of that, he brought modern art from France to the United States. As a dealer and propagandist, he brought forward and pushed along the whole first generation of American moderns. Today, Marin, Demuth, Hartley, Dove, and O'Keeffe are valued at Steiglitz's estimation. He should be pleased, but you can be sure he would object.

Yet his achievement was remarkable. The eight painters in this book are precursors, though not the parents, of part of what we see today. The triumph of modern art has been complete, and, in this country, the Stieglitz group paved the way.

# Chronology

**1864.** Alfred Stieglitz born in Hoboken, New Jersey.

**1868.** Alfred Maurer born in New York City.

**1870.** John Marin born in Rutherford, New Jersey.

**1877.** Marsden Hartley born in Lewiston, Maine, as Edmund Hartley.

**1878.** Abraham Walkowitz born in Siberia.

**1880.** Arthur G. Dove born in Canandaigua, New York.

**1881-90.** Stieglitz in Germany, principally Berlin, where he taught himself photography. Began writing for photographic magazines and winning prizes at international exhibitions.

**1881.** Max Weber born in Russia.

**1883.** Charles Demuth born in Lancaster, Pennsylvania.

**1884.** Maurer studied at the National Academy of Design in New York.

**1887.** Georgia O'Keeffe born near Sun Prairie, Wisconsin.

**1889.** Walkowitz came to New York.

**1890.** Stieglitz returned to New York, went into lithography business, very active in photography.

**1891.** Weber came to New York.

**1897.** Maurer to Paris.

**1900.** Weber graduated from Pratt Institute in New York, where he studied with Arthur Wesley Dow. Hartley studied at the National Academy of Design.

**1901.** Maurer awarded First Prize and gold medal at Carnegie International. Marin studied at the Pennsylvania Academy of the Fine Arts in Philadelphia, where he met Arthur Carles.

**1902.** Stieglitz founded the magazine *Camera Work.*

**1904.** Demuth studied at the Pennsylvania Academy and made his first trip to Paris. Walkowitz exhibited at the National Academy of Design, where he had previously studied.

**1905.** Stieglitz opened Photo-Secession Gallery at 291 Fifth Avenue, New York.

**1905–10.** Marin in Paris.

**1906.** Walkowitz to Paris.

**1907.** O'Keeffe studied at the Art Students League, New York. Walkowitz returned to New York. Demuth's second trip to Paris. Dove to Paris.

**1908.** Stieglitz exhibited Rodin drawings and the work of Henri Matisse at his gallery. Hartley painted in Maine.

**1909.** Stieglitz exhibited the work of Alfred Maurer and John Marin, the first American exhibition at his gallery. Gave Hartley his first exhibition anywhere. First exihibition of Toulouse Lautrec lithographs in the United States. Weber returned to New York.

**1910.** Stieglitz held group show of "Younger American Painters," including Carles, Dove, Hartley, Marin, Maurer, Steichen, and Weber. Marin returned to States for good. First Marin one-man show at 291. Dove moved to Westport, Connecticut and bought a farm.

**1911.** Stieglitz gave Max Weber his first one-man show anywhere.

**1912.** Second Hartley exhibition at 291 Fifth Avenue. First Dove exhibition anywhere. First comprehensive Walkowitz show. First Matisse sculpture show anywhere. First exhibition of children's art anywhere. Demuth's third trip to Paris, where he met Hartley and Gertrude Stein. Hartley's first trip to Europe, where he exhibited with the *Blaue Reiter* group in Munich and *Der Sturm* in Berlin.

**1913.** Demuth to Berlin.

**1914.** Hartley in Berlin. Maurer returned to the States for good. O'Keeffe studied with Arthur Wesley Dow at Teachers College in New york. Stieglitz held first exhibition of Negro sculpture anywhere. Third Harley exhibition. Demuth had one-man show of watercolors at Daniel Gallery. Marin made first trip to Maine.

**1915.** Demuth had second one-man show at Daniel Gallery.

**1916.** O'Keeffe included in a group show at 291 Fifth Avenue without her knowledge.

**1917.** One-man O'Keeffe exhibition, the last at 291 Fifth Avenue. Demuth and Hartley in Bermuda. End of Walkowitz's association with Stieglitz.

**1919.** Hartley to New Mexico.

**1920.** Dove left his family and went to live on a boat in Long Island Sound.

**1921.** Stieglitz mounted one-manshows of O'Keeffe and of his own work at the Anderson Galleries. Stieglitz arranged a successful auction of Hartley's pictures at the Anderson Galleries which allowed him to return to Europe. Demuth to France.

**1924.** Stieglitz and O'Keeffe were married.

**1925.** Recent paintings by Demuth at the Intimate Gallery, which Stieglitz ran in the Anderson Galleries.

**1926-29.** Yearly exhibition of O'Keeffe at the Intimate Gallery.

**1929.** O'Keeffe to Taos, where she stayed with Mabel Dodge Luhan. Marin to New Mexico. Opening of An American Place, Stieglitz's last gallery.

**1930.** Hartley returned to United States. Marin in New Mexico. Hartley to Maine. Weber had retrospective at Museum of Modern Art.

**1931.** O'Keeffe painted first bone paintings.

**1932.** Hartley to Mexico. Maurer died.

**1933.** Hartley in Bavaria.

**1934.** Marin bought house at Cape Split, Maine. Dove worked the family farm in Geneva, New York.

**1935.** Demuth died in Lancaster, Pennsylvania.

**1936.** Stieglitz put on Marin retrospective at Museum of Modern Art.

**1938.** Dove moved back to Long Island. Hartley had first exhibition at the Hudson D. Walker Galleries.

**1939.** Walkowitz had retrospective at Berkeley Museum.

**1943.** Hartley died in Ellsworth, Maine.

**1946.** Death of Dove and Stieglitz.

**1950.** Closing of An American Place by O'Keeffe.

**1952.** O'Keeffe had one-man show at Downtown Gallery in New York.

**1953.** Marin died.

**1961.** Weber died.

**1965.** Walkowitz died.

**1970.** O'Keeffe retrospective at Whitney.

**1974.** O'Keeffe working in New Mexico.

# Bibliography


Ames, Scribner. *Marsden Hartley in Maine.* Orono, Maine, 1972.

Baur, John I. *Revolution and Tradition in Modern American Art.* New York, 1951.

Brown, Milton W. *American Painting from the Armory Show to the Depression.* Princeton, 1970.

———. *Story of the Armory Show.* Greenwich, Connecticut, 1963.

Bullitt, J.C. *Apples and Madmas.* Chicago, 1930.

Cahill, Holger, and Barr, Alfred H. Jr., eds. *Art in America in Modern Times.* Freeport, New York, 1934.

Cheney, M.C. *Modern Art in America.* New York, 1939.

Columbus Gallery of Fine Arts. *American Paintings in the Ferdinand Howald Collection.* Columbus, Ohio, 1969.

Demuth, Charles. *America and Alfred Stieglitz.* New York, 1934.

DuBois, Guy Pène. *Artists Say the Silliest Things.* New York, 1940.

Farnham, Emily. *Charles Demuth: Behind a Laughing Mask.* Norman, Oklahoma, 1971.

Frank, Waldo. *The Rediscovery of America.* New York, 1929.

———, Lewis Mumford, Dorothy Norman, Paul Rosenfeld, and Harold Rigg, eds. *America and Alfred Stieglitz: A Collective Portrait.* New York, 1934.

Geldzahler, Henry. *American Painting in the Twentieth Century.* New York, 1965.

Goodrich, Lloyd. *Pioneers of Modern Art in America.* New York, 1963.

———, Doris Bry, *Georgia O'Keeffe.* New York, 1970.

Green, Samuel M. *American Art: A Historical Survey.* New York, 1966.

Hapgood, Hutchins. *Victorian in the Modern World.* New York, 1939.

Hartley, Marsden. *Adventures in the Arts: Informal Chapters on Painters.* New York, 1924.

———. *Selected Poems.* New York, 1945.

Helm, MacKinley. *John Marin.* New York, 1970.

Kootz, S. M. *Modern American Painters.* New York, *ca.* 1930.

Kuhn, Walt. *The Story of the Armory Show.* New York, ca. 1938.

LaFolette, Suzanne. *Art in America.* New York, 1929.

Larkin, Oliver. *Art and Life in America.* New York, 1949.

Luhan, Mabel Dodge. *Movers and Shakers.* New York, 1936.

———. *Edge of Taos Desert.* New York, 1937.

Marin, John. *Letters.* New York, 1931.

———. *Selected Writings.* New York, 1949.

McCausland, Elizabeth. *A. H. Maurer.* New York, 1951.

———. *Marsden Hartley.* Minneapolis, Minnesota, 1952.

McCoubry, John. *American Tradition in Painting.* New York, 1963.

Mellow, James R. *Charmed Circle: Gertrude Stein & Company.* New York, 1974.

Norman, Dorothy. *Alfred Stieglitz: An American Seer.* New York, 1973.

Phillips, Duncan. *A Collection in the Making.* Washington, D.C., *ca.* 1926.

Reich, Sheldon. *Alfred H. Maurer 1868-1932.* Washington, 1973.

———. *John Marin: A Stylistic Analysis and Catalogue Raisonné,* vol. 2. Tucson, Arizona, 1970.

Reid, B.L. *The Man from New York: John Quinn and His Friends.* London and New York, 1969.

Richardson, Edgar P. *Painting in America.* New York, 1956.

Rosenfeld, Paul. *Port of New York.* New York, 1924.

Seligmann, H.J. *Alfred Stieglitz Talking.* New Haven, 1966.

Steichen, Edward. *A Life in Photography.* New York, 1963.

Stein, Gertrude. *Autobiography of Alice B. Toklas.* New York, 1933.

Tomkins, Calvin. "Georgia O'Keeffe," *The New Yorker,* March 4, 1974 (pp. 40-66).

Tucker, Marcia. *American Paintings in the Ferdinand Howald Collection.* Columbus, Ohio, 1969.

Wight, Frederick S. *Arthur G. Dove.* Berkeley and Los Angeles, 1958.

Zigrosser, Carl. *The Complete Etchings of John Marin.* Philadelphia, Pennsylvania, 1969.

# Index


Abbey, Edward Austin, 12
*Adventures in the Arts*, 22
Aix-en-Provence, France, 17
An American Place, 11, 22, 64
Anderson Galleries, 11, 13, 22, 138, 142
Anderson, Sherwood, 118
Anshutz, Thomas, 12
Armory Show, 10, 13, 92, 116
Art Institute of Chicago, Illinois, 22
Art Students League, New York, 12, 22
*Aucassin and Nicolette*, 58
Auden, W.H., 26

Barr, Alfred, 102
Berenson, Bernard, 11
Biddle, George, 14
Bittinger, Charles, 12
*Blaue Reiter*, 17
Bluemner, Oscar, 120
Brancusi, Constantin, 11
Braque, Georges, 10
Bullitt, William C., 17

*Camara Work*, 11
Carey, Elizabeth Luther, 12
Carles, Arthur, 12, 14, 20
Carnegie International, 20, 116
Cézanne, Paul, 11, 12, 15
Cleveland School of Art, Ohio, 16
Cook, George Cram, 15

Daniel, Charles, 13, 15, 17
Dasburg, Andrew, 114
Daumier, Honoré, 50
Davies, Arthur B., 17, 64
Davis, Stuart, 116
Degas, Edgar, 16, 50
Demuth, Charles: biographical data, 14-15; color plates, 47-67
Dôme, Paris, France, 14, 66
Dove, Arthur G.: biographical data, 18-19; color plates, 91-112
Dow, Arthur Wesley, 21
Duchamp, Marcel, 91
Duncan, Isadora, 21

Educational Alliance, New York, 21

Fisher, William Murrell, 136
Frank, Waldo, 10
Franklin and Marshall Academy, Lancaster, Pennsylvania, 14
Frieseke, Frederick Carl, 117

Galleries: An American Place, 11; Anderson, 11; Intimate, 11; Photo-Secession, 10, 11
Glackens, William, 16, 68
Glaspell, Susan, 15
Goncourt, Edmond, 12
Goncourt, Jules, 12
Gurdieff, Georges Ivanovich, 10

Hapgood, Hutchins, 15
Hart, William S., 19
Hartley, Marsden: biographical data, 16-17; color plates, 69-89
Hartpence, Alanson, 16
Haskell, Ernest, 13
Hemingway, Ernest, 17
Homer, Winslow, 32
Howald, Ferdinand, 13, 15, 19, 22, 30

Intimate Gallery, 11, 13

James, Henry, 15
Jerome, Leonard, 11
*Jugend*, 16

Kandinsky, Vasili, 17
Kelly, Ellsworth, 140
Kreymborg, Alfred, 10
Kuhn, Walt, 80

Lachaise, Gaston, 20
Lawson, Ernest, 70
Luhan, Mabel Dodge, 13, 22

McAlmon, Robert, 17
McBride, Henry, 12, 15, 18
Man Ray, 10
Manet, Edouard, 16

Marin, John: biographical data, 12-13; color plates, 25-45
Matisse, Henri, 10, 21, 22
Maurer, Alfred: biographical data, 20; color plates, 115-119
Mellquist, Jerome, 16
Meryon, Charles, 12
Morgan, J.P., 11
Mumford, Lewis, 10
Museum of Modern Art, New York, 13, 102

Nadelman, Elie, 20
*Nana*, 15
National Academy of Design, New York, 16, 20, 21
*New York Herald*, 118
New York School of Art, New York, 16
Notre Dame Cathedral, Paris, France, 14

Obermeyer, Emmeline, 11
O'Keeffe, Georgia: biographical data, 22; color plates, 133-151
O'Neill, Eugene, 15
O'Sheel, Seumas, 16

Pater, Walter Horatio, 136
Pennsylvania Academy of the Fine Arts, Philadelphia, Pennsylvania, 12, 14
Phillips, Duncan, 13, 19, 98, 104, 110
Photo-Secession Gallery, 10, 11, 16
Picabia, Francis, 91
Picasso, Pablo, 10, 21, 22
Pratt Institute of Art, 21
Prendergast, Maurice, 16, 70, 128
*Primitives*, 122
Proust, Marcel, 15

*Remembrance of Things Past*, 15
Rockwell, Norman, 18
Rodin, Oliver, 11
Roosevelt, Franklin, 17
Rosenfeld, Paul, 10, 12
Rousseau, Henri, 21
Ryder, Albert Pinkham, 16, 72, 76

Salon d'Automne, Paris, France, 18, 21
*Saturday Evening Post*, 118
Segantini, Giovanni, 16
Seligman, Herbert, 42
Sheeler, Charles, 10, 14
Sloan, John, 16, 68
Steichen, Edward, 10, 12, 18, 21
Stein, Gertrude, 11, 12, 15, 17, 18, 118
Stein, Leo, 20, 114
Stevens Institute of Technology, Hoboken, New Jersey, 12
Stieglitz, Alfred: biographical data, 10-11
Strand, Paul, 13

*Tristan und Isolde*, 11
Turner, William, 32
*Turn of the Screw*, 15

University Settlement House, New York, 21

Van Gogh, Vincent, 12

Walkowitz, Abraham: biographical data, 21; color plates, 127-131
Watkins, Franklin, 14
Waugh, Frederick, 28
Weber, Max: biographical data, 21; color plates, 121-123
Wehye, Erhard, 20, 118
Whistler, James McNeil, 12
Williams, William Carlos, 14, 15
Wright, MacDonald, 20

Young, Mahonri, 20

Zola, Emile, 15
Zorach, William, 128

Edited by Claire Hardiman
Designed by Bob Fillie
Composed in 11 point Souvenir by Gerard Associates/Graphic Arts
Printed by Rochester Polychrome
Bound by Riverside Press